Praise for *Venezuela in Crisis*

"Easy praise of the Hugo Chávez era always concealed a more complicated scenario on the ground. But for well over a decade it has been impossible to deny the depth of the mire into which the Bolivarian process has sunk. One option among former celebrants on the international left has been to go mute and turn attention elsewhere. This path sometimes includes a dose of honesty, but with little reckoning or integrity. Another option has been to double down and defend bureaucratic sclerosis and authoritarian consolidation under Nicolás Maduro. Rather than turning one's head, this requires burying it in the sand. Down this road, no truth, no reckoning, no integrity. *Venezuela in Crisis* is the first collection in English to genuinely grapple with the crisis—its origins, character, scale, depth, trajectory—from socialist perspectives that take democratic self-determination seriously. This book is a crucial contribution toward our collective understanding of what went wrong in the Bolivarian experiment, which is the first step toward the monumental work of rebuilding a genuinely socialist alternative future."

—**Jeffery R. Webber**, coauthor of
The Impasse of the Latin American Left

"This book, coordinated under the attentive and careful eye of professor Anderson Bean, combines contributions from the editor himself alongside some of the most prominent leftist thinkers in Venezuela. The book explores over a quarter century of Venezuela's sociopolitical experience, highlighting the advances and setbacks associated with the Bolivarian process during two distinct periods: the first under Chávez, from 1999 until his death in 2012; the second the period under Maduro, from 2013 to the present. The latter contrasts sharply with the former in terms of leadership, achievements, and both national and global impact. Through the perspectives provided by each contributor, readers can form their own understanding of the ongoing struggle in Venezuela to realize the ideals of the Bolivarian homeland."

—**Jorge Giordani**, Marxist engineer-economist,
former planning minister under Hugo Chávez

"An invaluable book that helps us all better understand how a country that was once the most exciting social laboratory for change descended into such a profound crisis. Written amid rising US aggression and internal repression, this collection of insightful essays critically foregrounds the often-silenced voices of Venezuelan leftists seeking a democratic and anticapitalist path out of the crisis, making it essential reading for anyone interested in genuinely grappling with the complex realities of Venezuela today."

—**Federico Fuentes**, editor of *LINKS: International Journal of Socialist Renewal*

"Unlike the schematic, polarized takes that dominate discussion of Venezuela, this book offers a well-informed, reflective examination that aims not to persuade but to probe—critically and in depth—the political, economic, and environmental dynamics of the current Venezuelan process. Newcomers will find enough context to form a solid, integrated picture of what's happening, while readers seeking more will find rigorous, up-to-date analysis of Venezuela's complex reality today. I highly recommend this book."

—**Edgardo Lander**, retired professor, Venezuela Central University

"Coming at a time of global capitalist crisis and escalating geopolitical conflict, *Venezuela in Crisis* could not be more timely and urgent. These essays, written by Venezuelan socialists themselves, make clear that US economic warfare and rightwing counterrevolution are not enough to explain the Venezuelan crisis. Notwithstanding its socialist rhetoric, the Maduro regime has turned to authoritarian control in its drive to deepen a model of extractivist and rentier capitalism that has sacrificed the working class to local and transnational capital. The degeneration of the Bolivarian process is both a tragedy and a lesson for popular struggles from below throughout the Americas and beyond: would-be socialist projects cannot serve both capital and the working class. The international left must stand in solidarity with the Venezuelan popular classes by opposing both US intervention and the Maduro regime."

—**William I. Robinson**, distinguished professor of sociology, global, and Latin American studies, University of California at Santa Barbara

Venezuela in Crisis

Socialist Perspectives

Edited and translated by

Anderson M. Bean

Haymarket Books
Chicago, IL

Published in 2026 by
Haymarket Books
P.O. Box 180165
Chicago, IL 60618
www.haymarketbooks.org

ISBN: 979-8-88890-464-0

Distributed to the trade in the US through Consortium Book Sales and Distribution (www.cbsd.com) and internationally through Ingram Publisher Services International (www.ingramcontent.com).

This book was published with the generous support of Lannan Foundation, Wallace Action Fund, and Marguerite Casey Foundation.

Cover design by Abby Weintraub. Book design by Jamie Kerry.

Printed in the United States.

Library of Congress Cataloging-in-Publication data is available. Library of Congress Control Number: 2025948029.

10 9 8 7 6 5 4 3 2 1

For Carlos Carcione

Contents

Abbreviations

AD	Acción Democrática
ALBA	Bolivarian Alliance for the Peoples of Our America
AMO	Arco Minero del Orinoco
AN	National Assembly
ANC	National Constituent Assembly
BANFAN	Bank of the National Armed Forces
BCV	Central Bank of Venezuela
CAMIMPEG	Military Mining, Oil, and Gas Industries Company
CAN	Andean Community of Nations
CANTV	Venezuelan National Telephone Company
CAP	Carlos Andrés Pérez
CBST	Bolivarian Workers' Union
C-CURA	Autonomous, Revolutionary, Unitary Class Tendency
CIA	Central Intelligence Agency
CELAC	Community of Latin American and Caribbean States
CIF	Cost, Insurance, and Freight
CLAP	Local Committees for Supply and Production
CNC-TL	National Committee for Workers in Struggle
CNE	National Electoral Council
COPEI	Independent Political Electoral Organization Committee (Social Christian Party)
CORDIPLAN	Central Office for Planning and Coordination of the Presidency of the Republic

Corpoelec	National Electricity Corporation
CRBV	Constitution of the Bolivarian Republic of Venezuela
CSSL	Committees on Occupational Safety and Health
CTR	Collective of Workers in Revolution
CTV	Confederation of Workers of Venezuela
DEA	US Drug Enforcement Agency
DGCIM	General Directorate of Military Counterintelligence
DSA	Democratic Socialists of America
FANB	National Bolivarian Armed Forces
FAPUV	Federation of Associations of University Professors of Venezuela
Fedecámaras	Venezuelan Federation of Chambers of Commerce
FONDEN	National Development Fund
FPO	Faja Petrolífera del Orinoco
FSBT	Bolivarian Socialist Worker Force
FTAA	Free Trade Agreement of the Americas
FUTPV	Unitary Federation of Oil Workers of Venezuela
FUTSEB	United Front of Socialist Workers of Bolívar State
GDP	Gross Domestic Product
HR	Human Rights
ICC	International Criminal Court
ICJ	International Court of Justice
ICSID	International Centre for Settlement of Investment Disputes
ILO	International Labor Organization
IMF	International Monetary Fund
INE	Statistics National Institute
INPSASEL	National Institute for Prevention, Health and Safety
INSOPESCA	Socialist Institute of Fisheries and Aquaculture

IRE	Employee Remuneration Index
ISI	Import Substitution Industrialization
LAB	Anti-Blockade Law
LOPCYMAT	Organic Law on Prevention, Conditions, and Work Environment
LOT	Organic Labor Law
LOTTT	Organic Law of Labor, Work and Workers
MAS	Movement for Socialism
MBR-200	Revolutionary Bolivarian Movement 200
MDME	Ministry of Ecological Mining Development
Mercosur	Common Southern Market
MPPC	Ministry of Popular Power for the Communes
MVR	Fifth Republic Movement
NAFTA	North American Free Trade Agreement
OAS	Organization of American States
OHCHR	United Nations High Commissioner for Human Rights
OPEC	Organization of the Petroleum Exporting Countries
OPF	Orinoco Oil Belt
PCV	Venezuelan Communist Party
PDVSA	Petroleum of Venezuela
PNC	People's National Congress (Guyana)
PNC-R	People's National Congress Reform (Guyana)
PPP	People's Progressive Party (Guyana)
PROVEA	Venezuelan Program of Education-Action in Human Rights
PSL	Socialism and Freedom Party of Venezuela
PSUV	United Socialist Party of Venezuela
PUD	Democratic Unitary Platform
SEBIN	Bolivarian Intelligence Service

SEZ	Special Economic Zone
SIDOR	Siderúrgica del Orinoco
TeleSUR	New Television Station of the South
TSJ	Supreme Court of Justice
UCMs	Unilateral Coercive Measures
UF	United Force party (Guyana)
UNASUR	Union of South American Nations
UNETE	Venezuela's National Workers' Union
UNHCR	United Nations Refugee Agency
WPA	Working People's Alliance of Guyana

Translator's Note

With the exception of the introduction and afterword, all endnotes are the authors' original bibliographic citations and clarifying notes, and all footnotes are translator notes, unless otherwise noted. In the introduction, since the author is the translator, all endnotes and footnotes are translator/author notes. In the introduction and afterword, the endnotes are bibliographic citations, and the footnotes are clarifying notes.

Introduction

Anderson M. Bean

Throughout the first decade of the twenty-first century, Venezuela was an inspiration across the world, particularly so for the left. Venezuela's Bolivarian process—the shorthand used for the revolutionary struggle and newly formed state institutions created following the election of Hugo Chávez in 1998—improved Venezuelans' material well-being, brought greater social equality, and empowered sectors of society that were traditionally excluded from the political process through flourishing sites of participatory democracy that empowered ordinary people to engage actively in the decisions that affected their lives. The Bolivarian process inspired anti-imperialists across the globe as it challenged US hegemony in the region, particularly by rejecting the US-sponsored Free Trade Agreement of the Americas and through the creation of alternative institutions that promoted regional integration, such as the Bolivarian Alliance for the Peoples of Our America, the Bank of the South, the New Television Station of the South, and the Andean Community of Nations.

The Bolivarian process, which had its roots in sectors of the military and in Venezuela's long tradition of grassroots movements, began in earnest with Hugo Chávez's presidency in 1999. The Bolivarian process was made up of three key components. The first was the rewriting of the constitution, which with its promotion of broad citizen participation and comprehensive human rights protections was considered by many as the most progressive constitution in the world at the time.[1]

The second component was the redistribution of oil profits through various social programs called "missions." Partly because of the redistribution of oil wealth through missions, poverty was reduced by 37.6 percent, and extreme poverty dropped by 57.8 percent from the start of Chávez's first presidential term in 1999 until 2011.[2] By 2008, Venezuela also had the highest minimum wage in all of Latin America, and inequality in the country dropped to one of the lowest in the Americas.[3] By 2011, Venezuela was the second most equal country in the Western Hemisphere. Only Canada had lower levels of inequality.[4]

The third and perhaps the most transformative component of the Bolivarian process was the transfer of power from traditional nodes of power to the popular sectors through the creation of new forms of popular assemblies and experiments with workers' controls, communal councils, and communes.

Fast forward to today, and Venezuela is in crisis. The crisis is the most severe in Venezuela's history and is one of the worst in Latin American history. From 2013 to 2021, Venezuela's gross domestic product declined by more than 75 percent. Inflation has been a persistent problem, reaching 130,000 percent in 2018, the highest in the world. The percentage of households classified as poor increased from 48.4 percent in 2014 to 81.5 percent in 2022.[5] The monthly minimum wage is the equivalent of US$2.23, the lowest in all of Latin America.[6] After adding the government food bonus, the monthly minimum salary is roughly US$4.47, or about US$0.15 a day, eight times less than the United Nations's limit for absolute poverty of US$1.25 a day.[7] For comparison, the monthly minimum wage under Chávez was US$300, over sixty times higher than what it is today.[8] Four dollars is about what two pounds of meat costs. In other words, the monthly minimum wage is barely enough to buy two pounds of meat. And even this number changes daily, as prices go up regularly, sometimes several times a day. Minimum wage is insufficient to cover basic needs, and one simply cannot survive on minimum wage alone.*

---

* Minimum wage in Venezuela has been highly variable, depending on the oscillations of the exchange value of the bolivar, the monetary conversions, and the increases granted that sometimes placed the minimum wage between US$5.00 and

As a result of and compounding this economic shock, Venezuela is also experiencing a migration crisis. Since 2016, millions of Venezuelans have fled the country looking for a better life; most are seeking work abroad in order to send money back home. In 2019 and 2020, between three thousand and five thousand Venezuelans left the country every day.[9] Today the number of Venezuelan refugees and migrants worldwide is estimated to be around 7.7 million, meaning that around 20 percent of all Venezuelans now live abroad.[10] By 2020, Venezuela had become the country with the highest number of displaced people in Latin America and the second highest in the world, just behind Syria.[11] Since 2014 the number of Venezuelans who have applied for asylum in other countries has increased by 4,000 percent.[12] The crisis seems to have no end in sight. What was once an inspiration is now a nightmare.

How did Venezuela go from the highest minimum wage in Latin America to the lowest? How did Venezuela go from being seen as a model of social progress to the site of perhaps the deepest crisis in the history of Latin America? What factors led to and contributed to this crisis? From the perspective of the US state (regardless of party affiliation), as well as Venezuela's domestic right wing, the crisis is a result of socialism. As Donald Trump expressed in a 2018 address to the United Nations General Assembly, "Not long ago, Venezuela was one of the richest countries on Earth. Today, socialism has bankrupted the oil-rich nation and driven its people into abject poverty." For them, the crisis is a product of the Bolivarian Revolution's attempt to usher in a socialist project. Socialism, or any attempt to create any society that diverges from capitalism, is always doomed to fail.

Meanwhile, much of the left, particularly the Anglophone left, argues that the crisis can be explained primarily by the US sanctions imposed on Venezuela, coupled with other attempts by the US state, in collaboration with the domestic Venezuelan right-wing opposition, to intentionally undermine the Venezuelan economy in order to carry out a regime change to unseat Nicolás Maduro and put a complete end to the Bolivarian process.

US$7.00 but which quickly degraded with the inflation and fluctuations of the currency (in terms of its equivalent in foreign exchange).

Both of these perspectives miss the mark. Both of these perspectives view Venezuela as a socialist country, or at least on the path toward building socialism. One side sees this as precisely the cause of the crisis—socialism always fails. The other argues this is why the Maduro regime must be defended at all costs—socialism needs protection.

To understand the crisis in Venezuela, it is helpful to start with what is often called the "commodity boom." Like many other left-of-center progressive presidencies in Latin America, much of Chávez's time in office coincided with a boom in commodity prices driven by demand from emerging markets like China and India. The price of primary commodities such as soy, iron ore, copper, and, most importantly, oil reached new highs. With the price of oil and natural gas so high, even a modest increase in royalties and taxes created a huge influx in state revenue. This increased revenue enabled Chávez to increase social spending, create various distribution programs, and improve the standard of living of the majority of Venezuelans. But this increased revenue also meant Chávez was able to increase social spending without having to confront the capitalist class in any serious way. There was no real meaningful transformation of social property relations, no transformation of the international division of labor, and no challenge to the prerogatives of transnational capital.[13] Importantly, there was also no break with extractivism (a mode of natural resource appropriation characterized by the extraction of large volumes of unprocessed or minimally processed raw materials, primarily for export) and no break with the country's dependence on the export of minerals and hydrocarbons.[14] In fact, Venezuela's dependence on oil exports increased during the Chávez and Maduro era, leaving the country more beholden to global financial and oil markets.[15]

Because of the commodity boom, Chávez was able to reduce poverty and inequality and to expand a variety of different social programs without confronting capital or the global capitalist order in any serious way.[16] Seventy percent of the economy remained in the hands of private capital throughout the Chavista era.[17] Wealth may have been redistributed to some extent, but there was no change to society's underlying class structure or serious confrontation with private property or profitability.[18]

This model and its mutually beneficial relationship between capital and labor rested on a fragile base and was only temporary and entirely contingent on high commodity prices. This delicate balance sustained itself until 2011–12, when China's economy began to slow down. China's rate of growth dropped to its lowest since the 1990s. Once the Chinese economy, far and away the largest market for resource exports, began to slow, the high commodity prices that sustained the Chávez government began to fall, and crisis ensued. The ability to appease both labor and capital came to an end with the end of the commodity boom. By 2015, commodity prices hit a twelve-year low.[19] The slowdown hit Venezuela particularly hard since increased dependence on oil meant that oil exports accounted for 95 percent of its export earnings and oil revenues made up more than 90 percent of the government's budget. The end of the commodity boom forced the Chavista government to make a decision they had managed to delay while commodity prices were high. Now in a situation of austere state revenues, who was going to pay for the crisis? Was it going to be labor and regular working people, the social bases that supported and voted Chávez into power? Or was there going to be a conflict with capital that had been delayed for years? This, as history would have it, was not a decision that Chávez had a chance to make. Chávez got sick with cancer in 2012, the same year the boom went bust, and died at the beginning of 2013. Shortly afterward, Nicolás Maduro was elected to replace Chávez, and the burden of resolving these questions fell on his new government.

Here, it is important to clearly define what Maduro inherited to contextualize his administration's response to the situation in Venezuela. Throughout the Chávez years, even during the apex of the Bolivarian process and the height of the commodity boom, and despite the gains that were made during these years, Venezuela remained a capitalist country and remains so to this day. Throughout the Chávez and Maduro years, the overwhelming majority of the means of production remained in the hands of the private sphere and the capitalist class.* The control

* The means of production are the physical, nonhuman inputs required for producing goods and services in an economy. This can include the instruments of labor: tools, machinery, equipment, and infrastructure used in the production process; or

of the economy still remains in the hands of private capital. In fact, between 1999 and 2011 the private sector's share of economic activity actually increased from 65 percent to 71 percent.[20] Production for private profit dominates the economy. The production and distribution of the majority of goods and services, including key industries like major food import and processing operations, pharmaceuticals, and auto parts, are still controlled by the private sector. The bourgeoisie state apparatus still endures; the fundamental structure and function of the state remains rooted in a system that serves capitalist interests and preserves class hierarchies. Even in instances where the state does own the means of production, for example, the state-owned oil and natural gas company Petroleum of Venezuela (PDVSA) and the concrete and asphalt industries, it is the state bureaucracy that controls and makes all decisions in these industries, rather than the workers. And in the instances of state control of industry, in particular PDVSA, production and distribution are shaped by the logic of capital and capital accumulation. While there were expropriations and state takeovers under Chávez, the underlying property relations and the profit motive in major sectors of the economy remain largely intact. The oil industry represents 95 percent of the country's total exports sold on the world market and is thus beholden to its capitalist logic. Decisions in state-controlled industries like PDVSA are driven by the imperatives of profitability (which has often meant laying off workers and freezing wages to cut costs) and the need to compete in global markets, rather than by the prioritization of social- or worker-oriented goals. In other words, in neither the large extant private sector nor in the majority of state-owned industries do workers exercise control of the means of production. Moreover, despite the progressive language of participatory democracy and human rights, the 1999 Chavista constitution gives significant protection to private property (Article 15).

Even Chávez openly spoke about how the transition to socialism had yet to come to fruition, nor would it in the near future, and that Venezuela remained a capitalist country. In an address on his weekly radio and television show *Aló Presidente*, he said,

---

the subjects of labor: raw materials, natural resources, and land that are acted on or processed to create goods.

> Who would think to say that Venezuela is a socialist country? No, that would be to deceive ourselves. We are in a country that still lives in capitalism, we have only initiated a path; we are taking steps against the world current, including towards a socialist project; but this is for the medium or long term.[21]

If socialism was never achieved at the peak of the Chávez era, then it is far more difficult to argue that socialism exists in Venezuela today. While there may have been openings to struggle for socialism within the Bolivarian process during the Chávez era, Maduro has reversed this process and become an obstacle to the struggle for liberation.

However, the fact that Venezuela has remained a capitalist country has certainly not protected the country from US aggression. The US state saw Chávez and the Bolivarian process as a threat, a threat that needed to be dealt with. Preceding the Chávez era, the United States had close relations with Venezuela, one of its major oil suppliers. But Chávez quickly became an adversary of the US following several acts deemed unacceptable to Washington. These included Chávez's renationalization of the nation's oil production, Venezuela's role in the defeat of the Free Trade Agreement of the Americas (a trade agreement pushed by the US that was aimed at extending the terms of NAFTA throughout North and South America, effectively deepening US economic, political, and military dominance in the region), and the creation of South-South regional integration agreements as alternatives to US-sponsored and -dominated free trade agreements. Further, more broadly speaking, the US was displeased with Venezuela's radical redistribution programs and anti-imperialist rhetoric and that it was distancing itself from the US's sphere of influence.

Maduro has largely abandoned Chávez's explicitly anti-imperialist and redistributionist policies but has nonetheless drawn the ire of the US for strengthening Venezuela's ties with US adversaries, namely Iran, Russia, and China. Maduro has chosen to side with one imperialist bloc (particularly China and Russia) against another, an unforgivable act in the eyes of the US state. US interference in Venezuelan affairs has the explicit goal of installing a head of state more compliant to US interests.

Since the early years of the Bolivarian process, the US has taken measures to undermine the Bolivarian project and destabilize the economy, and in several cases it launched efforts to overthrow both Chávez and Maduro. In 2002, the US, in collaboration with the Venezuelan business class, attempted a coup to overthrow Chávez. He was removed from office for forty-seven hours, before being reinstated by mass popular mobilizations. From late 2002 to early 2003, the US supported an oil lockout to bring oil production to a halt with the stated goal of forcing Chávez to resign. In 2014, the US backed the Venezuelan right-wing again in violent street protests called the *guarimbas*, demanding la salida, or the "exit," of Maduro. The US, again in collaboration with the sections of the Venezuelan right wing, attempted yet another coup in January 2019, when Juan Guaidó unconstitutionally declared himself president of Venezuela. After the January coup failed to overthrow Maduro, Guaidó tried again in April of 2019 but was thwarted once more. Of all these efforts to undermine the Bolivarian process—and the list above is by no means exhaustive—the most relevant to understanding the current crisis in Venezuela are the US-imposed sanctions, which began in 2014 and are still in place today.

Although the crisis in Venezuela precedes US sanctions, the sanctions have exacerbated already dire conditions and have caused untold pain and misery for hundreds of thousands of Venezuelans. The Venezuela Defense of Human Rights and Civil Society Act, passed under Barack Obama in December of 2014, imposed targeted sanctions on the country, including visa restrictions on various Venezuelan officials and their family members. Just a few months later, on March 9, 2015, Obama signed an executive order declaring Venezuela an "unusual and extraordinary threat to the national security of the United States" and expanded the sanctions further. This executive order, which was the ostensible justification for Obama's second round of sanctions, set the stage for the sanctions that were to come under Donald Trump. Then, as one of Obama's last acts as president, in January of 2017, he extended the sanctions on Venezuela yet again.

Picking up where Obama left off, Trump in his first month of taking office renewed and expanded the sanctions implemented under the remit of Obama's earlier executive order. Over the course of Trump's first presidency, his administration continued to expand and deepen the sanctions on the Venezuelan government. Most notably was Executive Order 13884, which froze all Venezuelan government assets in the United States and banned Americans from doing business with the Venezuelan government.

The illegal economic sanctions have imposed a litany of debilitating penalties on the Venezuelan government, driving the Venezuelan economy into even deeper problems than it was already in.* Under Trump's sanctions, US institutions and citizens were prohibited from trading in Venezuelan debt. All government assets were frozen. The country was prevented from restructuring its foreign debt or payment schedules. Payments sent by countries participating in its program for preferential payment of oil were blocked. The sale of billions of dollars in trade credits were banned.[22] Sanctions also closed off Venezuela to its most important oil market, the US, and confiscated properties abroad, like the US-based Citgo, which the state depended on for sources of income. These are but a few of the actions taken against Venezuela.

The August 2017 sanctions critically impacted Venezuela's oil production, causing a loss of $6 billion in revenue in just 2018 alone.[23] This figure is important because virtually every necessity (food, medicine, clean water, electricity, transportation, etc.) is funded through oil export revenue.[24] In the years since, the impact of the sanctions has continued, deepened, and compounded. Sanctions have frozen $17 billion worth of the country's assets and were expected to cost the country around $11 billion in export losses in 2019.[25] In other words, the sanctions are costing Venezuelans $30 million a day.

---

* The sanctions on Venezuela are illegal under US and international law. Domestically, the US government justified the sanctions by declaring a "national emergency" and labeling Venezuela an "extraordinary threat"—claims that are factually baseless, making the sanctions incompatible with US legal requirements under the National Emergencies Act. The sanctions constitute collective punishment, prohibited by the Geneva and Hague Conventions, due to their severe impact on civilians—including tens of thousands of deaths and widespread deprivation. The sanctions also violate the OAS Charter, which bars coercive economic measures intended to force political change in sovereign states.

The Washington, DC–based Center for Economic and Policy Research published a 2019 report detailing the effects of US sanctions on Venezuela.[26] The authors, economists Mark Weisbrot and Jeffrey Sachs, reported that "in the week of March 15th, US imports of Venezuelan oil fell to zero for the first time, and they remained at zero for two weeks." Oil export revenues in 2019 were projected to fall by an unprecedented 67.2 percent from 2018 because of the tightening sanctions. The authors also found that between 2017 and 2018 alone, the sanctions killed an estimated 40,000 Venezuelans and plunged many more into precarity. Over 300,000 people were put at risk because of the lack of medicine and health care, including 80,000 HIV-positive Venezuelans who have gone without antiretroviral drugs for years now. Additionally, obtaining needed cardiovascular medicine or insulin is a challenge for the 16,000 Venezuelans who need dialysis, the 4 million with diabetes and hypertension, and the 16,000 people who have cancer.[27]

The UN Human Rights Council adopted a resolution denouncing the US sanctions, and one of its human rights experts, Idriss Jazairy, said that "the use of sanctions by outside powers to overthrow an elected government is in violation of all norms of international law."[28] One UN rapporteur called the sanctions "economic warfare" and argued that they constitute crimes against humanity under international law.[29] The strategy of the US and the domestic right-wing opposition seems to be, to use the words of Richard Nixon, "to make the economy scream."

Despite the harm that the sanctions have wrought in Venezuela, and the various ways in which the sanctions have exacerbated and compounded the crisis, they are only a part of the picture of the crisis. It bears reiterating that the crisis began before the sanctions were imposed, which means that fully understanding the crisis and its origins requires analyzing another major component: the economic mismanagement and neoliberal program of the increasingly authoritarian Maduro government.

While the national and international opposition have not succeeded in taking political power in Venezuela, it has, to a large extent, managed to get the Maduro government to legislate and defend policies that Chavismo had long opposed. Venezuelan economist Luis Salas writes,

> There is not much difference between the economic program of the [right-wing] opposition and that of the [Maduro] Government. . . . The only difference with the opposition is that the Government wants to reach agreements with the Russians, the Chinese or the Turks; and the opposition, with the Americans and Europeans. They are capitalist alliances, but with different partners.[30]

This can be seen clearly in how the Maduro administration responded to the end of the commodity boom. In a situation of newly austere state revenues, the question stood as to who would pay for the crisis: workers or capital. Almost without exception, Maduro chose the working class, the sector that supported the Bolivarian process. Despite maintaining the socialist and anti-imperialist rhetoric of Chávez, Maduro carried out a regression and reversal of many of the most popular aspects of the Bolivarian project. As Roberto López argues later in this book,

> [T]he inauguration of Nicolás Maduro as president in 2013, meant the almost total abandonment of the anti-neoliberal program, and the return of the same economic policies implemented in the last decade of the twentieth century. Maduro maintained the same radical discourse as his predecessor and presented his government as a genuinely "workerist" and "socialist" one, which had the backing of the ruling class. However, in office, he has implemented a real change of economic course, opening the doors to neoliberal policies, in a framework of growing authoritarianism. The reality of the Venezuelan economy more than eight years into Maduro's rule ranks as the worst performance in the world.

This book explores in depth the many ways in which the Maduro government responded to the end of the commodity boom and the many ways that Maduro has contributed to the crisis through antiworker, neoliberal programs and increasingly authoritarian measures. For the purposes of this introduction, we will briefly discuss eight of them.

First is the Arco Minero project. In 2016, the Maduro administration opened the Orinoco Mining Arc for mineral exploitation. This territory, which makes up over 12 percent of the country's area, is a repository of minerals such as gold, oil, gas, bauxite, and coltan and is the country's principal source of fresh water. For the project, Maduro invited 150 multinational corporations from around the world, including the US, China, Canada, and Russia, to bid for concessions.[31] Extremely favorable conditions were offered to multinationals to exploit Venezuela's mineral resources. This massive privatization of the nation's extractive industries was an abandonment and reversal of Chávez's strategy of state control of resources and the socialization of its profits. Many of the multinational corporations that Maduro offered favorable contracts to were corporations that Chávez had excluded from the country years before. In fact, the first offer was made to Barrick Gold Corporation, a giant Canadian gold-mining corporation that Chávez had kicked out of the country a decade prior.[32] In 2011, when Chávez nationalized the mines, Barrick demanded hundreds of millions of dollars in compensation. To lure Barrick back into the country, Maduro not only agreed to pay this "debt" but also offered the corporation a ten-year tax holiday and pledged to develop the regional infrastructure at the state's expense.[33] Scholar Mike Gonzalez accurately describes the project as "colonialism by invitation."[34]

The project has been an environmental and social disaster, as it has displaced populations (particularly Indigenous communities), poisoned rivers and land, destroyed mountain ecologies, and disrupted the fragile ecosystem of the rainforests. The project was promoted as a solution to the country's declining GDP and depleted foreign currency reserves. Maduro was correct that something had to be done, but this solution was an abandonment of national sovereignty and a return to the same neoliberal, neocolonial arrangements that social movements, workers' movements, Chávez, and the Bolivarian process had been fighting against for decades. Venezuela was on the cutting edge of antineoliberalism in the region at the end of the century, and the Arco Minero is a major reversal and setback to that project. In fact, a similar plan was rejected by Chávez years before because of environmental concerns and in recognition of Indigenous communities' human and territorial rights.[35]

The 2021 Organic Law for Special Economic Zones (SEZs) is another important example of Maduro's reversals. This law was endorsed by both Maduro and the Venezuelan right-wing opposition, including Fedecámaras (Venezuelan Federation of Chambers of Commerce and Production), one of the principal organizers of the 2002 coup that temporarily overthrew Chávez. This SEZ law grants power to the president to designate spaces where existing fiscal, financial, commercial, labor, and environmental laws will not apply. This opened the country up to foreign investment by giving large tax breaks to corporations, giving favorable access to natural resources, relaxing environmental regulations, and weakening labor rights. Venezuela now has the cheapest labor force in the world.

The 2018 Memorandum 2792, which abolishes the right to strike, is a third example. The memorandum permits employers to unilaterally modify labor conditions and fire workers at their discretion. With it, Maduro dismissed *all* the collective bargaining agreements in the country, eliminating much of what had been achieved under Chávez. The memorandum also undermines virtually all the labor rights enshrined in the constitution and in the Organic Law of Labor, Work and Workers (LOTTT) agreement of 2012. Labor leader Orlando Chirino stated that no other government anywhere in the world has produced a legal instrument as reactionary and antiworker in the last thirty years as Memorandum 2792.[36] And when dozens of labor leaders criticized the memorandum, they were arrested. Essentially, all the legal gains achieved by workers through years of struggle were erased with the stroke of Maduro's pen.

Fourth is the 2020 Anti-Blockade Law, which effectively suspends the constitution and grants extra-constitutional authority to the executive branch for steering the economy. The law allows the president to relax and suspend legal and constitutional regulations and norms and for deals between the government and private capital to be carried out behind closed doors, without any public knowledge of the agreements, meaning unsavory backroom deals with capital are brokered without any legal or constitutional controls. This law has subsequently been used to open up the country to plunder by corporations, to grant transnational corporations enormous incentives to invest in the country, and to expand the extractivist and accumulation rentier model, which is a major factor in the crisis. It is also worth mentioning that while Maduro pursued these actions, the US sanctions—largely for political and geopolitical motives—paradoxically hindered Venezuela's integration into the global capitalist market. In doing so, the US, by imposing these sanctions, has missed out on the opportunity to take advantage of, and fully capitalize on, these new advantageous conditions provided by Maduro's new laws opening up Venezuela for the exploitation of its resources and cheap labor.

Fifth is Maduro's refusal to maintain a living wage policy. As mentioned before, under Chávez the minimum wage pushed above 300 USD a month, while today it hovers between $2 and $3 dollars a month. Venezuela went from having the highest minimum wage in Latin America to the lowest in less than a decade. For many workers their wages do not even cover the cost of commuting to their workplaces. A corollary of low wages is a reduction in domestic consumption, which further contributes to a depressed economy. Part of the reason over seven million Venezuelans fled the country was to get work abroad in order to send remittances back to Venezuela, since one can simply not survive on minimum wage alone. Maduro's minimum wage policy is in violation of Article 91 of the 1999 Chavista constitution, which guarantees that every worker has the right to a salary sufficient to cover basic material, social, and intellectual needs for themselves and their family. The constitution states that the minimum wage is to be adjusted annually using the basic market basket as a reference.* Maduro has not raised the minimum wage in years. Not only is the minimum wage below what is needed to provide a living income, but the average salary is also insufficient for basic survival.

The next policy to consider is the 2017 Constitutional Law Against Hate, which established prison sentences of up to twenty years for persons convicted of "hate speech" per its stipulations. The law was ostensibly passed to curb speech that "incites hatred" against any person or group on social media. But in practice, it makes it more difficult for journalists, media outlets, labor organizers, activists, political parties, and civil society leaders to be critical of the government. This law has been used to repress dissent, including imprisoning activists and labor leaders for criticizing actions of the government, as in the case of Dario Salcedo. Salcedo, a labor leader who was a worker at the

---

* The basic basket includes the cost of the amount of foodstuffs that is considered necessary to keep a person healthy and the cost of other necessities, such as housing and transportation.

Socialist Institute of Fisheries and Aquaculture (INSOPESCA), sent a tweet critiquing the privileges enjoyed by Maduro's minister of Fisheries and Aquaculture, Dante Rivas, in contrast to the precarious salaries and benefits of the workers. Later that day he sent a voice message on WhatsApp to the director of human resources at INOPESCA venting about the drastic increase in the cost of the food package to a value that is more than three months of wages for a worker making minimum wage. A few weeks later, Maduro's criminal investigation police raided his home, seized his laptop and cell phones, and arrested him. He was subsequently charged under Article 20 of the Law Against Hatred with the crime of promoting and inciting hatred.[37]

The gains during the Chávez era were not simply a result of reforms handed down from Chávez, but rather products of the complex and often contradictory relationship between the regime and massive popular mobilizations from below. Resistance and bottom-up struggle were essential in deepening and radicalizing the Bolivarian process. In his attempts to stifle these mobilizations, Maduro weakened perhaps the most important component driving the advances made during the early years of the revolutionary process. Repression—to say nothing of the Law Against Hate alone—cannot explain the recent waning of popular forces, but it has certainly contributed to the demobilization and weakening of the organizational capacities of the popular sectors.

Seventh is the high levels of corruption that long preceded Maduro but have only worsened during his time in power. But when we talk about corruption in Venezuela, we are not simply referring to the abuse of power for the personal benefit or enrichment of individuals in government positions, of state officials across various institutions and agencies, or of those who head public companies and manage project execution. We are speaking of a pattern of capital accumulation by a social caste and a bureaucracy that thrive on the plunder of resources and exploit state transactions to the detriment of the people. It is not a matter of individual corruption alone but rather a mega-corruption that exists as a system and a web of complicities, sustained and enabled by the monopolization of power.

Corruption in Venezuela takes many forms, including bribes and kickbacks, embezzlement and fraud, overbilling, smuggling, illicit capital flight, nepotism and influence peddling, dispossession and the direct appropriation or exploitation of public and private property under the protection of power and judicial corruption. But at its core, corruption is intrinsically tied to the rentier capitalism that has characterized Venezuela both before and after the Bolivarian process, which failed to transform this system and was instead engulfed and assimilated by it. Oil rentierism has turned the Venezuelan state into a piñata, where, alongside individual and group ambitions, the political-military caste must distribute resources, privileges, and financial benefits to secure loyalty and maintain its hold on power.

This dynamic creates a subjective phenomenon—a "consciousness," culture, or habit—that perpetuates itself through clientelism, authoritarian leadership, state coercion of the working class, and the persistence of poverty and inequality. It is further reinforced by the inefficiency of institutional mechanisms to address problems, the lack of transparency that makes public and citizen oversight impossible, and the weakness of independent organization among marginalized social groups. Corruption, coupled with prevailing impunity—where reporting wrongdoing can result in repression—further corrodes political life, leading to significant losses that undermine economic and social development. While corruption stems from an exploitative, class-based economic system, it simultaneously magnifies its worst effects, deepening the hardships faced by society as a whole.

Eighth is Maduro's policy of privatization, which more closely resembles the policies of the Fourth Republic (the era that preceded Chávez) than those of Chávez. The Maduro government privatized major branches of industry, including oil, iron, aluminum, gold and diamonds, and petrol distribution, despite the fact that the last one, petrol distribution, is a function reserved to the state by law. Many of Maduro's privatizations targeted the very same industries that Chávez had previously nationalized, in effect carrying out a reverse appropriation that restored former state-owned assets to capitalist ownership. Ironically,

US sanctions have impeded this process to some extent by restricting the investment of new capital and new businesses to varying degrees.

All of which should make clear that the crisis taking place in Venezuela is not the result of socialism—the collective and democratic control of the means of production—nor of attempts to achieve socialism. Rather, it is a crisis produced by pursuing a strategy of conceding to powerful sectors of the capitalist class *instead of* directly confronting them. The crisis, which had begun before US sanctions, has been profoundly exacerbated by their imposition. In trying to explain the crisis, we can't ignore these crippling sanctions, the sharp decline in oil prices, or the range of economic and political moves by Maduro that have fueled the crisis. Nor should the left defend any of these incendiary policies as necessary responses to external factors like US aggression or the collapse of key commodity prices. There was another path not pursued, and rather than confront the domestic capitalist class in any serious way, rather than push for any meaningful transformation of social property relations, rather than challenge the prerogatives of transnational capital, rather than break with an extractivist strategy for growth and its dependence on the export of minerals and hydrocarbons, the Maduro government has made the working class pay for the crisis

Such a confrontation with the capitalist class could not be pursued purely as a political, legal decision taken by a Maduro or even a Chávez. A serious confrontation capable of meaningfully challenging social property relations would depend on the kind of radical massive popular mobilization from below that deepened the Bolivarian process during the Chávez era. This would require, on the governmental level, making decisions to unlock, support, and rely upon that radical mobilization from below and allowing it to contest, transform, and attack capitalist social relations and the regime of private property. It is not simply the decisions of governments that could confront the capitalist class, but rather that the decisions of government that could allow the forces from below to carry on that confrontation. This more revolutionary change could be supplemented, expanded, and defended through the actions of a left government like Chávez's, but the principal actor has to flow through extra-parliamentary channels, through powerful movements from below capable of implementing democratic workers' power.

One specific example is the militant working-class response to the oil lockout of 2002. This lockout, orchestrated by PDVSA executives, Fedecámaras, and the old Confederation of Workers of Venezuela (CTV) bureaucracy, sought to economically cripple the Chávez government by halting oil production and paralyzing the industry. In response, oil workers mobilized to take over production and restart operations at various small- and medium-sized enterprises, aiming to prevent closures and secure unpaid wages. Recognizing the importance of this worker-led mobilization, Chávez supported and encouraged the growing wave of worker organization and began to promote new models of comanagement. The oil workers' collective action, and Chávez's support of these actions, was central in defeating the right-wing opposition's efforts to undermine Chávez.

Contrast this with Maduro's response to another right-wing attempt to destabilize the government in 2014. In February of that year, a wave of violent right-wing protests known as the *guarimbas* erupted. Though different in some respects, these protests were similar to the 2002–2003 oil lockout in that they aimed to overthrow the president. The protesters targeted state-run health clinics, burned buses, and even decapitated motorcyclists. Maduro's approach to resolving the guarimba violence was to negotiate with the business elite. In a bid to reconcile with sectors of the traditional capitalist class, these so-called peace negotiations brought Maduro to the table with business leaders and powerful private capitalists, including Fedecámaras—an organization that had played a key role in the failed 2002 coup against Chávez. Notably absent from these negotiations were representatives of the working class and popular sectors, leaving only the right-wing voices at the table.

Another example is Maduro's response to a proposal by the National Network of Comuneros. In an effort to address the severe crisis of food shortages, malnutrition, and hunger, the National Network of Comuneros proposed creating a national communal enterprise for the production and distribution of food. The plan called for government investment in the communes to produce and distribute food locally, ensuring that affordable provisions reached those in need. This initiative aimed to reduce reliance on foreign imports, diversify the economy to make it less vulnerable to global market fluctuations, and expand the communes—arguably the country's most democratic institutions.

However, Maduro rejected the proposal in favor of establishing Local Committees for Food Distribution and Production (CLAPs). Despite the term *production* in their name, all food distributed through CLAPs is imported. This includes products from major capitalist companies, such as Polar, but also products of dubious origin, quality, and sanitary conditions, which were imported without bidding processes and involved fraud and overbilling. Unlike the democratic decision-making processes of the communes, CLAPs are government-controlled entities overseen by local United Socialist Party of Venezuela (PSUV) officials, allowing for tighter central control. This system enables officials to dictate actions, whereas decisions within the communes are made collectively in citizens' assemblies. Faced with a choice between continuing to provide preferential dollars and subsidies to the business class for food imports or investing in the communes—the cornerstone of the Bolivarian process—Maduro opted for the former.

Unfortunately, some sections of the left have struggled to adequately grapple with the complexities of the Maduro regime and its impact on Venezuela, which often takes the form of dismissing or ignoring the realities on the ground. There are two common errors on the left that have shaped recent responses to Venezuela's crisis. The first is the tendency to unwittingly lend credibility to a regime that uses the language of socialism to obscure its own oppressive and antiworker practices. The second is the overreliance on a framework that views all criticism of Maduro through the lens of US imperialism, as if acknowledging the regime's rightward turn undermines opposition to imperialism itself. While these errors are deeply problematic, they often stem from an instinctive opposition to US hegemony—a reaction that, while understandable in its intentions, can sometimes cloud judgment. By failing to reckon with the realities of Venezuela's crisis, such positions inadvertently sideline the struggles of the Venezuelan people, who are fighting both the consequences of the Maduro government and the suffocating sanctions imposed by the United States.

In the summer of 2021, the largest socialist organization in the history of the United States took one of these missteps when they sent a delegation to Venezuela to attend the Congreso Bicentenario de los Pueblos (Bicentennial Congress of the Peoples of the World). The International Committee of the Democratic Socialists of America (DSA) described its eight-person delegation as part of its "international solidarity front." This congress was explicitly organized by President Nicolás Maduro to give a façade of national and international support for his government. On the government's web page, it says that the purpose of this congress was to "express support for the Bolivarian Revolution."

The DSA delegation met with Maduro and publicly expressed its support for his government and for what it considered to be the "construction of a socialist project." One member of the DSA International Committee wrote, "How can we properly be in solidarity with [workers]? In the case of Venezuela, the answer is the PSUV, the largest party in Venezuela."[38] Delegations such as these give legitimacy to President Maduro from the left, while Maduro represses the domestic left and continues to implement capitalist policies in the country. In practice this delegation serves to give solidarity with a capitalist government instead of solidarity with the Venezuelan people, who are suffering the rollback of gains won during the Chávez era, who are dealing with increased political repression and the dismantling of their unions and organs for worker militancy, and, most importantly, who are struggling against the consequences of Maduro's political choices and strategy and the stifling sanctions regime imposed by the US. Others on the left, like Max Blumenthal from the "independent news website" *The Grayzone*, and Ben Norton from the site *Geopolitical Economy Report* (formerly *Multipolarista*), deny the humanitarian crisis and say that it is only propaganda from the US State Department.[39] These types of perspectives and errors are by no means limited to organizations and outlets like the DSA, *The Grayzone*, and *Geopolitical Economy Report* but reflect much broader patterns of analysis on the left and illustrate how they manifest in practice as well as in political consequences.

This book aims to serve as a corrective to both mainstream perspectives of the crisis, which blame it on currently existing socialism or attempts to build socialism, and some left perspectives that at best ignore the role of the Maduro government and at worst defend and justify its antiworker, neoliberal program. Each chapter in the book was written by Venezuelan Marxists, socialists, or anticapitalists. Some contributors served in Chávez's cabinet and have now become critics of the Maduro government. Bringing these voices to an English-speaking audience will allow readers to engage with the current debates and perspectives of the Venezuelan left.

Though the chapters in the book represent different perspectives and highlight important debates, two common themes are apparent. One is that the international left must oppose the sanctions imposed on Venezuela, which have significantly curtailed Venezuela's international trade and severely affected national revenue, and consequently caused untold pain and misery for hundreds of thousands of Venezuelans. The second common theme is that to stand in solidarity with Venezuelans and their struggle for liberation, the left cannot stop at just opposing sanctions. Maduro has proven to be more of an obstacle to socialism than a vehicle for its implementation. The international left should stand in solidarity with the Venezuelan people, not with a corrupt and repressive capitalist government, even if it cloaks itself in socialist and anti-imperialist rhetoric. Participating in events like the Congreso Bicentenario de los Pueblos or unconditionally supporting Maduro more broadly undermines our ability to support and stand in solidarity with genuine worki36ng-class movements in Venezuela, which are organizing against both US imperialism and Maduro's authoritarian rule and antiworker neoliberal economic program. The left should fight against neoliberal economic programs regardless of whether the regime carrying it out uses capitalist, socialist, or anti-imperialist rhetoric.

Organization of Book

This book brings together some of the most important Marxist, socialist, and anticapitalist thinkers in Venezuela, representing a range of left political traditions and organizations. Through its translation, it introduces the dynamic and ongoing debates among Venezuelan socialists to an Anglophone audience. While there is broad agreement among the authors on the right-wing character of the Maduro regime, there are notable divergences on how to characterize the Chávez government that preceded it and the factors that shaped Maduro's neoliberal, antiworker policies today. Gonzalo Gómez, Carlos Carcione, and Juan García, for example, were founding members of Marea Socialista, a socialist organization that critically supported Chávez and saw openings within the Bolivarian process to push for revolutionary socialism. During their time in the PSUV, Marea maintained its own independent press and actions and promoted a radical revolutionary current within Chavismo, alongside other critical sectors of the left. Eventually, Marea split with the PSUV in 2015, citing political and methodological divergences with the PSUV's leadership, its direction under Maduro, and the constant exclusion and repression Marea experienced within the party. The group criticized the PSUV's authoritarian tendencies, corruption, and deviation from the revolutionary principles of grassroots democracy and worker empowerment. By 2015 Marea believed that the opening to struggle for socialism within the PSUV had closed.

Simón Rodríquez and Omar Vásquez were prominent members of the Socialism and Freedom Party (PSL), a socialist organization that remained independent of the PSUV throughout the Chávez (and subsequent Maduro) era and saw the Bolivarian process as fraught from the start. The PSL from the beginning had the perspective that socialists should maintain independence from the Chávez/Maduro governments. The PSL and Marea Socialista came from the same previous political organization: the Party of Revolution and Socialism (PRS), which was the result of the convergence of several Trotskyist groups after the 2002 coup. Together, they created the C-CURA (Classist, Revolutionary, and Autonomous Union Current), led by Orlando Chirino and Stalin Pérez, which by 2006 had become the main tendency in the National Workers' Union. This name was retained by the tendency led by Chirino (who would later be one of the founding members of the PSL) when Marea parted ways due to differing tactics regarding Chávez's government and the PSUV and different approaches to influencing Chavista workers and the popular movement.

A third prominent organization represented in this book is the Citizen Platform for the Defense of the Constitution. The group is a collective composed of socialists from different political traditions, former Chavista officials, and academics and activists whose central organizing tenet is upholding the principles of the 1999 Chavista constitution. Members of the Platform agree on the neoliberal, antiworker character of Maduro but fall on different sides of the debate about the extent to which there is continuity and rupture from the Fourth Republic to Chávez to Maduro. Oly Millán, a prominent left-wing economist and former Chávez minister of Popular Economy; Gustavo Márquez, former president of the party Movement for Socialism in the 1990s and former Chávez minister of Industry and Commerce; Juan García, founding member of Marea Socialista and the left-wing news website *Aporrea*; Ana Viloria, longtime political activist and founder of *Aporrea*; and Roberto López, former guerilla, former member of both Proyecto Nuestra América and Marea, and founder of the National Union of Workers–Zulia, are all members of the Platform.

Emiliano Terán is the only contributor, other than the editor, who is not a member, nor has he ever been a member, of any of these three formations. Terán is a researcher at the Center for Development Studies, a member of the Observatory of Political Ecology in Venezuela, and one of the foremost experts on extractivism and the Arco Minero in Venezuela.

In the debate about continuity or rupture, those that emphasize the continuities (Milan, Rodríguez, Vázquez, and Márquez) tend to stress Chávez's and Maduro's failure to depart from a rentier model of capital accumulation and their failure to alter the inherent exploitation of capitalist social relations. Rentier economies are economic systems where a country or countries rely heavily on income derived from the extraction and export of natural resources, rather than from productive activities like manufacturing or agriculture. In Venezuela, this model manifests through its dependence on oil revenues. This reliance has led to economic vulnerabilities, such as exposure to fluctuating global oil prices, underinvestment in other sectors, and a centralized state that allocates wealth. This model created a clientelistic system where political elites use resource wealth to maintain political loyalty through patronage and subsidies. Chávez's and Maduro's failure to depart from this model hindered efforts to foster self-sufficiency and structural transformation. These critiques suggest that Venezuela's reliance on rents from an oil industry heavily penetrated by US, European, and Chinese capitals stymied the deeper economic and political changes promised by the Bolivarian process, while shaping processes such as the emergence of a new bourgeois sector linked to the Chavista state apparatus.

Others (García, Viloria, López, Carcione, and Gómez), while recognizing the continuation of the rentier model and capitalist relations of production, place their emphasis on the drastic ruptures, or breaks, that Chávez made with the previous governments and that Maduro made from Chavismo. The Chávez administration's break from the Fourth Republic can be seen in its antineoliberalism, its progressivism, and its expansion of worker rights and participatory democracy. This perspective then argues that the Maduro regime represents another break, in which Maduro abandoned all the progressive aspects of Chávez and reversed virtually all the gains that were won during the Chávez period. This remains a live debate and one that this book is meant to give insights into, rather than answer it definitively.

The book is divided into two parts. Part 1 (covering chapters 1 to 4) broadly discusses the continuities and ruptures between the Fourth Republic, the Chávez era, and the Maduro era. Chapter 1 analyzes the ruptures and continuities between the Fourth Republic, the Chávez era, and the Maduro era as they relate to each period's distinct political model. Gustavo Márquez examines how each of these models should be characterized. In Márquez's analysis of these different political models, he discusses the causes and consequences of the downward trajectory of the revolutionary project. Chapter 2 discusses the economic transitions and shifts from the Fourth Republic through the Chávez era to the Maduro era. Oly Millán argues that despite many of the changes that Chávez was able to achieve, the Bolivarian process was unable to overcome its dependence on an extractivist model centered around oil. In fact, during the Bolivarian process, rent-seeking was consolidated, so despite a discourse around national sovereignty, the country became more dependent on extractivism and more vulnerable to powerful international capital. Chapter 3 identifies two major ruptures. The first is when Chávez broke with the Fourth Republic's neoliberalism, and Roberto López provides an analysis of Chávez's nationalization policies, expansion of social programs, construction of the Constituent Assembly, and creation of regional political and economic integration initiatives, such as the Bolivarian Alliance for the Peoples of Our America and the Community of Latin American and Caribbean States. The second rupture López addresses is Maduro's break from, and reversal of, Chávez's antineoliberal policies. This chapter concludes with a discussion of the various ways Maduro oversaw the return to the neoliberalism of the Fourth Republic. Chapter 4 analyzes the changes and continuities in the labor movement during the era of the Bolivarian process. In this chapter, López explores the crisis and fall of the Confederation of Workers of Venezuela and the birth and development of Venezuela's National Workers' Union, and later, the Bolivarian Workers' Union. This chapter also gives a critical analysis of the adoption of new labor legislation during the Chávez era and the reversal of much of this legislation under Maduro.

Part 2 (chapters 5 to 11) discusses specific aspects of the Venezuelan crisis today and the struggles surrounding them. Chapter 5 examines the role that sanctions play in the crisis today. Omar Vázquez Heredia argues that the criminal sanctions imposed by the United States have exacerbated the dire economic crisis in Venezuela and have impeded the prospects and scale of its recovery. Heredia also offers a critical analysis of how the Maduro government has responded to the sanctions. Chapter 6 analyzes the Maduro administration's poor economic management and its role in the economic crisis in Venezuela. Gonzalo Gómez discusses a variety of different economic policies and strategies that characterize the Maduro era, including embezzlement, corruption, capital flight, collaboration with the capitalist class, prioritization of paying the illegitimate foreign debt, and bureaucratization. Chapter 7 discusses Maduro's authoritarian turn. Carlos Carcione analyzes the antidemocratic actions and policies carried out against liberal bourgeois democratic norms. Critically, these attacks were waged against the very protagonistic and participatory democracy that defined the Chávez era of the Bolivarian process.* In chapter 8, Emiliano Terán analyzes extractivism in the Orinoco Belt—specifically the Minero project. This chapter gives an in-depth analysis of the origins of the Arco Minero projects up until today. Terán explores the ways in which the project has been an environmental and social disaster, as it has displaced populations, poisoned rivers and land, destroyed mountain ecologies, and disrupted the fragile ecosystem of the rainforests.

Chapter 9 discusses human rights violations committed by the Maduro regime. The centerpiece of this chapter is Ana Sofia Viloria and Juan García's critical analysis of several reports published by various human rights organizations, specifically the most recent International Criminal Court's report on Venezuela. Simón Rodríguez provides further discussion on salaries, minimum wage, and fiscal policy under the Maduro administration in chapter 10. Rodríguez analyzes salary deterioration under the Maduro regime and examines the unconstitutional salary and wage policies that have resulted in starvation wages. Chapter 10 also discusses the Essequibo conflict with Guyana. Rodríquez begins this chapter with a history of the conflict and concludes by arguing that conflict is alien to the needs of the peoples and the working classes of Venezuela and Guyana and that the Venezuelan and Guyanese states both pose as nationalists and invoke sovereignty while competing to hand over natural resources to transnational corporations. The book concludes with a perspective piece written by Gonzalo Gómez, which ties together the central themes of the book.

Overall, the chapters in this book present the debates and perspectives of important and vibrant socialist voices within Venezuela that are seldom heard. Collectively, these chapters make a positive case for standing in solidarity with Venezuelan worker struggles against both imperial aggression and oppressive regimes.

---

* Protagonistic democracy refers to a political framework championed during the Bolivarian Revolution under Chávez, emphasizing direct participation of citizens in governance and decision-making processes. The goal was to move beyond representative democracy by empowering people, particularly workers, marginalized communities, and grassroots organizations, to actively engage in shaping policies and managing resources.

PART 1

Continuities and Ruptures in the Bolivarian Process

CHAPTER ONE

Continuities and Ruptures in the Bolivarian Process

Gustavo Márquez Marín

Ideological and Programmatic Foundations

The ideological foundation of the Bolivarian project did not originate from discussions within the Patriotic Pole, the electoral coalition that supported Chávez in 1998.[1] It was Hugo Chávez himself who summarized the ideological framework, encompassing various leftist currents and outlining the programmatic direction of the government. Initially, Chávez's discourse centered on three significant historical figures: Simón Bolívar, and his republican, nationalist, and anti-imperialist thought; Simón Rodríguez, embodying educational, republican, and civic principles; and Ezequiel Zamora, who advocated for justice, anti-oligarchic values, and democracy. These three aspects of nineteenth-century Venezuelan emancipation, symbolically portrayed as the "tree of the three roots," formed the basis of the Bolivarian movement. Additionally, the ideology and practices of revolutionary Christian movements played a role, as did the long-standing tradition of the left's struggle for national liberation and socialism.

The economic program of the Bolivarian project was structured around the five imbalances of the Venezuelan capitalist crisis, as outlined in the Economic and Social Development Plan of the Nation 2001–2007. This plan aimed to establish a model of sustainable and inclusive development with various objectives. These goals included addressing social inequality and fostering human development, democratizing both the market and capital through the promotion of the social economy. Economically, the plan sought to stimulate self-sustaining economic growth through diversification of productive sectors and international competitiveness. On the political front, it aimed to encourage citizen participation, strengthen social stability, decentralize decision-making at the national and regional levels, and create a new institutional and legal framework to support participatory and protagonistic democracy. In terms of territorial development, the plan envisioned a shift in settlement patterns, production methods, investment strategies, distribution mechanisms, and revenue collection over the medium and long term. Additionally, it emphasized the incorporation of environmental considerations into the overall development strategy. Lastly, on the international stage, the plan aimed to achieve a more balanced global presence and promote greater integration among Latin American and Caribbean nations toward the formation of a regional community of nations.

Stage 1 (1999–2000): Constituent Process

The initial years of the Bolivarian government were marked by significant economic challenges and immense social pressure. This situation arose as tax revenues sharply declined, primarily due to historically low oil prices, which had plummeted to just seven dollars per barrel. This drop in oil prices was a consequence of the Oil Opening policy implemented by the preceding administration.

In response to the pressing needs of local communities, the government launched Plan Bolívar 2000, leveraging the logistical capabilities of the National Armed Forces.[2] This strategy involved circumventing the bureaucratic inefficiencies of the state apparatus to achieve immediate, tangible outcomes. However, it came at the expense of introducing a form of "military management" into public administration, which created a false dilemma between effectiveness and proper oversight of governance. The frequent practice of bypassing administrative regulations under the pretext of an "emergency" facilitated the misallocation of public resources for clientelistic and questionable purposes. Consequently, there were numerous allegations of corruption associated with the implementation of this emergency plan, with many directed at the newly established revolutionary government.

Given the prevailing fiscal constraints, the government's primary focus was to reverse the adverse effects of the Oil Opening policy, which had led to the decline in crude oil prices and the weakening of the Organization of Petroleum Exporting Countries (OPEC). To achieve this objective, President Chávez spearheaded the convening of the second OPEC summit in Caracas.[3] This initiative, led by President Chávez, proved to be successful. In fact, it marked the beginning of the recovery of oil prices, thereby generating additional revenue for the national treasury.

During this period, the central political endeavor of the revolution was to promote the constituent process, with its most significant achievement being the people's approval of the Constitution of the Bolivarian Republic of Venezuela. This process catalyzed the emergence of a diverse array of social movements, representing an unprecedented expression of various sectors of Venezuelan society. These movements actively participated by presenting their demands and viewpoints, contributing to the creation of a new legal framework that governed the social and political life of the nation. This framework promised to transition from a bourgeois liberal democracy to a more profound, inclusive, participatory, and protagonistic democracy. The constitution encompassed a range of political, economic, social, cultural, and environmental rights, all integrated into a system of citizen guarantees.[4]

The debate between the government, represented by the Patriotic Pole, and the opposition, composed of the traditional parties from the previous Fourth Republic, predominantly revolved around the question of whether it was appropriate to convene a constituent assembly, a concept not explicitly outlined in the existing constitution at that time.[5] This debate was resolved by the Supreme Court of Justice, which mandated the election of a National Constituent Assembly tasked with drafting the new constitutional text. Subsequently, the proposed constitution underwent a consultative referendum in 1999, resulting in its adoption. Once the new constitution was officially promulgated in 2000, Chávez proposed the legitimization of the five public powers established in the new constitution for a new period extending from 2001 to 2006. This marked the conclusion of this stage of democratic validation, the reaffirmation of Chávez's leadership, and the preparation for the second phase of the Bolivarian Revolution. This period heralded optimistic changes aimed at moving away from the bipartisan clientelistic model that was intrinsic to the dependent, extractive, rentier capitalist economy. All of this transpired with the support of a population that, for the first time, began to engage in direct, participatory, and protagonistic democracy through an unprecedented constituent process.

Chávez's national leadership gained strength, and on the international stage, he emerged as a prominent figure in Latin America and the Global South. In the Latin American and Caribbean region, he set the tone for a shift toward left-wing politics and progressivism, championing the right to human development for countries in the Global South. He consistently confronted the neoliberal model embodied in the Free Trade Area of the Americas in various international forums.[6]

To grasp the nature of the Bolivarian Revolution and its dynamics, it is crucial to consider some background information. The political movement that gave rise to this process was a coalition of left-wing parties and groups. They coalesced under the leadership of Hugo Chávez, who had been one of the commanders during the military rebellion of February 4, 1992.[7] His party, the Fifth Republic Movement, had its roots in the MBR-200.[8] This alliance adopted the Bolivarian Alternative Agenda as its program.[9] According to Chávez, this agenda aimed not only at restructuring the state but also at overhauling the entire political system, from its philosophical foundations to its constituent elements and relationships that governed it. Hence, the resort to constituent power was deemed necessary to establish the Fifth Republic.[10]

According to this strategic approach, addressing Venezuela's social crisis, marked by high levels of poverty and marginalization, required more than just political-system transformation. It necessitated a transformation of the economic model while simultaneously addressing the social and environmental crises. The proposal was described as "humanistic, integral, holistic, and ecological." This agenda served as a roadmap for the transition toward regime change, with a primary focus on addressing the most pressing needs of the population and regaining state sovereignty, particularly in the realm of hydrocarbons, to revive an economy suffering from declining oil revenues.

In this context, two critical issues were identified: poverty and denationalization. Consequently, the top priority was to address the substantial social debt left behind by the Fourth Republic, which required resources that were not readily available. To secure these resources, it was necessary to abandon the Oil Opening policy inherited from the prior regime, which had been tailored to the interests of international oil corporations.

Another key aspect of the agenda involved a transformation of the economic model aimed at achieving broader societal equilibrium. This transformation would entail fostering the social economy by promoting the establishment of family businesses, microenterprises, and cooperative units. These initiatives represented a starting point toward the creation of a new diversified, endogenous, and sustainable production model.

In addition to uniting various left-wing factions and presenting a program to win the support of the significant majority marginalized by the Fourth Republic's bipartisan rule, the charismatic figure of Hugo Chávez played a pivotal role. He symbolized a new leadership dedicated to bringing about democratic change, eradicating corruption, and delivering justice to a population that had been impoverished and disillusioned due to the deception and demagoguery of a "political class" that had abandoned them. By raising the banners of Bolívar, Zamora, and Rodríguez, Chávez and the Bolivarians achieved political power, an accomplishment that had eluded the left for over half a century of tireless struggle.

Background

The unexpected announcement made by the social democratic leader (AD), Carlos Andrés Pérez (CAP), who had recently begun his second term in office (1989–93), that he intended to implement the neoliberal economic adjustment "package" designed by the International Monetary Fund was a stark contrast to his earlier campaign promises of a return to the "Great Venezuela," a symbol of his first government during an oil boom (1974–78).[11] This announcement left the people feeling deceived once again. The initial measures of the "CAP package," particularly a hike in public transportation fares, triggered a massive uprising known as the "Caracazo."[12] This uprising escalated into widespread looting in the city of Caracas, which subsequently spread to other parts of the country.

In response to these events, the Pérez government suspended constitutional guarantees and imposed a curfew. Military forces were deployed to the streets, leading to a tragic massacre in Caracas. Official figures reported more than 360 casualties, although some human rights organizations estimated the death toll to be around 2,000. This unprecedented incident severely undermined Pérez's hold on power not long after he assumed office. Consequently, his government became unstable and was unable to fulfill its program. In the end, President Pérez faced embezzlement charges and was replaced by an interim president appointed by Congress.

The events of the Caracazo in 1989 marked the beginning of a prolonged period of political instability that persisted until the late 1990s. During this time, political parties, leadership, and democratic institutions lost credibility and legitimacy, leading to the emergence of an "antipolitical" sentiment among the population. While Carlos Andrés Pérez was still in office, a military uprising occurred on February 4, 1992, involving lower- and middle-ranking members of the armed forces, with Hugo Chávez playing a prominent role. Although this rebellion did not succeed in overthrowing the Pérez government, it inflicted upon it a fatal wound that resulted in his premature exit from power.

Dr. Rafael Caldera, the founder of the Social Christian Party (COPEI), won the subsequent presidential election in 1993.[13] He received support from a coalition of left-wing parties that included the Movement for Socialism, the People's Electoral Movement, the Communist Party of Venezuela, and Convergencia.[14] Caldera's victory was closely linked to his endorsement of the young military insurgents from the February 4, 1992, uprising and his self-critical remarks regarding the Puntofijista democratic system, despite being one of its principal architects.[15] His presidency marked a "transition" from the Fourth to the Fifth Republic.

Notably, the government's decision to release the military rebels, including Chávez, had a significant impact on subsequent events.

Amid the collapse of the Fourth Republic, the leadership of Hugo Chávez and the political emergence of the MBR-200 project became prominent. This political initiative originated from the February 4, 1992, military uprising and later transformed into the Fifth Republic Movement (MVR) through a coalition of civilian and military actors.[16] It aligned itself with the Patriotic Pole, a coalition comprising the major left-wing parties in Venezuela.

Stage 2 (2001–2006): Participatory Democracy, Oil Sovereignty, and Economic Revival

During this phase, the recovery of government revenues commenced as a consequence of shifting from the "open oil" policy to the "complete oil sovereignty" strategy. This resurgence was attributed to the government's assumption of control over the oil industry, which had previously been under the authority of Petroleum of Venezuela (PDVSA), the state oil company of Venezuela, technocrats aligned with the interests of multinational corporations. The increase in oil income translated into an economic recovery, beginning in the first quarter of 2003.

The following graph shows key events in the conflicts that unfolded between the government and the right-wing opposition, which sought to restore its power with support from the US government.[17] Notably, there is a clear connection between the decline in GDP and disruptive political incidents. This linkage is particularly evident between 2002 and the first quarter of 2003, when the economic impact of the April 2002 coup d'état, orchestrated by private media, the business consortium (Fedecámaras), the Venezuelan Workers' Union affiliated with the Democratic Action party and COPEI, the ecclesiastical hierarchy, and the US government was registered.[18] This coup attempt involved officers from the military high command of the armed forces and aimed to install businessperson Pedro Carmona as the president, serving the interests of the business elite.

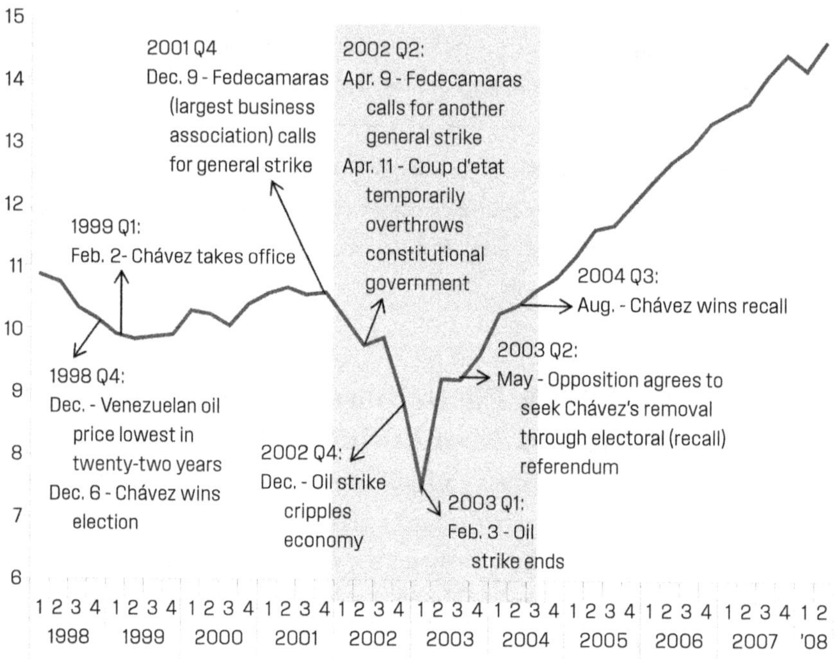

The shaded region indicates the recession and recovery of 2001-2004.

Figure 1.1
Source: Central Bank of Venezuela (BCV)

Following the unsuccessful coup attempt in April 2002, the opposition retaliated within the oil industry when the managerial technocrats associated with foreign oil companies declared a work stoppage.[19] Their objective was to halt hydrocarbon production and exports, with the intention of forcing Hugo Chávez to resign or compelling the military to remove him from office. Although the strike ultimately failed after sixty-two days, it resulted in estimated losses of $20 billion and a twenty-point drop in GDP. In 2004, the opposition made another attempt to oust Chávez from power through a recall referendum, but they were also defeated in that electoral process.[20]

Beginning in the third quarter of 2003, there was an uptick in GDP due to increased production by PDVSA, eventually reaching its peak at 3,329 mbd in 2007. With favorable economic conditions, the government had the resources needed to implement its plans. By the end of this initial phase, Chávez had solidified his position as a national and international leader. He enjoyed widespread popular support and had the backing of the Bolivarian National Armed Force, which had been restructured and united around the Bolivarian military doctrine.[21] Chávez's legitimacy was further bolstered by his return to power after the coup d'état, a restoration made possible through mass popular mobilization and his undefeated record in all the electoral processes up to that point.

It is possible that due to these factors, Chávez believed the conditions were ripe to accelerate the advancement of the revolutionary process and declare the revolution's "socialist" nature, which he did during a meeting of the São Paulo Forum in 2005.[22] There, he introduced the concept of "21st-century socialism" with Venezuelan nuances, later detailed in the Plan for the Homeland (2007–12).[23] Chávez's stance on socialism did not emerge from a thorough debate or a critical self-assessment of the first phase, which would have involved identifying progress, errors, successes, and lessons learned. It also did not address the specific type of socialism to be constructed, a discussion essential for building consensus within the revolutionary base of support. This oversight ultimately narrowed the scope of the political project as one solely defined by Chávez and his party, which contributed to the defeat suffered by the Bolivarian government in the constitutional reform referendum of 2007.

One of the keys to understanding this second phase of the revolution was Chávez's initiative to propose a constitutional reform to the National Assembly, leveraging the control held by the governing parliamentary bloc. The objective was to establish the legal framework for constructing a "revolutionary democracy" during the transition to socialism. The term "revolutionary democracy" represented a distinct concept from the "participatory and protagonistic democracy" outlined in the constitution. This was presented as an evolution toward a more advanced form of democracy.

Another key element of the proposed constitutional reform was the adoption of a new state model characterized by a concentration of power in the executive branch, while limiting direct citizen participation in decision-making. Additionally, the reform proposed indefinite reelection for the president and other popularly elected positions. When examining both proposals together, it becomes evident that the intention was to create a mechanism that would hinder leadership rotation and diversity, influenced by a notion of hegemony reminiscent of the Soviet revolutionary process. This concept assumed the irreversibility of the established revolutionary regime, the enduring presence of the ruling party, and the continued leadership of the maximum leader in power.

A third crucial aspect was Chávez's call for alliance parties to merge into a single organization, forming the "single socialist party of Venezuela." This request was made without a shared political or ideological identity and without consensus on the strategic direction of the process. Only the MVR, which later evolved into the current governing party, the United Socialist Party of Venezuela (PSUV), accepted this request. The objective now was to construct a unified vanguard around the singular leader and revolutionary ideology, following a model akin to the Soviet and Cuban examples. The course of the revolution was redirected toward a form of socialism where the party and the state converged, distinct from the twenty-first-century socialism centered on participatory and protagonistic democracy, autonomous popular power separate from the state, and a new endogenous, diversified, sustainable, and self-managed socioeconomic model during the transition to a post-capitalist society.

Although the constitutional reform was narrowly defeated, the revolutionary bloc later succeeded in a referendum that approved the constitutional amendment, permitting indefinite reelection. This allowed Chávez to seek a third term as president.

The economic indicators at the conclusion of this period provide insight into the significant improvement in the economic landscape. The rise in oil prices played a pivotal role, propelling economic growth until 2008. However, in 2009, GDP declined by 3 percent, primarily due to the aftermath of the Wall Street financial crisis. The following graph (covering the years 1996–2011) illustrates the fluctuations in GDP alongside the oil price.

GDP Growth (in percentages) **and Oil Prices** ($USD) **for 1996-2011**

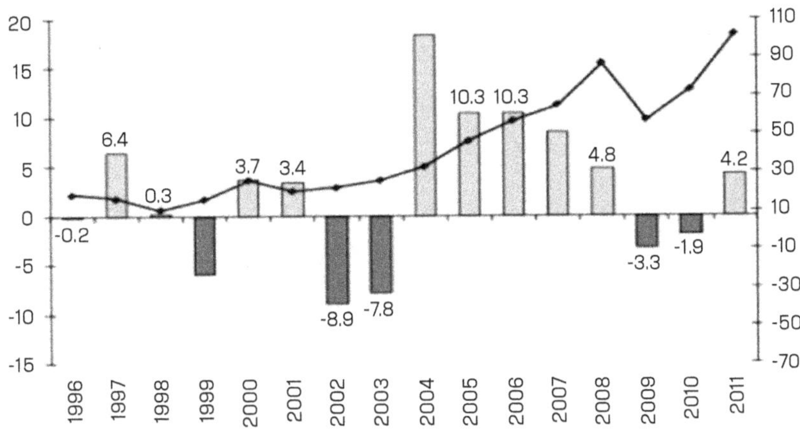

Left Y Axis: GDP; right Y Axis: $USD

Figure 1.2 This graph shows how, starting in 2004, the economy begins to grow as the price of oil increases, except in the years 2009 and 2010, in which there was a decline due to the abrupt fall in the price of oil as a consequence of the Wall Street crisis. *Source: BCV, PDFVSA*

The fiscal "bonanza" resulting from increased oil prices allowed for a substantial uptick in public spending and social investment, leading to significant improvement in social indicators. The evolution of poverty and extreme poverty rates are shown in Figure 1.3.

These outcomes align with the principles of the Bolivarian Alternative agenda, which prioritizes addressing "macrosocial imbalances over macroeconomic imbalances" as a means to address the social debt. What remained less clear, however, was the specific approach to achieve this goal without encountering insurmountable challenges, given the nature of Venezuela's dependent rentier capitalist system.[24]

Figure 1.4 illustrates the reduction in both overall and extreme poverty levels from 1990 to 2021, encompassing the final two administrations of the Fourth Republic and the first twenty-two years of the Bolivarian Revolution during which Chávez and Nicolás Maduro held presidential office.[25]

Population Living in Poverty and Extreme Poverty by Geographic Area (percentage of the total population in each geographic area)

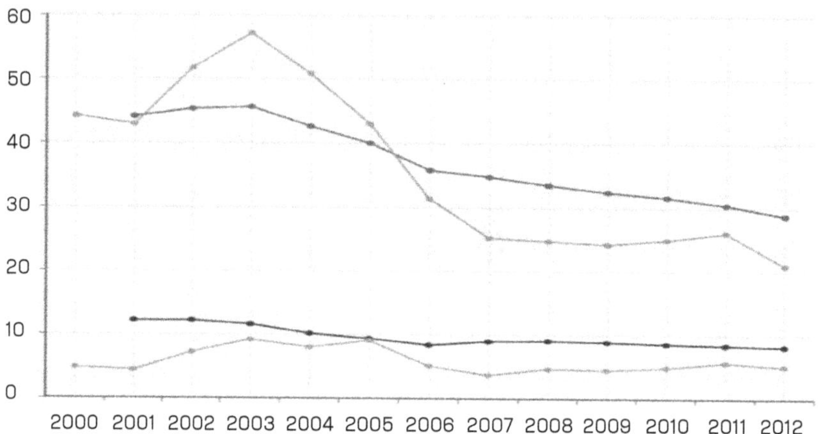

Top to bottom: Latin America, Poverty; Latin America, Extreme Poverty; Venezuela, Poverty; Venezuela, Extreme Poverty

Figure 1.3 UN Economic Commission for Latin America (ECLAC). Graph of the evolution of the population in poverty and extreme poverty of LA/Venezuela from 2000 to 2012, from CEPALSTAT.
Source: Economic Commission for Latin America and the Caribeean–United Nations

Extreme and Total Poverty as a Percentage of GDP

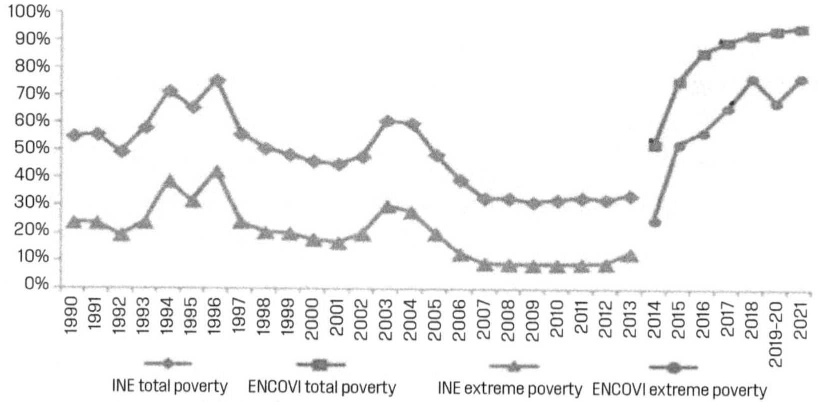

Figure 1.4
Source: 1990–2013 (INE); 2014–2021 (ENCOVI)

Stage 3 (2007–2012): The Deepening of the Revolution, Revolutionary Democracy, and Oil Socialism

This phase began with the consolidation of Chávez's leadership and his political party, the PSUV, despite his initial electoral setback in the narrowly defeated constitutional reform referendum. Shortly thereafter, he secured his fourth consecutive presidential term, signifying that Chávez retained the support of the majority, even though the proposed "socialist" model within the constitutional reform was not endorsed. An analysis of the referendum results revealed that the loss was not due to an increase in opposition votes but rather stemmed from abstention within the government's support base.

Despite the failure of the constitutional reform, the government persisted in pursuing its objectives, leveraging its control over the National Assembly. To facilitate this, an alternative budget, distinct from the regular budget, was established, tapping into extraordinary resources managed directly from the presidential office. Additionally, the Ministry of Popular Power for the Communes promoted the formation of "communes" and "communal cities" as new territorial political structures aligned with the socialist agenda, which overlapped with and contrasted with the older territorial political organization established in the Fourth Republic and still enshrined in the constitution.[26] The underlying goal of this hegemonic strategy was to circumvent the conventional public administration and advance the development of "communal socialism."

Another indication of the shift toward socialism was the renaming of ministries as "People's Power" ministries, a symbolic move aimed at projecting the idea of alignment between popular power and the government. The underlying concept assumes the existence of a politically homogeneous popular power that is integrated into the state's structure and is often blurred with the ruling party and its leader. In practice, the financing, direction, and formation of grassroots organizations are dependent on the Ministry of Popular Power for the Communes, an established governmental entity. Consequently, this conception of popular power lacks independence from the state and the government, which results in it not truly representing the will and diversity of the constituent power within democratic society or different social classes, but rather reflecting the interests of the state bureaucracy.

Another characteristic of this approach was the disregard for the popular vote when the executive branch appointed regional and local authorities described as "protectors" to govern in regions where the party-government had lost elections, effectively establishing parallel governments alongside legitimately elected authorities. In the event that the municipal or state elections were lost, the Bolivarian government, acting outside the constitution and the law, undemocratically created and installed a parallel authority under the control of the National Executive.

The shift toward "socialism" also involved establishing the "single party of the revolution" under the supreme leadership of Chávez, creating a symbiotic relationship between the party and the government, where the actions of both became intertwined in an environment characterized by extreme polarization and the need to respond to various electoral challenges.[27] Building hegemony under this regime, without obtaining the approval of at least half of the Venezuelan population, was constrained by the legal framework set forth in the Bolivarian Constitution. This led to calls for constitutional reform. Even when the popular vote did not endorse these changes, the "radicalization" of the process continued, setting the revolution on a path toward an authoritarian-leaning regime.

To respond to the dilemma of addressing short-term social urgencies while advancing structural transformations of the dependent rentier capitalist economy and the clientelistic liberal democracy model, the government adopted a strategy that paradoxically reinforced political clientelism and the petro-dependent extractivist rentier model. This strategy revived the old policy of "sowing oil" as a transition toward "petro-rentist socialism."[28] The approach involved using substantial oil revenues to underpin the structural transformation of the rentier capitalist system and the development of socialism. In the weekly national broadcast program *Aló Presidente*, Chávez addressed this dilemma.[29]

> We are dedicated to constructing a socialist model that significantly diverges from the 19th-century vision of Karl Marx. Our model is unique, given the presence of our abundant oil wealth. Oil socialism, in our context, is inseparable from oil-related activities. This resource plays a distinctive role in shaping our economic model. It should enable us to advance the Venezuelan socialist system, recognizing oil as one of the most influential drivers for establishing networks linked to the oil sector or complementary to overall economic development.

To utilize oil revenue as a catalyst for driving change, the government redefined the methods for distributing oil income, channeling it toward projects focused on restructuring and transformation, bypassing the traditional bureaucratic apparatus of the bourgeois state. A pivotal instrument within this new framework for redistributing oil income was the National Development Fund (FONDEN).[30] This fund was established using surplus international reserves, contributions from PDVSA's social investments, and budget credits. FONDEN was initially endowed with around $140 billion to finance projects related to the "sowing of oil," and an additional $60 billion was contributed from the Chinese Fund, obtained through credits from the China Development Bank repayable with oil, totaling approximately $200 billion.[31] These substantial resources were managed as an "alternative budget" and were not subject to regular administrative procedures. However, it became evident that this strategy was ineffective due to unmet expectations regarding its achievements and widespread corruption undermining its mechanisms.

The Fruits of the Sowing

The objectives of "oil socialism" in this third stage can be encapsulated in the idea of "sowing" oil revenue to address the social debt and propel the development of a new sustainable and diversified production model rooted in social ownership of the means of production.[32] Additionally, it aimed to establish a new territorial power structure based on communes and communal cities, transforming Venezuela into an energy powerhouse to support the process and contributing to the creation of a regional geopolitical bloc in Latin America and the Caribbean.

Regarding addressing the "social debt," specialized United Nations agencies have reported improvements in various indicators, including poverty, inequality, human development, social security, health, education, culture, sports, housing, science, citizen security, employment inclusion, access to clean water, infant mortality, and malnutrition, among others.[33] These achievements were the outcome of an extensive and impactful social policy aimed at fostering social inclusion.[34] This policy was implemented through the "National System of Missions," which operated alongside the regular public administration and was funded by surplus oil revenues and PDVSA's "social investment" portfolio. Chávez described the missions as follows:

> The Missions are an extraordinary effort to cancel the social debt, which no previous government had ever tackled. We will continue expanding and deepening them, and, most importantly, creating a new institutional framework: a new social state of law and justice.[35]

However, when comparing the outcomes of the social policy during Chávez's tenure with the subsequent decline of the social missions caused by falling oil revenues, it becomes apparent that there were underlying conceptual flaws in the revolution's social policy.

The revolution proposed to advance in the construction of "revolutionary democracy" and foster the development of a new domestic socialist economic model as an alternative to the rentier model. Funding for various productive programs and projects in this phase primarily came from FONDEN and the Chinese Fund. However, the massive volume of investments undertaken during this period resulted in a trail of failures and disappointments. This was evident in numerous unfinished infrastructure projects, industrial facilities, and technological systems that did not align with initial planning, were not adapted to the country's reality, or simply did not come into operation because of corruption.

The numerous failed multimillion-dollar projects and investments, tainted by corruption in contracting or execution, raise questions about the political and economic effectiveness of the strategy to transition from rentier capitalism to "rentier socialism" through governance. This approach employed a statist and authoritarian model reminiscent of traditional Cuban socialism. In objective terms, the social economy was overshadowed by the growth of the capitalist economy, which expanded. However, due to the nature of Venezuela's extractive rent-based model, this growth translated into external capital accumulation through capital flight.

This third stage of the revolution concluded with the reelection of Chávez for a new constitutional term (2013–19), but due to his death, Nicolás Maduro temporarily assumed the presidency and was subsequently elected to complete that constitutional term.

Stage 4 (2013–present): The Decline and Retreat of the Revolution—Emergence of a Neoliberal Authoritarian Regime

Nicolás Maduro won the presidential election by a narrow margin in 2013, while the opposition candidate initially contested the results and alleged fraud, without formalizing the accusations. Thus, Maduro assumed leadership of the Bolivarian Revolution, facing challenges such as the absence of Chávez's charismatic leadership and an economy burdened by previous policies. One of the key aspects of these policies was the strategy of "exchange anchoring," which, although initially implemented as a temporary measure following the 2002 coup attempt and the 2003 oil strike to control inflation and capital flight, eventually became a permanent feature of economic policy, with unintended consequences.[36]

The currency's stability was not achieved, inflation remained high, and capital flight increased over time. Price controls also failed to effectively curb inflation. Instead, the freezing of fuel prices led to corruption and extensive smuggling activities, fostering transnational criminal organizations engaged in money laundering, drug trafficking, and organized crime. This situation exacerbated insecurity issues and placed a significant financial burden on PDVSA and public finances. The indiscriminate subsidy freezes negatively affected the performance and productivity of state-owned enterprises, rendering them financially unsustainable and draining resources that could have been allocated to social investments.

Figure 1.5 illustrates the evolution of GDP during the Bolivarian Revolution, depicting the period of economic prosperity under Chávez and the subsequent decline under Maduro, beginning in 2013, driven by reduced oil production and falling oil prices.[37]

Economic Expansion with Chavez, Retraction with Maduro

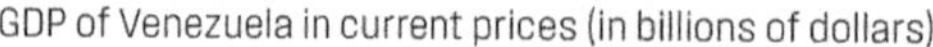

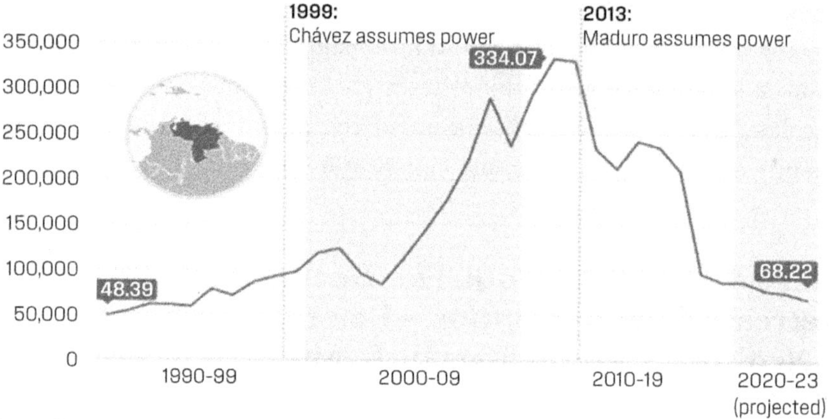

Figure 1.5 This graph compares the evolution of the main macroeconomic and social indicators between the periods of Chávez and Maduro. *La economía de Venezuela desde la muerte de Chávez en cinco gráficos*, Banca y Negocios, June 3, 2018.
Source: International Monetary Fund

Indeed, the oil boom made it possible to address the social crisis inherited from the Fourth Republic and to fulfill the expectations of addressing the "social debt," leading to a significant reduction in poverty and social inequality. However, the focus on welfare-oriented policies, combined with the unrealistic assumption of continuous and sustained growth in oil revenue, left these policies economically vulnerable when oil prices began to decline. Moreover, due to the rigidity of social spending, the inadequacy of its funding became evident through the fiscal deficit, which affected the overall macroeconomic stability. This underscores the fact that macrosocial imbalances cannot be rectified by disregarding their interconnectedness with economic variables, as was assumed in the Bolivarian Alternative Agenda. Figure 1.7 shows the sharp fluctuations in poverty levels during both the Chávez and Maduro periods.

Production and Exportation of Crude in Venezuela (millions of barrels per day)

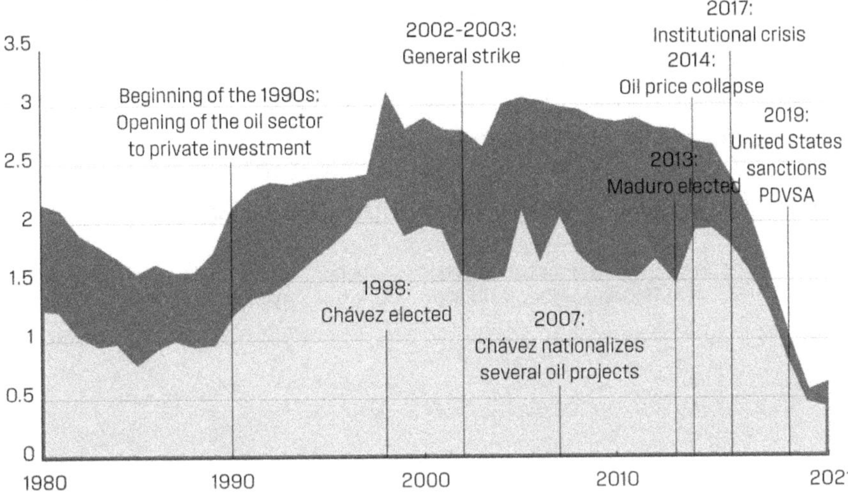

Figure 1.6 The changes in Venezuela's crude oil production and exports from 1981 to 2021 are illustrated in Figure 1.6, offering a comparison between the eras of Chávez and Maduro.[38]
Source: Alvaro Merino (2022), OPEC (2021)

Evolution of Poverty in Venezuela, Measured by the Poverty Line

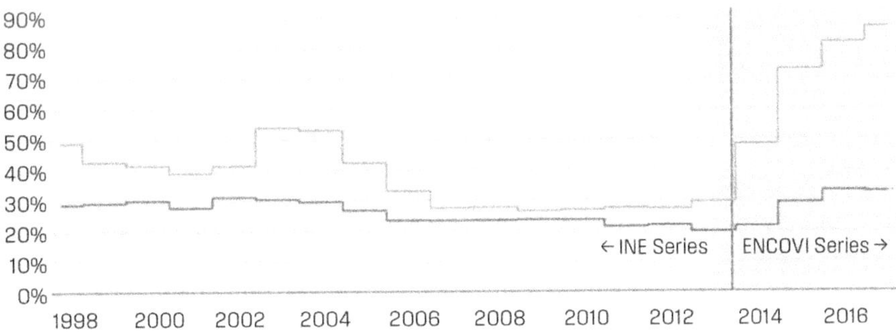

Upper line: Poverty rate (poverty line)
Lower line: Poverty rate (NBI)

Figure 1.7 This graph contrasts the evolution of poverty using two INE/ENCOVI sources in both periods.
Source: ENCOVI, INE

Figure 1.8 illustrates a sharp decline in the real minimum wage relative to the cost of the basic basket, highlighting how the Maduro-led neoliberal authoritarian regime placed the entire burden of the crisis and neoliberal adjustments on the shoulders of the working class. This is one of the factors contributing to the significant emigration of Venezuelans to other regions in search of refuge.

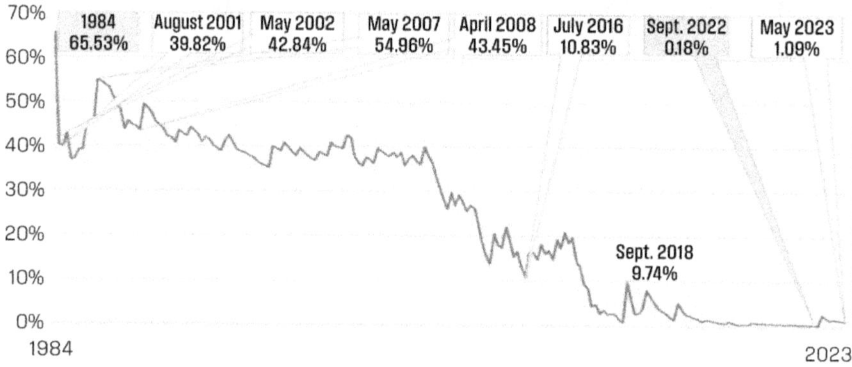

Figure 1.8 This graph shows the abrupt decline of the salary/basic basket relationship in the Maduro period. The idea of a basic basket is used in the field of economics to name a set of products and services that are considered essential for the subsistence and well-being of family members. Generally, the basic basket is made with the objective of estimating the expense that a family group must bear to satisfy its basic needs. *Source: BCV, INE, Agroplan, TSJ gazette*

Confronted with an ongoing political and institutional crisis with seemingly no resolution in sight and an uncertain economic environment marked by a significant decrease in income and deteriorating living and working conditions, a staggering 7.7 million Venezuelans, including a notable number of young people from various social backgrounds, made the decision to emigrate to other countries in search of better opportunities to support themselves and their families. This mass exodus, as reported by the United Nations Refugee Agency (UNHCR), constitutes the second-largest displacement crisis globally, despite Venezuela not experiencing a war.[39] The repercussions of this tragic event are profound, resulting in the loss of skilled human talent that had been cultivated over decades at a substantial cost to the nation and the fragmentation of countless Venezuelan families.[40]

The primary factors contributing to the deepening economic crisis during the Maduro administration include not only the decline in hydrocarbon production and oil prices but also inefficiencies and corruption within the system, compounded by the imposition of unilateral coercive measures (UCMs) by the United States and its allies.[41] Figure 1.9 illustrates the trajectory of Venezuela's oil production from 1960 to 2019 and the impact of UCMs on its decline.[42]

Total Oil Production in Venezuela (1960-2019)

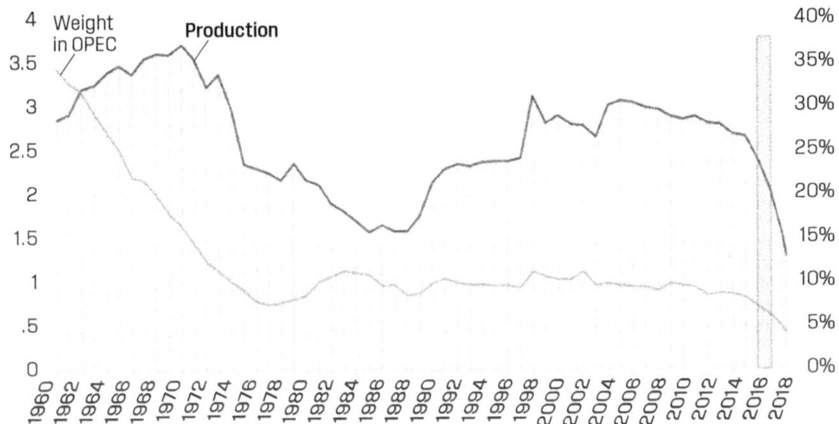

Left Y Axis: Millions of barrels a day; right Y Axis: Weight in percentage. Shaded area indicates US sanctions.

Figure 1.9
Source: OPEC, Direct Communication, Elaboration Economipedia

Comparison of Oil and Non-Oil Exports by Venezuela (1986-2015)

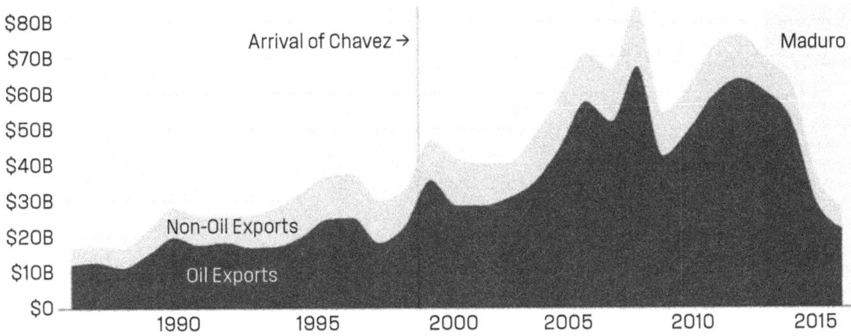

Figure 1.10
Source: Atlas of Economic Complexity, Harvard University

In Figure 1.10, you can observe the fluctuations in the value of oil exports spanning the years 1986 to 2015.[43] The boom in the Chávez period and the decline in the Maduro period are evident. Following President Obama's executive order in 2015, which declared Venezuela "an unusual and extraordinary threat to the United States," and the subsequent arrival of Donald Trump to the White House in 2017, the use of UCMs escalated, violating international law.[44] Similar to their application on Cuba and Iran, these measures proved unsuccessful but came at the cost of adversely affecting the Venezuelan people. The country has endured an unprecedented economic blockade, which, while not the root cause of the existing crisis, has exacerbated it to unimaginable depths. The authoritarian and neoliberal regime under Maduro's government has exploited this "blockade" as a cover for its role in the crisis, justifying its authoritarian and neoliberal drift to retain power at any cost.[45] The ruling party exercises centralized control over all public branches, has criminalized dissent and social protests, and has normalized actions that run counter to the constitution, legality, and rule of law. Using the blockade as a pretext, the Maduro government has implemented an indefinite regime of exception, adopting the slogan "until the blockade ends." To this end, it introduced the unconstitutional Anti-Blockade Law, which essentially allows Maduro to govern outside constitutional bounds, without constraints, and without accountability.[46] With the blockade as a justification, Maduro attempted to legitimize and justify the violation of human rights, freedom of expression, freedom of association, the right to strike, the right to peaceful demonstration, and other fundamental rights and guarantees enshrined in the constitution.[47]

In response to the social protests driven by the overwhelming and unbearable living and working conditions experienced by the majority of the population, the Maduro government has attempted to quell them through repression and intimidation, resorting to the reprehensible practices of imprisoning and torturing political leaders and social activists. This marks a departure from the democratic tolerance that characterized the Chávez era.

Maduro assumed office as the oil-rentist and extractivist economic model was nearing its collapse. He faced the daunting task of governing a country gripped by an economic recession and dwindling oil revenues caused by the PDVSA crisis, disinvestment, debt, corruption, inefficiencies, and external market factors. He grappled with an escalating economic crisis, evidenced by soaring public debt, dwindling international reserves, and the ineffectiveness of exchange and price control policies in the face of mounting inflation and speculative pressures.

Confronted with this unfavorable reality, Maduro's initial response during the early years of his administration was to adhere to the existing economic policies, even as it became increasingly apparent that a severe economic crisis was looming. Rather than acknowledging the impending economic "storm" facing the country, he chose to maintain a façade of normalcy and acted as if nothing out of the ordinary was happening. An example of this unrealistic approach was the prioritization of servicing the burdensome debt, rather than seeking to renegotiate it to allocate those resources toward urgent social and economic needs.

Two significant events in his third year of governance (2015) had a profound impact on Maduro's decision-making. First, there was President Obama's executive order, and second, the 2015 parliamentary elections in which the opposition emerged victorious. Faced with an economic crisis that had pushed 80 percent of the population into poverty and an opposition pursuing a policy of "regime change" that refused to recognize his legitimacy as president, Maduro chose to veer toward the right and solidify his hold on power. This marked a clear shift toward an authoritarian and neoliberal character within the developing regime.[48] Subsequently, the opposition's insurrectional activities intensified in 2017, coinciding with the Trump administration's escalation of UCMs.

For over seven years, the US government has been implementing UCMs against the Venezuelan oil industry, aiming to restrict both imports and the sale of Venezuelan oil, not only to the US but also to other global destinations. This has led to a collapse in oil production and tax revenues from oil. The situation was further exacerbated by the COVID-19 pandemic, which accelerated the economic downturn, causing the economy to shrink to less than one-seventh of its size in 2016. Figure 1.11 shows the sharp decline in Venezuela's oil-dependent rentier economy and the impact of the UCMs.

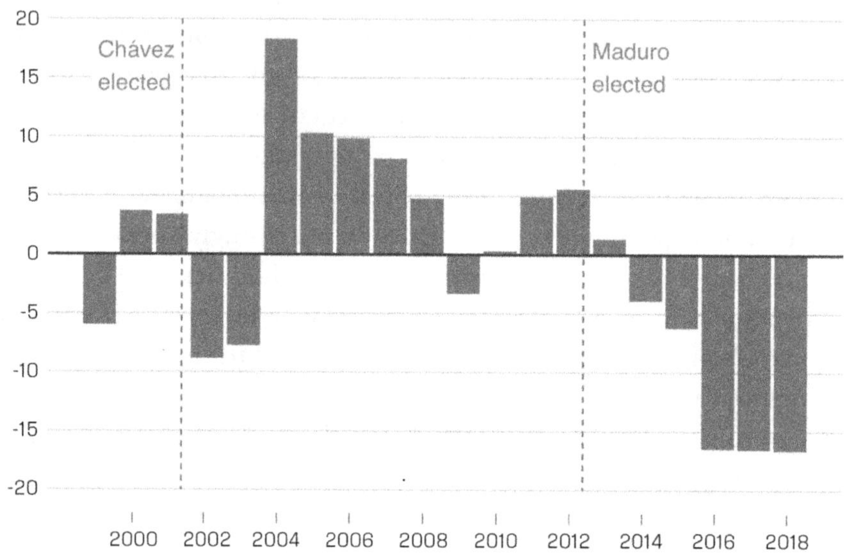

Figure 1.11
Source: Banco Central de Venezuela

In 2015, the opposition-controlled National Assembly gave President Maduro a six-month ultimatum to step down, signaling the opposition's refusal to recognize him as the legitimate leader. The government viewed this as a declaration of war, leading to a confrontation between branches of government. With the support of the Supreme Court of Justice, Maduro began ruling by decree, essentially operating outside the bounds of the constitution. Attempts by the extremist *piti-yanqui* opposition, such as calling for a presidential recall referendum in 2016 and advocating for abstention in the 2018 presidential elections, failed to achieve their goals, as the government continually changed the rules to its advantage.[49] This marked the country's shift toward an openly authoritarian regime, with the executive branch dominating other branches of government. To consolidate power further, Maduro organized the election of a National Constituent Assembly outside the constitutional framework, with the aim of altering the constitution and neutralizing the opposition-controlled National Assembly elected in

2015.[50] This allowed him to centralize power under the ruling party's leadership. When the National Constituent Assembly was established in 2017, it had supraconstitutional authority that enabled it to legislate, effectively taking over the legislative functions of the National Assembly. In response, the opposition continued to operate the 2015 National Assembly with the recognition of the United States, the European Union, and the Lima Group, creating a situation of dual legislative bodies.[51] This crisis unfolded alongside increased financial sanctions imposed by the US government starting in 2017, targeting credit to the Venezuelan oil industry and the state.

In the 2018 presidential elections, Maduro was reelected as president, despite the opposition sector of the G4, which followed the abstention policy promoted by the US government, supported the UCMs, and demanded US military intervention in Venezuela, did not participate.[52] Another opposition faction, which distanced itself from this policy and ran its own candidate in the elections, was defeated, securing Maduro's reelection for a new term. At the beginning of 2019, when the National Assembly was convened, the opposition became divided into two groups. One group, backed by the US government and following an abstentionist and insurrectional approach that refused to recognize Maduro (G4), designated Juan Guaidó as president of the parliament. Guaidó, upon taking office, violated the constitution by proclaiming himself interim president during a massive rally. He quickly garnered support from the United States, Canada, several European nations, and some Latin American countries.

This move solidified the insurrectionary strategy of creating a "dual government" orchestrated by the US government, with the aim of bringing about a regime change in Venezuela, either by forcibly removing Maduro from power or compelling his unconditional surrender and replacing him with Guaidó in an "interim" capacity. By the end of 2019, this strategy appeared to have run its course, as assassination attempts, coup efforts, and US military intervention had all failed. Consequently, the US government and the extremist opposition reevaluated their approach, shifting back toward a "dialogue," while intensifying financial sanctions. President Biden, under the influence of the collateral effects caused by the conflict in Ukraine, which impacted US imports of Russian oil, initiated direct talks with the Maduro government, effectively recognizing him as the de facto head of state. In response, the opposition faction known as the Democratic Unitary Platform returned to the electoral path.[53] Currently, direct negotiations between the US and Venezuelan governments have deepened. Guaidó, the former "interim president," eventually went into exile in Miami after the US government granted him the authority to manage all of Venezuela's assets abroad, including financial holdings and state-owned companies like Monómeros del Caribe in Colombia, CITGO, and PDVSA International, amidst allegations of significant corruption.[54]

While the party-government continued to adopt the revolutionary and anti-imperialist rhetoric of the Bolivarian Revolution, with Hugo Chávez as a reference, Maduro started signaling a shift in the course of the process shortly after his election. His primary objective became holding on to power at any cost, regardless of the social and political consequences. As a result, he began to downplay the importance of respecting popular sovereignty, the rule of law, and the constitution. In 2016, through an unconstitutional executive decree for the Arco Minero del Orinoco, he introduced an authoritarian, neoliberal, and denationalizing style of governance.[55] This decree marked the beginning of a new direction for the party-government leadership, characterized by institutional, environmental, labor, jurisdictional, sociocultural, and territorial deregulation.

Following this, the Maduro administration deepened this model by promoting special economic zones modeled after the Arco Minero del Orinoco, implementing a policy of hydrocarbon denationalization with the "new Oil Opening" and establishing a regime that involved the repression and persecution of dissent, including political parties, movements, and social activists from the left who had previously supported Chávez and the Bolivarian Revolution but distanced themselves from the Maduro regime.[56] The stark contrast between the Maduro regime and Chávez's legacy is seen in the continuous violation of human rights and due process and the persecution of workers' leaders fighting for their rights that have been violated by the regime.[57]

Continuities and Ruptures Between the Fourth and Fifth Republics

Continuities

To sum up the continuities and ruptures between the Fourth Republic and the Bolivarian Fifth Republic, let us first begin with the continuities. The strategy of "oil socialism" based on the rentier model continued and ultimately led to the failure of the Bolivarian Revolution.[58] This strategy perpetuated the dependent rentier capitalist system and maintained the populist clientelistic political model.[59] It exacerbated polarization, frequent elections, discretionary resource management, and administrative opacity, which, in turn, facilitated the growth of corruption to unprecedented levels.[60] Corruption became a significant factor in the collapse of the system, ultimately contributing to its downfall. This also nurtured the emergence of a new bourgeoisie that benefited from corrupt practices.

Ruptures

A significant break from the Fourth Republic occurred with the initiation of the constituent process, which facilitated a peaceful transition from the Puntofijista representative democracy to a participatory and protagonist democracy. This transition established a new programmatic framework aimed at enhancing democracy and creating a comprehensive system of social and citizen rights and guarantees.

In contrast to the previous regime, Chávez prioritized the direct distribution of oil revenues for substantial social investments aimed at combating poverty, inequality, and social exclusion. This approach temporarily reduced poverty and social exclusion during the oil boom cycle.

Another significant rupture was the reassertion of control over the oil industry and the assertion of sovereignty over hydrocarbons through the adoption of the "full sovereignty" policy, abandoning the denationalizing Oil Opening policy inherited from the Fourth Republic.

Additionally, the Bolivarian government departed from the neoliberal model employed in the Fourth Republic, which was based on the Venezuela Agenda. Instead, it pursued public policies guided by the Bolivarian Alternative Agenda, with a focus on developing a new sustainable endogenous productive model.

Finally, Chávez implemented an international policy that diverged from the foreign policy of the Fourth Republic, which had primarily revolved around the geopolitical interests of the United States. The new policy aimed to consolidate the nation's independence and sovereignty, foster multiple alliances in the region and among the Global South, and establish cooperative and complementary relationships. The goal was to contribute to the construction of a multipolar world, ensuring balance and peace, strengthening multilateralism, and respecting the self-determination of peoples.

Continuities and Ruptures in the Revolution

To sum up the continuities and ruptures within the Bolivarian Revolution, let us first begin with the continuities. In many ways the revolution is a singular and continuous process, even though it has been segmented into stages for analytical purposes, corresponding to various political circumstances influenced by class struggle, economic developments, and geopolitical factors. There exists a progressive inertia bridging the two phases of Chávez's leadership. This continuity can be observed in fundamental policies.

Continuities

The development of a political model rooted in Cuban "revolutionary democracy" persisted throughout the Bolivarian Revolution. During Maduro's administration, the mechanisms of social and political control established around the party-government were further strengthened. At the same time, corruption remained a pervasive issue in the Fifth Republic, expanding to unprecedented levels. While serious acts of corruption occurred during Maduro's government, many others were incubated and took place during Chávez's era. This highlights corruption as a cross-cutting problem characterized by common factors such as impunity, the absence of checks and balances, a lack of transparency, ineffective and independent social auditing, and the absence of separation of powers.

Ruptures

In 2016, as the political and economic crisis worsened, a significant rupture occurred when the Maduro government shifted toward right-wing policies. This shift led to the establishment of an authoritarian, neoliberal, unconstitutional, and repressive regime that violated human rights, democratic freedoms, and due process.

Another departure from Maduro's policies involved the reversal of the full oil sovereignty policy in favor of returning to the Oil Opening approach from the Fourth Republic.[61] Additionally, Maduro abandoned the sustainable, diversified, endogenous development project that was part of the Bolivarian vision, opting instead for externalization and neocolonization of the expanded extractive economy. This shift was manifested through the creation of special strategic zones, within a framework of denationalization, the surrender of sovereignty, and an intensified neocolonial model.

Epilogue

The Bolivarian revolutionary movement, as outlined in the Bolivarian Alternative Agenda, had two immediate goals: addressing the social debt accumulated during the Fourth Republic and eliminating corruption from public administration. The core strategic objective was to reestablish the republic through a constituent process, creating a democratic, participatory, leading society governed by the rule of law and justice. Despite significant resources and efforts dedicated to this cause for more than two decades, the revolution fell short of achieving its aims. This latest setback prompts revolutionaries to engage in profound introspection and to draw lessons from this experience. It's not the ideas and objectives that the Bolivarian Revolution represented that failed, but rather the historical implementation. It is imperative to delve deeper into the underlying causes of the failure, critically reevaluate the concepts of power, democracy, and socialism, and, most importantly, reconsider the transition necessary to advance toward a new postcapitalist society through the establishment of a liberating democratic hegemony.

CHAPTER TWO

The Venezuelan Economy During the Bolivarian Process, 1999–2024

Oly Millán Campos

The current situation in Venezuela has sparked interest worldwide, not only among academics but also among leftist activists. One of the main reasons for this interest is that the Bolivarian process in Venezuela was undeniably the first attempt to build socialism for the twenty-first century. For Venezuelans, the present state of our country is marked by a deep multidimensional crisis, encompassing social, economic, political, and cultural dimensions. This reality compels us to adopt a comprehensive historical analysis to understand and explain its causes, development, and potential outcomes.

To begin, let us briefly summarize the current situation in Venezuela. Venezuela is currently facing an unprecedented and complex societal crisis, encompassing various aspects of its economy and society. This crisis can be characterized by significant economic contraction, with the GDP declining by more than 75 percent between 2013 and 2021. The country has also experienced an oil collapse beginning in 2014, leading to a sustained decrease in oil production, reaching levels below 700,000 barrels per day (between 2017 and 2021). This stands in stark contrast with the 3.23 million barrels per day achieved in 2008.[1] Inflation has also been a persistent issue, with monthly consumer prices rising by an average of over 50 percent. The situation has now transitioned into hyperinflation, with a 440 percent interannual inflation rate recorded in January of 2023.[2] Furthermore, the percentage of households classified as poor has increased from 48.4 percent in 2014 to 81.5 percent in 2022.[3] Venezuela has also witnessed significant migration, with the number of Venezuelan refugees and migrants worldwide reaching 7.1 million people, surpassing 15 percent of the projected total population, according to the United Nations Refugee Agency as of September 5, 2022.[4]

This crisis, which represents the convergence of various complex and interconnected factors both domestic and international, presents a harsh reality that appears to lack short-term solutions and offers little hope for improvement of the precarious living conditions of the Venezuelan population. However, it is crucial to avoid falling into simplistic and binary interpretations of this situation that embrace the all-too-common errors inherent in certain sections of the campist left.[5] Similar to the philosophical "law of excluded middle," which is based on a binary logic of either-or, or black and white, this approach oversimplifies the complex reality of the country by reducing it to a dichotomy of enemy versus friend.

The essential question arises: How did a "process of political change" that promised to bring about the utmost happiness for the population culminate in a crisis as profound as the one currently plaguing Venezuela today?

To answer this question, it is imperative to adopt an unbiased perspective, devoid of ideology, when examining the political and economic trajectory of Venezuela over the past few decades.[6] This approach guides us methodologically toward understanding the phenomenon within a historical framework, ensuring that we do not oversimplify reality and inadvertently overlook the fundamental issues that have persisted throughout more than a century of Venezuela's oil-driven history. By acknowledging these core problems, we can undertake the responsible and necessary changes demanded by our society and effectively confront the challenges we face as a country, a region, and members of humanity in the twenty-first century.

This chapter will conduct a critical assessment of the Venezuelan economy during the course of the Bolivarian process. Our aim is to discern both the continuities and ruptures between the government of Hugo Chávez and its predecessors, as well as the subsequent administration under Nicolás Maduro. By examining these factors, we highlight certain critical issues that the country must address in the near future, particularly regarding the imperative and time-sensitive need to transition away from fossil fuel–dependent production.

With the initiation of the Bolivarian process in Venezuela following Hugo Chávez's assumption of the presidency in 1998, a new political era emerged, challenging the existing bipartisan system established by the Punto Fijo Pact in 1958.[7] This pact shaped Venezuela's political landscape, predominantly led by the Democratic Action and Social Christian Party parties for four decades in the twentieth century. However, it is important to note that, in terms of economic structure, the Bolivarian process has so far been unable to overcome the crisis of the oil-dependent extractive model that emerged at the end of the previous century. This chapter aims to demonstrate, contrary to expectations, that Venezuela failed to transcend the rentier economic model during the Bolivarian process. Consequently, despite discourse emphasizing national sovereignty, Venezuela experienced an increased dependency on oil extraction, rendering it more vulnerable to the power dynamics and interests of global geopolitics, which today holds the stability of the world in suspense.

This chapter gives a comprehensive historical analysis of the Venezuelan economy during the Bolivarian process, spanning from 1999 to the present. This requires examining the underlying structural causes that led to the deep crisis facing Venezuela today. Additionally, this chapter aims to understand the strategies implemented by the Maduro government to overcome this crisis.

The Bolivarian process marked the beginning of an economic transition that signified the culmination of a distinct stage in the country's economic history. This stage is characterized by a fossil fuel–centered accumulation model that exercised significant influence on national production. This almost century-long stage of oil exploitation not only shaped the profile of the state but also that of the economic and social structures of the country. Oil played a crucial role in Venezuela's distinctive form of integration in the world system.

Consequently, Venezuela finds itself in a transitional phase known as the "post-oil" era. This transition has been prompted by two major factors: the exhaustion of the oil-based model, hastened by the collapse of the national oil industry, and the shifts unfolding in the global energy landscape. As a result, the country is compelled to undergo a process of transformation, which revolves around two mutually exclusive strategies.

The first strategy revolves around maintaining income through continued extractivism, while also pursuing economic restructuring guided by neoliberal principles—an approach that enjoys consensus among the national political and economic elite. The other strategy involves exploring alternatives that challenge the extractive and rentier model. Thus far, the first strategy dominates national discourse, facing little to no opposition from the country's political and economic elite. Nevertheless, it is our hope that this book will contribute to fostering a robust regional, national, and international discourse that forms part of the second strategy, as the urgent demands of the climate crisis require us to do.

The term *extractivism* emerged in Latin America in the 1950s and was initially associated with "extractive industries." During that time, international organizations such as the World Bank played a significant role in promoting the connection between these industries and mining activities. These industries are characterized by the extraction of natural resources that are sold on the global market, the requirement of substantial capital investments, and their limited lifespans.

As it is commonly known, in both Latin America and other countries in the Global South, there is a long history of the exploitation of natural resources.[8] This experience is shaped by the role these countries play in the international division of labor, primarily as suppliers of raw materials.

In the early years of the twenty-first century, the term *extractivism* began to regain popularity and gained traction in the social sciences, academic institutions, research centers, and social resistance movements. This resurgence was a result of growing awareness around climate change, characterized by the escalating destruction of nature and the limited capacity for its replenishment. One particular concern within this discourse is the energy mix (the composition or combination of different sources of energy the country uses to meet its energy needs), primarily focused on fossil fuels, and its direct impact on climate change.

In this context, we define extractivism as a mode of accumulation that focuses on the primary extraction of natural resources for global commercialization. While it aligns with countries' roles in the international division of labor, its impact extends far beyond mere economic considerations. Extractivism becomes an institution, shaping and solidifying relationships, habits, customs, and even culture between the state—which benefits from the commercialization of natural resources and gains income—and the various sectors composing society.

In the economic realm, extractivism finds expression in what Asdrúbal Baptista referred to as rentier capitalism, as is the case in Venezuela.[9] This model is based on rent, defined as follows:

> It is, therefore, an income not generated within the country, meaning it lacks the economic presence of labor and capital on the other side of the balance sheet. Strictly speaking, it is an income without a productive counterpart.[10]

The mechanisms for transmitting and distributing oil rent have played a significant role in shaping the entire history of the Venezuelan political economy throughout the twentieth century up to the present time.

This chapter is structured around two significant moments. The first pertains to the historical context leading up to the Bolivarian process, while the second focuses on the Venezuelan economy during the Bolivarian process itself. With the latter, we will distinguish between the period under Hugo Chávez spanning from 1999 to 2013, and the subsequent period under Nicolás Maduro, which began in 2013 and continues to the present day. Finally, we will conclude with some overall reflections and considerations.

Background of the Bolivarian Process

To understand the ongoing Venezuelan crisis, it is necessary to take a look at the historical background. This involves identifying the fundamental issues within the country's economic and social structure that existed prior to the Bolivarian process, specifically between 1980 and

1997. Additionally, it is important to consider Venezuela's connection to global geopolitics and the resulting impacts stemming from evolving dynamics of the world-system. Particularly significant is the exhaustion of what Armando Córdova called the Fordist-Keynesian accumulation regime, which was the postwar model of capital accumulation.[11] In its place the monetarist neoliberal regime emerged, with its roots tracing back to the late 1970s.

It is within this context that the recent shifts in the Venezuelan economy are taking place. In 1974, the Central Office for Planning and Coordination of the Presidency of the Republic extended an invitation to the economist Celso Furtado to visit the country. The purpose was to gather insights on the situation in Venezuela and the potential pathways for development. Furtado gives a summary of his reflections:

> An economic system has been established that generates limited surplus in terms of savings and taxes, as well as a low return on the substantial investments made possible from oil surplus. Consequently, this economic system is primarily geared towards consumption and wastefulness, while income is highly concentrated and likely to remain concentrated in the long term. As a consequence, there is an extraordinary diversification in consumption patterns leading to negative secondary effects on the system's productivity. The relatively small size of the domestic market, coupled with the demands of a highly diverse consumer base, hinders integration of the industrial system, which remains heavily reliant on foreign markets.[12]

Furtado's statement describes an economy in which oil revenue fueled an expansion of domestic demand, primarily driven by consumption patterns commonly seen in developed nations. However, this growth has not been accompanied by a corresponding increase in national productive capacity. Despite significant investments made possible by the oil surplus, productivity levels remain low. It is important to note that throughout Venezuela's history in the oil sector, this substantial surplus has shaped an "oil state" that acts as a mediator in distributing income among various economic groups, both traditional and emerging, as well as the wider Venezuelan society. The connection between oil revenue, the oil state, and power elites within society has been shaped by the emergence of an extractivist and rentier culture.[13] This culture has acted as the binding agent that has created an economic system reliant on extracting income, following the capital accumulation model prevalent in the Global South.

As these events unfolded within Venezuela, simultaneous changes were occurring in the world-system. These changes eventually exposed the exhaustion of the industrial accumulation model, specifically the Fordist-Keynesian model, as a result of structural issues within the system. This led to the decline in support for the import substitution industrialization (ISI) model in Latin American nations, including Venezuela. The ISI model had been instrumental in guiding public policies and the implementation of "development" plans in the country since the 1960s.[14]

The Fordist-Keynesian model experienced a definitive decline in the mid-1970s, paving the way for the emergence of neoliberalism as a response to the crisis. In Venezuela, the 1980s marked the beginning of an era of economic uncertainty, characterized by the inability to sustain the previous pattern of accumulation that supported fiscal income.[15] As a result, the balance of key macroeconomic indicators became increasingly precarious. Additionally, there was a significant deterioration in the living conditions of the Venezuelan population, leading to a substantial rise in poverty.[16] Moreover, the excessive corruption of state institutions, including the National Armed Forces, created tensions and further undermined the stability of the country.[17]

The progressive deterioration of the Venezuelan economic model's structural crisis was exacerbated by the poor performance of its economic dynamics. During that period, the proposals put forward by various governments to address the crisis often failed to accurately comprehend the nature of the crisis or failed to recognize it altogether, as exemplified by the case of the Herrera Campins government.[18] As Córdova points out, "[T]he government of Luis Herrera Campins was responsible for overseeing an economic crisis without realizing its severity until the final year of his administration."[19] Structural adjustment programs aligned with the principles of the Washington Consensus, such as the "El Gran Viraje" proposed during the second government of Carlos Andrés Pérez (CAP) also contributed to this situation. It is important to remember that CAP's victory in the presidential elections was fueled by the collective imagination of Venezuela society, as it symbolized a return to the prosperous era of the "Greater Venezuela" experienced during his first term in office (1974–79). However, it was during this period of oil boom that the underlying crisis was silently brewing.

This crisis, initially observed in the economic sphere, progressively evolved into a broader societal crisis, as it eventually manifested itself in the political, social, and institutional spheres. This was demonstrated by significant historical events like the popular uprising known as the Caracazo in 1989 and the military rebellion in 1992.[20] These events were expressions of the loss of trust and credibility among Venezuelan society toward the institutions established and represented by the political class that emerged from the Punto Fijo Pact.

It is important to note that the loss of trust in the leadership and political elite of Venezuela during that period also instilled in the collective consciousness of ordinary citizens a desire for change. This sentiment found resonance and strategic political direction in the slogans and messages of Hugo Chávez. Consequently, it paved the way for the political process that commenced with Chávez assuming the presidency of the republic in 1998.

The Venezuelan Economy During the Bolivarian Process

As previously mentioned, a new political process emerged at the beginning of the twenty-first century. However, this process did not address or resolve the underlying structural crisis in the economy. Instead, the crisis continued to unfold, with the debates and discussions on its causes and potential solutions receding into the background. The national focus shifted toward the institutional and political realm, centered around the deliberation and adoption of a new constitution. Simultaneously, a political crisis and power struggle took hold, leading to deep polarization within Venezuelan society. This polarization created a stark division, often characterized as "us versus them," with Chavistas representing the "us" and anti-Chavistas representing the "them."[21] This division persisted throughout a significant portion of the first two decades of the century.

The crisis was closely linked to the exhaustion of the petroleum-centered accumulation model, as noted by economists Maza Zavala, Armando Córdova, Asdrúbal Baptista, and many others since the late twentieth century.[22] Baptista stated that "oil income has no future. And it goes without saying that if this is the case, it can also be said that rentierism does not have a future either."[23] Zavala expressed a similar sentiment, stating,

> In the case of Venezuela, it is clear that the pattern of accumulation, which relies heavily on the fiscal utilization of oil income, has reached its limits. The avenues for further accumulation through this method have been exhausted, leading to the challenge of identifying alternative sources of accumulation that align with the changing economic conditions. It is crucial to reduce dependence on declining oil income and explore new avenues for economic development.[24]

The factors contributing to the decline in oil income, as argued by Baptista and Zavala, can be attributed to two interconnected variables. First, as Carlos Mendoza Pottellá pointed out, relates to Venezuela's oil production, where oil wells experienced a natural depletion process beginning in the mid-1970s (see annex, Figure 2.3).[25] Second, as Córdova has argued, since Venezuela is an oil-producing nation, it has a unique connection with the global market, which enabled it to benefit from substantial oil revenues for many years.[26] However, by the end of the last century, the world-system once again encountered the crisis of capital reproduction. Consequently, the Venezuelan economy was adversely affected, even during periods of oil boom, such as those experienced in a significant part of the first decade of this century. Córdova aptly expressed this phenomenon in the following statement:

> In short, a temporary increase in global energy prices would only provide a temporary lifeline to the struggling Venezuelan economy. It would not have significant qualitative impact and would merely serve as a short-term remedy by boosting oil income. However, once the income stabilizes or declines, the economy would inevitably revert back to its previous state, underscoring its underlying structural exhaustion.[27]

This is effectively what is happening right now. The contradictions surrounding capital's pursuit of profit are becoming increasingly apparent, particularly in relation to the environment. This dynamic is a crucial aspect of ongoing civilizational changes. Edgardo Lander explains it as follows:

> We face, as humanity, a deep civilizational crisis. The terminal crisis of the Promethean model of colonial modernity. It is a complex and multifaceted crisis, characterized by its anthropocentric, patriarchal, colonial, classist and racist dimensions and whose prevailing systems of knowledge, science, and technology, instead of providing solutions to this civilizational crisis, actually contribute to its deepening.[28]

Thus, the Bolivarian process emerged as a response to an economic crisis rooted in the worn-out petro-dependent extractive model. This crisis is intricately connected to the larger systemic complexity of the world-system and its ongoing civilizational crisis.

The Venezuelan Economy in the Period of Chávez, 1999–2013

The Bolivarian process, from the beginning, failed to fully embrace or understand this in-depth discussion regarding the root causes of the Venezuelan economic crisis. A review of the various documents formulated during the Chávez era (1999–2013), from his initial proposal as a candidate in 1996 to the Plan de la Patria 2007–2013, reveals a common thread of transformative goals for the country.[29] These documents begin with a characterization of the Venezuelan economy, which can be summarized as follows:

> Venezuelan society remains marked by the existence of a state that exerts significant control over the country's oil resources, playing a crucial role in shaping internal affairs. The nation's economy continues to be structurally dependent on oil, with this resilience shaping its trajectory. The economic dynamics of Venezuela have been closely tied to the surplus generated by a limited range of export products, transitioning from a historical period of mono-production focused on

> agricultural exports to a current state of mono-production centered around oil exports.[30]

As you can see, this program does not talk about the crisis itself, nor do subsequent plans, but it does describe the elements that define the economy, such as its oil dependence, the role of the state, and the economy's reliance on a single product for both production and exports. Consequently, the plans in subsequent years were primarily centered around implementing an oil policy. This involved strengthening OPEC's leadership to influence global price increases and seeking mechanisms to boost national oil production.[31] It is worth noting that the planning of what Francisco Mieres termed the "PDVSA mega-blunder," as mentioned by Mendoza Pottellá, played a significant role in these efforts:

> The process continued to intensify with the introduction of the "PDVSA mega-blunder," a term coined by Francisco Mieres—presented with great fanfare in 1983 during a gathering of the international oil community by Guillermo Rodríguez Eraso, the president of Lagoven, at the Saint Regis Hotel in New York. This ambitious initiative aimed to invest $100 billion in the Orinoco Oil Belt over the next two decades. However, this "megaproject" was short-lived as it coincided with the end of the price boom that began in 1973. Subsequently, there were further attempts at expansion through the Oil Opening projects between 1993 and 1998, followed by the formulation of the "Planes de la Patria" in 2005, 2008, 2010, 2013, 2015, and 2018.[32]

In this context, the Bolivarian process witnessed a strengthened OPEC, coupled with a significant rise in oil prices, which set the stage for a political process that needed to be "defended" amidst growing polarization fueled by critical events in the country. These events included the coup in 2002, the uprising of high-ranking military officers seeking refuge in Plaza Altamira in the same year, the oil and business strike from 2002 to 2003, and the recall referendum, among others. Furthermore, the opposition's choice to abstain from the parliamentary elections in 2005 contributed to a decline in trust and confidence in the electoral process as a mechanism for transferring power. This complex situation created a backdrop of political and institutional crisis during Chávez's tenure.

In 2005, Chávez publicly declared the socialist nature of the Bolivarian process, which not only contributed to the existing polarization but also brought about significant changes in the factors shaping the government's economic policy. This shift was reflected in the General Lines of the National Economic and Social Development Plan for the period 2007–2013. It is worth examining the differences and similarities between this plan and its predecessor, the National Plan for 2001–2007.

National Plan, 2001–2007, and the General Lines of the National Economic and Social Development Plan, 2007–2013

The 2001–2007 plan aimed to establish a "Venezuelan model" by attending to five key areas: political, economic, social, territorial, and international. This plan was designed to be implemented from 2001 to 2010, serving as a transitional phase toward a subsequent consolidation period projected to span from 2010 to 2020.

From an economic perspective, the plan proposed the development of a productive and competitive economic system that is open to international markets, acknowledging the significance of private initiative and investment in driving growth while fostering efficiency and productivity in business activities. The state's role was reserved to primarily focus on strategic industries, ensuring their protection to address instances of unfair competition, particularly in agriculture and industry sectors.

The plan, as outlined in the 1999 constitution, also stipulated the state's responsibility to foster and safeguard the growth of the social economy and its various components, including microenterprises, family businesses, and cooperatives.

In broad terms, the plan referred to the significance of coordinating fiscal, monetary, and exchange policies. It outlined a strategy to control fiscal resources, manage public expenditures, and tackle speculative currency attacks. The defined objectives were as follows:

- Attain consistent economic growth. This involved promoting private enterprise to produce goods and services for both the domestic and international markets. Emphasis was placed on strengthening the industrial sector, with the state playing a clear role as promoter and supporter of productive development. The plan aimed to achieve fiscal stability and generate foreign currency from non-oil activities.
- Eliminate economic volatility. This required achieving a harmonious relationship between fiscal and monetary policies. The goal was to avoid procyclical public spending that could disrupt the currency market. To maintain stability, an exchange rate policy served as a nominal anchor, preventing currency shocks in the foreign exchange market. With this in mind, a focus was placed on prioritizing the control of public expenditures, pursuing an efficient and transparent state, and preserving the autonomy of the Central Bank and the band system for determining exchange rates. This policy remained in place until 2003, when an exchange control system was introduced.
- Internationalization of hydrocarbons. The plan emphasized the need to attract national and international private investment for the downstream development of the hydrocarbons industry, as well as advancements in science and technology. It recognized the significance of strengthening OPEC as a crucial institution for safeguarding international oil prices. Additionally, it aimed to establish a robust legal framework that would ensure legal stability and foster partnerships between the private sector and the government for the overall development of the hydrocarbons industry.
- Develop the social economy. The objective in this area was to increase the productivity and management capabilities of the social economy sector. To support this, the plan introduced a microfinance system and provided comprehensive assistance, including educational and technical support, to empower and uplift the social economy.
- Attain fiscal sustainability. The plan aimed to achieve fiscal sustainability through improved efficiency in the collection of oil and non-oil reserves. It emphasized the need for greater coordination, harmonization, efficiency, transparency, and accountability

between the nation's plans, budget, and public spending. An important aspect of this objective was addressing subsidies, including adjusting rates for public services to enhance efficiency and effectiveness. Managing the public debt responsibly and in alignment with the state's major investment objectives was also highlighted.

- Increase savings and investment. The plan recognized the significance of stimulating domestic savings as a means to foster investment and drive economic growth. By encouraging savings, it aimed to create a favorable environment for increased investment, leading to improved economic performance.

Now we will examine the prominent aspects of the 2007–2013 plan, to identify the key differences between the two plans.

It is first essential to consider the context in which this plan was developed. It was proposed after Chávez declared the socialist nature of the Bolivarian process in 2005, referring to it as "21st century socialism."[33] This declaration took place amid significant political polarization within the country. It is also noteworthy that, at the time, Latin America was witnessing a surge in what is known as "progressive governments," which reflected the aspirations of the region's people for left-wing political leadership. This shift was prompted by the failures of neoliberal policies implemented in the late twentieth century, which led to increased poverty, inequality, and deteriorating living conditions.

The 2007–2013 plan outlined seven strategic guidelines that would shape the country's path toward building socialism. These guidelines were the following: The cultivation of new socialist ethics, the pursuit of supreme social happiness, the promotion of a leading democracy with a revolutionary spirit, the establishment of a socialist productive model, the development of a new national geopolitics, the positioning of Venezuela as a global energy power, and the reshaping of international geopolitics.

The plan, therefore, was not based on an analysis of the economic situation of the country, nor did it provide a critical assessment of whether the objectives of the previous plan were achieved. Instead, it presented a moral declaration of what should be done to achieve the construction of socialism in Venezuela, with a notable shift away from discussing private initiative, capital, and investment as emphasized in the 2001–2007 plan. The role of the central state is reinforced, and it emphasizes the crucial role of the oil sector in the development of "21st century socialism." One of the central goals is to transform Venezuela into a "world energy powerhouse" in the medium term. The following quote illustrates this perspective:

> Given the increasing global demand for fossil energy and the substantial reserves of oil that Venezuela possesses, it is evident that oil will continue to play a crucial role in shaping the country's future. *Its influence extends beyond the scope of resource acquisition from foreign sources, encompassing domestic investments, energy self-sufficiency, and the establishment of a new productive model [emphasis by author]*. Recognizing that the nation's natural wealth is the collective heritage of all Venezuelans, it becomes imperative to maintain state control over the key operations of the hydrocarbon industry. . . .
>
> *Considering the increasing global demand for oil, it is highly likely that the production of unconventional oils, particularly heavier oils, will experience significant growth. This presents an advantage for Venezuela since a substantial portion of its reserves consists of oils with these characteristics* [emphasis by author]. The upward trend in oil prices in the international market has rendered the extraction of heavier oils economically viable. In the long run, oil production worldwide will be concentrated primarily in the countries that are currently members of the Organization of Petroleum Exporting Countries (OPEC). . . .
>
> To enhance productive diversification and promote social inclusion, it is crucial to accelerate the expansion of oil cultivation while simultaneously focusing on the internalization of hydrocarbons.[34]

The foundation for achieving economic diversification, establishing a new productive model, and attaining social justice, as outlined in the plan, relies heavily on oil. The emphasis is placed on generating higher revenue, as indicated by the following quote: "The oil industry will prioritize maximizing income throughout the entire process and enhance tax contributions to revenue."[35] It is noteworthy that this vision of constructing a "new productive model" appears to overlook analysis and arguments regarding the climate crisis and the significant role of fossil fuels in exacerbating it. Furthermore, the ongoing societal crisis is not adequately addressed, and reinforcing an oil-driven extractivist model is certainly not an anticapitalist proposal.

In 2013, the economic outcomes vividly illustrated the unfolding crisis. The significant decline in oil prices, coupled with a decrease in national production, exposed the structural and systemic nature of the Venezuelan economy's crisis. This crisis, although temporarily concealed by the oil boom in the early 2000s wherein oil prices surged from around $30 per barrel in 2003 to over $100 per barrel in 2013, ultimately exposed the deep-rooted issues within the Venezuelan economy.[36] This situation is captured in the following quote from Oly Millán and Wilmer Torrealba:

> The economic dynamics fell into an inertia, driven by policy of excessive government spending, persistent fiscal deficits, and a significant increase in import which between 2007 and 2014, exceeded $40 billion USD. Concurrently, external debt, (both sovereign and of the state-owned PDVSA), went from less than 20% of GDP in 2000 to over 80% of GDP by 2015. The failure to effectively manage resources and conduct proper oversight resulted in unsuccessful plans for oil development, industrialization, infrastructure, and agricultural production. Additionally, the nationalization of companies added a substantial burden to state finances. This included the expansion of the state financial sector, exemplified by the creation of Banco de la Fuerza Armada National (Banfan), the acquisition of Banco de Venezuela, and the establishment of Banco Bicentenario.[37]

In the midst of this critical situation, the exchange policy implemented since 2003, characterized by exchange controls, did not achieve its intended objective. Instead of controlling capital flight, it inadvertently stimulated it, becoming the most noteworthy instance of embezzlement in Venezuela this century.[38] Moreover, this exchange policy, along with ineffective state management, had a detrimental impact on the financial and accounting status of PDVSA.[39] Combined with its substantial indebtedness, which increased from US$16 billion in 2007 to US$34.894 billion in 2021 (see annex, table 2.3), these factors contributed to the negative financial situation of the company.

The Venezuelan Economy in the Period of Nicolás Maduro, 2013–2021

Following the period of the oil boom, which due to the temporary boost provided by increased oil revenue kept the Venezuelan economy in an apparent state of good health, the underlying economic issues were unmasked. The signs of the crisis were evident prior to 2013, with imbalances in key macroeconomic indicators. This crisis was further exacerbated by negative expectations arising from the passing of Chávez and the reorganization of the ruling political elite.[40] It once again exposed the structural problems of an oversized and corrupt state, a collapsed oil industry (reflecting its dysfunction), and an economy heavily reliant on oil with limited capacity to withstand the decline in foreign currency. Initially, the new government under Nicolás Maduro struggled to grasp the severity of the situation and instead shifted blame to businesses, the political opposition, and hostility from the US State Department.[41] Although economic and financial sanctions escalated in 2017 and 2019, the crisis had already taken root prior to that period.[42]

The struggle for political power in Venezuela led to the erosion of the established institutions, including the current constitution, by both the government and the political opposition represented by the G4 coalition.[43] The situation reached a climax of deinstitutionalization when the Maduro government disregarded the outcome of the 2015 National Assembly elections, where the opposition secured a majority of legislative seats.[44] Subsequently, certain sectors of the opposition, with support from the US State Department and its allied countries, recognized Juan Guaidó, the president of the National Assembly, as the "interim president" in 2019, adopting a confrontational and violent strategy that pushed the country to the brink of civil war.[45]

On the other hand, the government responded by implementing permanent decrees of States of Exception and Economic Emergency and establishing the National Constituent Assembly in 2017.[46] These actions have been characterized by a greater neoliberal approach in economic matters and a noticeable drift toward authoritarianism in the political sphere.

The Maduro government recognizes the need to move away from relying solely on oil income as the driving force of the national economy. It recognizes the necessity of building a post-oil economic model, albeit one that remains deeply rooted in extractivism. A prime example of this shift is the development of the Orinoco Mining Arc project. This project designated 12 percent of the nation's territory for mining exploitation and involves significant economic and constitutional deregulation.[47] Additionally, the Maduro government implemented policies that allocated each Bolivarian governor a gold mine for exploitation, while laying the groundwork for neoliberal economic policies that promote market flexibility in areas such as labor, goods, services, and currency exchange.[48]

Furthermore, the Maduro government has made efforts to facilitate a "new opening" in the national oil industry sector. This "new Oil Opening" aims to provide multinational oil companies with various privileges, such as modifying the legal framework, reducing taxes, and recognizing international arbitration.[49] This proposed "new Oil Opening," which grants transnational companies significant prerogatives to "invest" in the country, is based on the unconstitutional Anti-Blockade Law.

It is important to highlight that the proposed Oil Opening is being formulated at a time when there is a widespread consensus on the necessity of transitioning away from hydrocarbons to mitigate global warming from surpassing predefined thresholds.[50] The International Energy Agency, for example, predicts a shift in the global energy landscape by 2050, with renewable energies experiencing significant growth (see annex, Figures 2.1 and 2.2).

As part of understanding the process to restructure the extractive model and seek diversification of oil revenue, it is essential to highlight the series of laws that have been introduced. Laws that, it is important to note, bypass constitutional provisions and disregard the existing constitution. One notable example is the approval of the Organic Law of Special Economic Zones in July of 2022.[51] Considering its significance, we would like to reproduce an excerpt of comments we previously made regarding the passage of this law:

> As we are aware, special economic zones refer to specific geographic areas that implement economic laws more favorable to foreign capital

> than to the general regulations of the country. These zones offer preferential treatment in terms of import and export goods, low-cost labor, and tax exemptions. Their main objective is to attract foreign investment by providing unique conditions not typically found in the country's constitution.
>
> This process involves an economic restructuring that revolves around deregulation in various areas such as finance, commerce, production, taxation, environment, and labor. It primarily aims to appeal to international capital by leveraging comparative advantages such as access to natural resources, cheap labor, and a liberal regulatory framework. Additionally, in the case of Venezuela, the government offers a productive infrastructure (e.g., roads, ports, airports) that may be lacking in other Latin American countries.
>
> It is noteworthy that while special economic zones have been dismantled in many Latin American countries due to their adverse effects outweighing their benefits, it is paradoxical that in Venezuela, despite previous antineoliberal discourse associated with the Bolivarian Process, government leaders now vigorously advocate for the establishment of these zones. It is as if they consider it the only viable solution to overcome the crisis.[52]

In summary, there is an ongoing development of an economic and political strategy through the implementation of several laws, such as the Anti-Blockade Constitutional Law for National Development and the Guarantee of Human Rights, the Organic Law of Special Economic Zones, and the Constitutional Law of Foreign Productive Investments. These laws aim to reorganize the economy by expanding and deepening the extractivist and rentier accumulation model. However, this strategy is also intertwined with the establishment of an authoritarian political system, which undermines the principles of justice, federalism, decentralization, and participatory and protagonistic democracy.[53] It contradicts the major challenges faced by our country, region, and humanity in the twenty-first century, such as transitioning to an economic system that embraces alternative energy sources beyond fossil fuels and achieving greater social and ecological justice. This approach is necessary for the cultural transformation required to break free from the complexities of capitalism.

Final Considerations

In attempting to respond to the hypothetical Venezuelan Zayalita who asks "At what moment did our country get fucked?," one could argue that Venezuela, from its discovery of oil to the present, has been entangled in a system shaped by values, customs, beliefs, and laws centered on oil extraction.[54] Over time, this system has established its own mechanisms, encompassing institutional and regulatory frameworks, cultural norms, political structures, social dynamics, and political practices. This system has perpetuated a rent-seeking pattern, centered on extracting wealth from oil resources. Unfortunately, this institution, closely tied to national and international oil dynamics, has become a major barrier hindering Venezuela's transition toward a diversified economy. Such a transition is necessary to offset the gradual loss experienced in oil revenue and effectively tackle the pressing need to shift away from fossil fuels as the core of our productive matrix.

Through the course of the Bolivarian process, Venezuela has further entrenched itself in a model of extractivism and rentier accumulation. Unfortunately, this is happening at the same time as an accelerating climate crisis, and we have failed to develop viable alternative proposals. It is clear that the commitment to constructing a "new productive model" that remains dependent on oil extractivism and that does not take into account alternative economic frameworks rooted in respect for human rights and the environment was destined to fail.

This dependency, despite numerous warnings about the exhaustion of the oil rentier model and the decline of the national oil industry, coupled with the challenges presented by the shift in the global energy matrix away from hydrocarbons, has been the driving force behind the magnitude of the Venezuelan crisis. It foreshadows the difficulties in overcoming this crisis by constructing a new way of life that challenges the consensus imposed by the dominant elite. This elite seeks to deepen and expand the extractivist model with a neoliberal approach, all while aspiring to achieve diversified income. Given this situation, one might wonder if we are destined to continue experiencing failures.

Annex

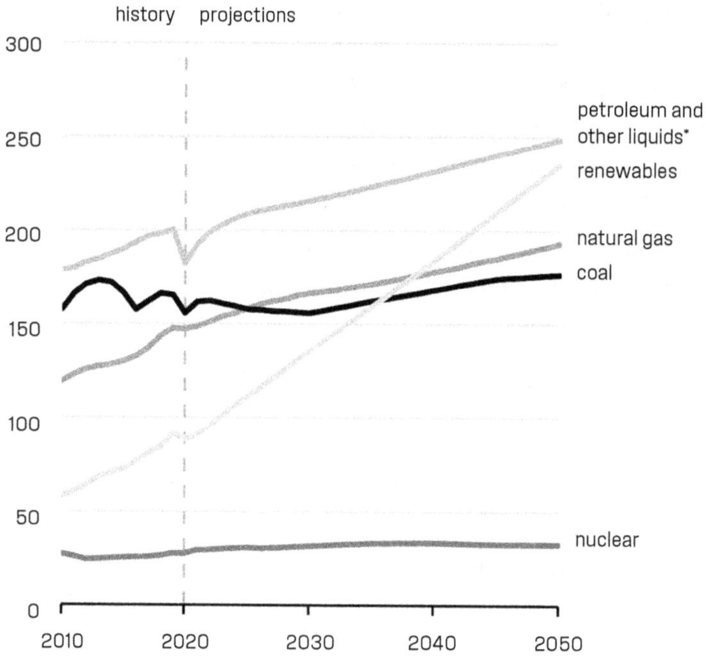

Figure 2.1
Source: U.S. Energy Information Administration, International Energy Outlook 2021 (IEO2021)

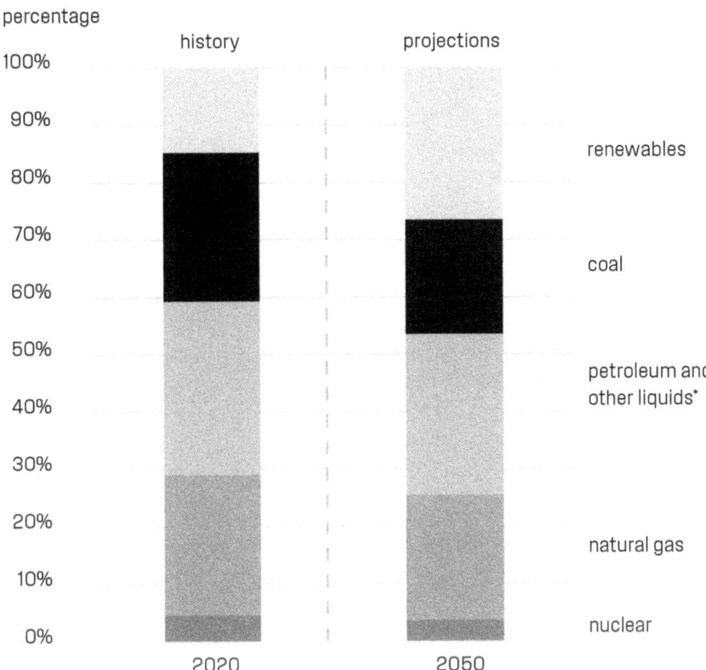

Figure 2.2
Source: U.S. Energy Information Administration, International Energy Outlook 2021 (IEO2021)

Venezuela Average Oil Production 1960-2021 (millions of barrels/day)

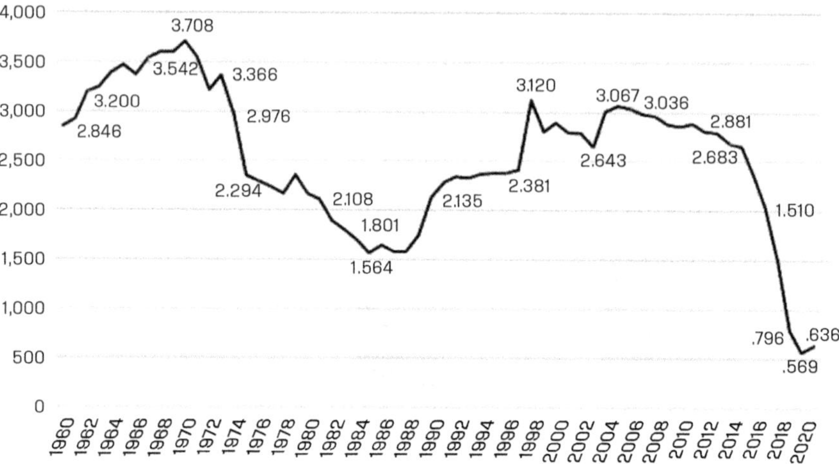

Figure 2.3
Source: OPEC

Table 2.1 Main economic indicators, 2013–2021

Indicators	2013	2014	2015	2016	2017	2018	2019	2020	2021
GDP % (constant prices)	1.34	-3.89	-6.22	-17.04	-15.67	-19.62	-28	-26	-3
Inflation (% BCV)	40.7	68.5	180.9	274	862.6	130,600	9,586	2,960	687
Exports (billions USD)	88,753	74,676	37,236	27,403	34,030	33,677	ND	ND	ND
Imports (billions USD)	57,183	47,255	33,308	16,370	12,023	12,782	ND	ND	ND
Monetary financing to PDVSA (% variation)	138	58	68	510	2,062	461.9	67.2	35.6	16.4
International reserves (billions USD)	21.4	22.08	16.4	10.9	9.6	8.8	6.6	6.3	10.9

Source: BCV, CEPAL (GDP 2019, 2020) and calculations by author

Table 2.2 Financial management of the central government, 2001–2009 (% of GDP)

Year	Total revenue	Total cost	Deficit or surplus
2001	20.78	25.14	-4.4
2002	29.5	26.12	-4.0
2003	23.39	27.78	-4.4
2004	34.39	31.91	2.5
2005	27.54	25.91	1.6
2006	29.57	29.62	-0.1
2007	28.86	25.83	3.0
2008	24.65	25.85	-1.2
2009	21.64	26.73	-5.1

Source: Ministerio del Poder Popular (Ministry of Popular Power) of Economy, Finance, and Foreign trade

Table 2.3 PDVSA financial debt and external debt

Year	Amount (billions USD)	External debt (billions USD)
2007	16.006	44.100
2008	13.418	44.103
2009	21.419	59.916
2010	24.950	71.800
2011	34.892	79.307
2012	40.026	130.785
2013	43.384	132.362
2014	46.153	135.767
2015	43.751	149.755
2016	41.027	149.859
2017	41.076	148.328
2018	34.555	148.432
2019	36.352	147.899
2020	34.494	ND
2021	34.894	ND

Source: PDVSA and CEPAL (external debt)

Table 2.4 System: Nine defining variables of the Venezuelan economic crisis, its causes, and its multiple relationships

Devaluation of currency • decrease in international reserves • decrease in exports • drop in oil production • exchange rate policy/corruption • drop in the price of oil • payments in debt service	**Fall in oil production** • without strategic direction and capacity • inefficiency and corruption • destruction of organizational culture • a progressive disinvestment process
Fall in GDP production • structural problems/characteristics of the Venezuelan economy • drop in PDVSA production • drop in imports • drop in raw materials imports • drop in consumption • drop in investments	**Fiscal deficit** • drop in tax revenue • increase in government spending • increase in corruption • state companies without economic viability • increase in state inefficiency
Political and institutional crisis • fracture of the constitutional framework • fracture of the structure of the state • generalized anomie in state institutions • loss of credibility in political leadership/no alternative political leadership • without credible, relevant, and coherent proposals to emerge in the short-/medium-term	**Capacity for popular struggle** • a majority rejection of the government's management, which does not translate into concrete actions that add up to a massive political position • a lot of dispersion in the leftist forces • fear of threats of loss of "social benefits" • migration became the escape valve for street protests • loss of credibility in the leadership of the right-wing opposition

<table>
<tr>
<td>Criminal capital flight<ul><li>design of the dual-denomination debt mechanism</li><li>elimination of controls and monitoring in institutions</li><li>elimination of the institutional profile of Moral Power</li><li>crisis in the administration of justice/corrupt judicial system</li><li>fracture of the structure of the state and the independence of institutions</li><li>political polarization and the permanent actions of political exit through nonconstitutional means</li></ul></td>
<td>Complex international plane<ul><li>SCM/NVA crisis correlation of forces; USA/Europe–China/Russia</li><li>political and economic crisis in Latin American countries; end of the rise of progressive governments and new progressive wave</li><li>strengthening neoliberal policies as proposals for exit and strengthening of the extractivist model</li><li>greater indebtedness of Latin American countries</li><li>resistance of the people</li></ul></td>
</tr>
<tr>
<td>Hyperinflation – high inflation<ul><li>characteristics of the Venezuelan economy, extractivist-rentier model</li><li>fall in foreign exchange income</li><li>monetization of the fiscal deficit</li><li>issuance of inorganic money</li><li>loss of the BCV profile</li><li>permanent devaluation of the currency</li><li>development of a spiral of inflationary expectations that actively affects the mechanisms of inflation propagation</li></ul></td>
<td></td>
</tr>
</table>

CHAPTER THREE

A Comparative Analysis of the Governments of Hugo Chávez and Nicolás Maduro

Roberto López Sánchez

Hugo Chávez won the presidential elections in December of 1998 after a decade of neoliberal policies in Venezuela. The previous period had seen two successive governments implement neoliberal economic programs. These programs were met with significant popular resistance, including a spontaneous popular uprising in February and March of 1989 that shook the two-party political system that had been in place since 1958; two nationalist and leftist military uprisings; and the removal of a sitting president from office by parliament on charges of corruption. The so-called Bolivarian process, which began in Venezuela with the electoral triumph of Hugo Chávez in 1998, was the popular response to the crisis of legitimacy of the political model of representative democracy that had been in place since 1958.[1] The failure of the productive model of import substitution, the foundation of representative democracy for thirty years, had become evident by the mid-1980s, with a profound economic crisis that worsened with the fall in oil prices in 1986.

An earlier version of this chapter first appeared in Mariana Mastrángelo, Ronaldo Munck, and Pablo Pozzi, eds., *Populismo: Una perspectiva latinoamericana* (CLASCO, 2023).

The spontaneous popular uprising on February 27–28, 1989, known as the Caracazo, revealed the great discontent the population had with a political-economic system that did not satisfy their fundamental needs.[2] The government's brutal repressive response caused hundreds of deaths in the neighborhoods of Caracas and nearby cities. It reinforced the view that those who governed did not deserve to enjoy the popular support that had sustained the ruling two-party political model for three decades. The two parties in question were Acción Democrática (Democratic Action [AD]) and Partido Socialcristiano (Social Christian Party [COPEI]).

However, in the absence of alternative political options, and with a left in crisis, both in its electoral versions and in the groups that maintained the armed struggle, the two-party system would remain in power for another decade. But the decomposition of the political model continued, and in 1992 two military uprisings followed one after the other. They both failed, but they showed that the ship of representative democracy was still sinking.

The military rebellions of 1992 marked a profound break in the dominant power bloc that had ruled since 1958.[3] A very large sector of middle-ranking officers in the armed forces, unhappy at having been used by the government as "executioners" of the people during the events of February 1989, decided to rebel, raising anticorruption slogans and promoting a diffuse nationalist and popular political change. The revolt was defeated, but the dominant bloc was now fragmented and unable to reconfigure in the following years.

In the decade before Chávez, the second government of social democrat Carlos Andrés Pérez (1989–93) had inaugurated the first fully neoliberal economic plan in Venezuela.[4] The package of measures implemented at the beginning of his government, such as the liberalization of prices and the elimination of subsidies (including the important subsidy on gasoline), was the trigger for the Caracazo. Pérez was finally dismissed in 1993 by the legislature, under the accusation of corruption. In reality, however, his dismissal was a maneuver by the ruling elite (AD, COPEI, and the business and military elite) in an attempt to contain the social and military discontent and to prop up a system whose legitimacy was in question.

The Pérez government was succeeded by the social-Christian Rafael Caldera (1994–99). This was also his second time in office, but despite being the founder of COPEI, he had now broken with it and won the elections with the support of the left-wing parties. But Caldera's government, instead of being consistent with its discourse, which was critical of the neoliberal plan implemented by his predecessor, applied the same economic prescriptions of the International Monetary Fund.[5]

Citizens' rejection of this new neoliberal turn was manifested in the elections of 1998 and allowed Hugo Chávez to present himself as the nationalist and popular alternative to twenty years of economic failure and forty years of a discredited two-party political model.[6]

Hugo Chávez: From the Third Way to Socialism

Lieutenant Colonel Hugo Chávez had led the February 4, 1992, "Bolivarian" military rebellion and planned the uprising of November 27, 1992, from prison. After his release, he decided to establish a legal party (Movimiento Quinta República) and entered the 1998 elections.

In a dizzying electoral surge throughout 1998, Chávez prevailed over the unified candidate of the AD and COPEI parties, which had taken turns in power since 1958. With a central aim to convene an assembly to draft a new constitution, Chávez had a political-economic program very close to the welfare state, in a global neoliberal context. His electoral proposal announced an endorsement of the diffuse "Third Way" formulated by British leader Tony Blair and others.[7]

However, his performance at the helm of government quickly transcended this framework, moving closer to models of "socialist revolution" such as Cuba. This was in the global context of the collapse of the socialist bloc in Eastern Europe a decade earlier, the failure in Latin America of attempts at political change through armed struggle (as in El Salvador and Guatemala), and the crushing of socialist attempts by "peaceful means" (Chile). Thus, Chávez, at the end of the twentieth century and the beginning of the twenty-first, followed a reexamined ideal of "socialist revolution" that linked the principles of national sovereignty and continental integration formulated in the War of Independence with the traditions of popular revolutionary struggle expressed in the last century. Chávez defined his revolution as "socialist" during his participation in the Porto Alegre Social Forum in January 2005.[8] The basic principles of this "socialism" were participatory and protagonist democracy of "popular power" (as opposed to liberal representative democracy), "equality and justice," and "civil-military" unity.

The general economic and political situation in Latin America at the end of the twentieth century included considerable citizen rejection of the neoliberal "shock" adjustments implemented in the previous two decades. There was also accumulated popular discontent at the disastrous results of these adjustments, which had led to a reversal of the labor rights won in the postwar period and a significant drop in the income levels of the working classes.[9] This reality forced many progressive parties and leaders to speak out against neoliberalism and its main promoter, the International Monetary Fund, and to postulate alternative paths that included Keynesian and socialist proposals.

Chávez's electoral triumph in 1998 contributed to reversing this process of falling income levels for the working class, as all the neoliberal plans that had been implemented since February 1989 began to slow down, and in some cases to be reversed, due to the explicit policies of the new government.[10] In particular, the processes of privatization of public companies were halted, including the "Oil Opening" proposed by Pérez and initiated by Caldera in 1995.[11]

In the economic sphere, Chávez's project was defined by antineoliberalism and the overcoming of oil rentierism and its replacement by a neo-developmentalist policy, with strong state intervention in strategic areas.[12] The trial was carried out in a process of polarized struggle between the government, the political right, and the traditional business sector (which emerged in the period 1958–98).

The first major transformative step taken by the government was the convening of a Constituent Assembly in April of 1999. The new constitution significantly expanded social rights and some new political rights, such as the midterm recall referendum for the president of the republic and other elected positions in the executive and legislative branches.

The Chávez period revitalized the workers' struggle, changing labor relations and forms of ownership. In terms of labor rights, the constitution, approved in December 1999, ratified fundamental workers' rights already enshrined in the 1947 and 1961 constitutions. These included the right to unionize; the autonomy of trade unions from the employer and the state; the right to collective bargaining; the right to strike; the right to social security as a public service and the obligation of the state to guarantee it; the right to work and the inclusion of new rights, such as equality and equity between men and women in the exercise of the right to work; the recognition of household work as an economic activity that creates added value and produces wealth and provides welfare; the right of homemakers to social security; the progressiveness of labor rights and their inalienable nature; and, finally, the reduction of the workweek from forty-eight to forty-four hours.[13]

These constitutional rights come from the most progressive visions of the welfare state, having the historical merit of being ratified after two decades of neoliberal policies at the global level, which had among their main objectives the annihilation of such rights and the "flexibilization" of labor relations.[14] In the years that followed, Venezuelan workers embarked on a process of profound reorganization of their trade union structures, raising demands and political proposals that confronted and transcended the previous neoliberal decade and opened up prospects for the anticapitalist direction of the Venezuelan political process.[15]

Chávez's Program of Nationalization

A failed coup d'état in April 2002 was closely followed by an employer-led general strike (known as the "oil strike" or "oil lockout") in December 2002, carried out by the Puntofijista elites. The strike was an additional failed attempt to overthrow the Chávez government. Resistance to that strike generated the rise of the workers' struggle throughout the country. Its failure was taken as a victory by the sectors of Bolivarian workers who were beginning to organize independently, outside of the Confederation of Workers of Venezuela (which was one of the organizers of the strike, together with Fedecámaras).

From 2003 onward, Venezuelan workers took back companies that had been paralyzed and demanded the nationalization/renationalization of industries in the hands of the national or foreign private sector. At the same time, the workers' struggle began to try out novel forms of organizing productive activity through workers' councils and workers' control, proposals that found an echo in the Bolivarian government and ended up becoming state policies.[16]

Workers' control, which emerged as a slogan for action during the 2002–03 strike, launched the slogans of "factory stopped, factory occupied" and "workers' control of productive activity," leading to the occupation by the workers of numerous companies that had ceased activity. This occurred in Venepal (Carabobo), Venezolana de Válvulas (Los Teques), Textiles Fénix (Guárico), Cristine-Carol Perfumes (Caracas), and others.[17]

From 2004, when Chávez ordered the expropriation of Venepal, workers' control began to be considered a policy of the Venezuelan state, although it was only in 2009 that it was included as a government guideline, in what became known as the Guayana Socialist Plan.[18] The aim of workers' control as a policy was to achieve the full exercise of participatory and protagonist democracy by the workers, inside and outside the factory.[19] It constituted an experiment in the workers' battle to replace the bourgeois state with a new state of transition to socialism and was designed not to repeat the fatal mistakes of the Soviet experience.[20] Another aspect of workers' organization was the Prevention Delegates and the Committees on Occupational Safety and Health, whose promotion was in the hands of INPSASEL, an institute that is in the Ministry of Labor.[21] These committees were set up throughout the country, in various companies, and in both public and private institutions, which made them an organizational tool almost as widespread as the trade unions themselves. Prevention delegates played a role as defenders of workers' rights, especially in small companies, where there were no trade unions.[22]

In May 2012, a new labor law (LOTTT) was passed, restoring the rights violated in the Caldera reform of 1997[23] and incorporating a series of new labor and political rights.[24] The approval of LOTTT was seen as an outstanding legal contribution to the workers' struggle against neoliberalism and against capitalist exploitation in general, according to the definition contained in its Article 25, which states: "The social labor process has as its essential objective to overcome the forms of capitalist exploitation."[25]

One of the starkest expressions of the antineoliberal program, implemented during the Chávez government, was the nationalization of a range of large companies throughout the country:[26]

- February 2007: Nationalization of the oil fields operated in the Orinoco Belt by transnational companies from the US, UK, France, and Norway.
- May 2007: Nationalization of the company Electricidad de Caracas, creation of the National Electricity Corporation (Corpoelec), and nationalization of regional private companies.
- May 2008: Nationalization of CANTV, buying the shares of the US company Verizon.[27]
- April 2008: Renationalization of Siderúrgica del Orinoco (SIDOR), which was owned by the Italian Argentine multinational Techint, a company closely linked to the Kirchner government.[28]
- 2008: Nationalization of the country's main cement industries, which were owned by Mexico's Cemex, Switzerland's Holcim, and France's Lafarge.
- May 2009: Nationalization of briquette companies, such as MATESSI, and the pipe factory TAVSA.
- 2009: Nationalization of seventy-six medium-sized companies that provided services to the oil industry.
- 2009: Nationalization of the sardine processing company La Gaviota and Café Fama de América.
- 2009: Nationalization of the Banco de Venezuela, which was owned by the Spanish Santander group.
- 2007–9: Occupation of idle land and nationalization of numerous large estates in various states of the country.

The highlight of this process was the renationalization of SIDOR, a product of a long struggle by the company's workers. In 1997, SIDOR had been handed over to a private Argentine consortium.[29] After fifteen months of struggle by its workers, President Chávez's decision to nationalize the company was the trigger for the strengthening of workers' control and the approval in 2009 of the Guayana Socialist Plan.[30]

The Plan Guayana Socialista represented the culmination of the efforts made during the government of Hugo Chávez to follow a path that would dismantle the neoliberal policies of previous decades and advance the definition of anticapitalist productive models.[31] From the outset, this plan was met with resistance and sabotage, from both the bureaucracy embedded in the structures of the state (companies and ministries) and the trade unions.[32] Both sectors reflected, to some extent, the interests of the large iron and aluminum multinationals that had been affected by the nationalizations, who were intent on recovering the business that the revolution had taken away from them.[33]

In general, all nationalized companies came under state control through various ministries. Although there were proposals and attempts to establish forms of co-management through workers' councils, the Chávez government ultimately imposed state management, appointing presidents, managers, and directors for each of the expropriated companies. For almost all of these expropriated companies, the state compensated their owners, as it did with Agroisleña, Banco de Venezuela (Grupo Santander), CANTV (telecommunications), the Caracas electricity company SIDOR, and most of the oil service companies in the state of Zulia. In the case of land expropriations, the state compensated for some, mainly the larger ones, but failed to pay for several dozen smaller expropriations.[34] The productive operations of almost all expropriations carried out under Chávez have seen a prolonged decline over the past fifteen years. Nearly all of these companies have incurred losses during this period; some have ceased operations entirely, while others continue to function thanks to state subsidies. Today, in 2024, the Maduro government plans to privatize around 350 companies that remain under state ownership, according to the president of Conindustria, Luigi Pisella.[35]

Final Considerations on the Chávez Period

Hugo Chávez's period of government contributed to the relative improvement of workers' incomes and living conditions by introducing the social missions, conceived as "social wages." Health programs in the neighborhoods, construction of popular housing, school feeding programs, access to vehicles and household appliances through pricing initiatives, expansion of the public university system, expansion of the pension system to homemakers and noncontributing workers, among others, all made it possible to improve the general living conditions of the working class. All of this despite the fact that real wages, although they experienced periods of increase between 1999 and 2001 and 2003 and 2006, saw an overall decline of 20 percent during the first decade of Chavismo (1999–2010).[36] It is important to emphasize this point: In the second half of Chávez's presidency (2006–12), real wages began to decline, a trend that accelerated under Nicolás Maduro's government, virtually disappearing altogether (wages under Maduro's government fell by over 95 percent).[37]

Although the program executed by Chávez was not, strictly speaking, a socialist or communist program, his performance at the head of the state was a 180-degree turn in relation to the previous governments of Venezuela since independence.

On the international front, Chávez moved away from the position of his predecessors, who had historically acted in subordination to the US government. He distanced himself from the so-called Western bloc (the United States and the European Union), moving closer to emerging powers such as China, Russia, Iran, and Turkey. He maintained a strong relationship with the communist government of Fidel Castro in Cuba. He confronted the traditional US hegemony in Latin America, challenging the Organization of American States and promoting the creation of alternative integration organizations, such as CELAC (Community of Latin American and Caribbean States) and ALBA (Bolivarian Alternative for the Americas). A highlight of his international actions was his opposition to the Free Trade Area of the Americas project, a US proposal to reduce or eliminate the trade barriers among all countries in the Americas, excluding Cuba. It was defeated at the Fourth Summit of the Americas in Mar del Plata (November 2005), with the prominent participation of the presidents of the Mercosur countries, who joined with Chávez to reject the US proposal and deliver a historic defeat to US interests, represented at the summit by both President George Bush and Secretary of State Condoleezza Rice.[38]

During Chávez's presidency, there was a rise of left-wing forces throughout Latin America, leading to a radical change in the entire Latin American political landscape. The anti-imperialist discourse, confronting the US government and its traditional influence in the continent, was strengthened as never before in history. This radical shift resulted in the electoral triumphs of Luiz Inácio Lula da Silva (2003–10) and Dilma Rousseff (2011–16) in Brazil;[39] Néstor Kirchner (2003–7) and Cristina Fernández de Kirchner (2007–15) in Argentina; Rafael Correa in Ecuador (2007–17); Evo Morales in Bolivia (2006–19); Tabaré Vázquez (2005–10) and José "Pepe" Mujica (2010–15) in Uruguay; Fernando Lugo in Paraguay (2008–12);[40] Michelle Bachelet in Chile (2006–10); Daniel Ortega in Nicaragua (2007–21); Mauricio Funes in El Salvador (2009–14); Manuel Zelaya in Honduras (2006–9);[41] and Ollanta Humala in Peru (2011–16).

Chávez's presidency in Venezuela brought about a radical transformation of the entire Latin American political landscape. The anti-imperialist rhetoric, opposing the US government and its traditional influence in the region, became stronger than ever before in history, contributing to the perception of Chávez and Chavismo as a "communist" political force, even though their policies and program were not defined as such. The influence of Chavismo throughout Latin America resurrected the language of the old Cold War in the discourse of US government spokespeople and their allies across the continent, even though the Cold War had ended in 1991 with the collapse of the Soviet Union.

The campaign mounted by the US government against Chávez and the spread of Chavismo in the region revived, in the twenty-first century, the fight against "communist expansion" that had been prominent during the 1960s, 1970s, and 1980s.

However, it must be emphasized that Chávez never outlined a truly socialist economic program. The measures he implemented fit perfectly within a Keynesian model of state intervention in the economy. Socialism was always present in his rhetoric, but it was rarely reflected in the actual governance. The expropriation of companies and land may have given the impression of a "socialist government," but in reality, they merely contributed to the formation of a relatively powerful state capitalism.

As early as 2009, during an event where forty intellectuals debated the most visible problems of the Bolivarian Revolution, warnings were raised about the formation of a new "Bolivarian" bourgeoisie.[42] This group emerged through the influence of the ruling party and numerous leaders of the revolution (governors, mayors, deputies, military commanders), who used their positions to seize numerous private companies, which simply changed hands due to the extortive power of those controlling the state.[43] A significant portion of the economic groups known as "bolibourgeoisie" (Bolivarian bourgeoisie) were established during Chávez's presidency, including figures like Raúl Gorrín (owner of the private TV channel Globovisión) and Wilmer Ruperti (owner of another private TV channel, oil entrepreneur, and professional baseball team owner). Major embezzlers of public funds, such as Lieutenant Alejandro Andrade (Chávez's private secretary and later national treasurer) and Claudia Díaz (Chávez's nurse and later national treasurer), fled Venezuela with hundreds of millions of dollars after Chávez's death. Both were detained in the United States in recent years, and their assets were confiscated.

The Return to the Neoliberal and Authoritarian Past Under the Government of Nicolás Maduro

Chávez's illness in mid-2011 weakened the forces that were fighting for alternative paths to the old neoliberal playbook, and in the course of 2012 the Guayana Socialist Plan began to be dismantled and abandoned by the ministries and companies involved.[44]

His death in 2013, and the inauguration of Nicolás Maduro as president later in 2013, meant the almost total abandonment of the antineoliberal program and the return of the same economic policies implemented in the last decade of the twentieth century. Maduro maintained the same radical discourse as his predecessor and presented his government as a genuinely "workerist" and "socialist" one, which had the backing of the ruling class. However, in office, he has implemented a real change of economic course, opening the doors to neoliberal policies in a framework of growing authoritarianism.[45]

The reality of the Venezuelan economy more than eight years into Maduro's rule ranks as the worst performance in the world, and one of the five worst performances in the history of capitalism over the past seventy years.[46] A contraction of more than 50 percent of GDP in seven years; closure of 60 percent of existing factories; a minimum wage of less than US$3 a month in the context of a monthly food basket of US$300; a society that had received a trillion dollars in the oil boom between 2004 and 2008 that, without having gone through a war, has today a totally destroyed economy.[47] All of this highlights the absence of a coherent economic plan and the adoption of measures that contradict each other and that deepen the collapse of the Venezuelan economy every day.[48]

The failure of endogenous development projects, due to state mismanagement of nationalized companies, combined with the fall in oil prices over the 2012–22 decade, has generated a drop in production and an increase in foreign borrowing to fund the state apparatus and the importation of manufactured goods and foodstuffs. This is the background to the current scenario of hyperinflation, overindebtedness, and falling oil production.[49]

It is important to note that this economic crisis has been exacerbated to the point of collapse by the blockade of assets and the economic and financial sanctions applied by the United States and its international allies beginning in 2017.[50]

The decision to grant a license to the Arco Minero del Orinoco (AMO) project is perhaps the starkest example of the return to neoliberal economics. It involved the approval of the extraction of minerals in the states of Bolívar and Amazonas, on a surface equivalent to 12.2 percent of the national territory, inhabited by 54,686 Indigenous people and with significant ecological biodiversity. This territory was handed over to multinational companies for the exploitation of gold, copper, diamonds, coltan, iron, bauxite, and other minerals.[51] The approval of the AMO did not comply with the constitutional requirement to consult the Indigenous communities living in the territory. The project also subordinates any disputes that may exist between the Venezuelan state and the contracting companies to international tribunals, despite express constitutional provisions that reject any interference by foreign courts in the national economy.[52] Similar to the maquiladora regions of traditional neoliberalism, the AMO does not recognize the validity of labor rights as laid out in the constitution and the LOTTT in areas subject to mining concessions. As Edgardo Lander puts it,

> The Venezuelan government is secretly taking strategic decisions that could be defining the future of the country for the rest of the century. . . . Through the presidential decree of the AMO, it was decided to create a . . . mining free zone, under military control, where many of the constitutional rights, among others, the rights of indigenous peoples, are pre-emptively suspended.[53]

In terms of wage policy, the performance of wages during the period 1999–2020 shows an upward curve in the first half of the period (1999–2007) and a downward curve in the following years (2008–23). The fall in wages in recent years has reached levels not seen in any other neoliberal administration on the continent. Real wages in 2020 have fallen by 96 percent since the period 2006–7.[54] The Federation of Associations of University Professors of Venezuela puts the fall in salaries in the period 2001–20 at 99 percent.[55]

This total collapse of real wages by 99 percent is what explains the enormous migration of more than seven million people from Venezuela in the past ten years. Javier Biardeau points out the wage regression of Venezuelan workers is so pronounced that, in 2020, a Venezuelan worker's monthly salary was almost equivalent to that earned by an oil worker in a day's work eighty-four years earlier at the time of the great oil strike of 1936 (5 bolivars a day is equivalent to US$1.57 a day).[56]

Maduro's government, with Memorandum 2792 of the Ministry of Labor in October of 2018, ignored all the collective bargaining agreements in force in the public administration and in the private sector, sweeping away, in a single act, all that had been achieved under Hugo Chávez.[57] As the class-conscious trade union leader Orlando Chirino states, "In the labor relations of the last 30 years a government had not produced a legal instrument as reactionary and anti-worker as Memorandum 2792."[58]

The government's policy has been to "flatten" the wage tables, establishing minimal differences between starting salaries and the highest pay scales, violating the constitutional principle of progressivity in labor rights and ignoring seniority, professional and technical training, degrees of responsibility, and the meritocracy of workers.[59]

As can be seen from the preceding, similar to the neoliberal programs put in place by the governments of Carlos Andrés Pérez and Rafael Caldera between 1989 and 1999, Maduro's government is following a neoliberal path in the design and implementation of its programs. The following are details of just some of these programs and their effects:

- Liberation of exchange control and free floating of the currency against the dollar. Since 2017 the bolivar has been devalued at the rate of hyperinflation.
- Import of food and other products free of tariffs. Import permits have been granted to businesses sympathetic to the government.
- Price liberalization of foodstuffs and other products from the basic food basket. When price regulations are established for a specific list of products, the amount needed to purchase that list is more than twenty times the official minimum wage.[60]
- Pulverization of real wages, which in relation to the dollar have been reduced by between 96 percent and 99 percent in twenty years.
- Maintenance of VAT (value-added tax) as a regressive tax that penalizes consumers.
- Privatization processes in major branches of industries, such as oil, iron, aluminum, and gold and diamonds, and in services such as petrol distribution, which by law is a function reserved to the state. The "unregulated" price of gasoline was set by the government at $0.50 per liter, introducing the dollar as the country's official currency.[61]
- Almost total labor flexibilization, with Memorandum 2792, which ignores the labor rights enshrined in the constitution itself and in the LOTTT.[62]

- Limitations of the "missions" social policies, which are most effective in the capital Caracas and are almost nonexistent in the rest of the cities and towns.[63] In recent years, the food box delivery service CLAP has been added to the social missions as has the *carnet de la patria*, which is random and irregular.[64]

At the same time, Maduro's government has developed a significant authoritarian profile, manifested in the following:

- The government has suspended the validity of the National Constitution through the so-called Anti-Blockade Law (LAB), approved by the unconstitutional Constituent Assembly (2017–20), which allows the president of the republic to relax and suspend legal and constitutional regulations and norms to advance a reorganization and restructuring of public entities and state-owned companies, including the modification of the business regime, business model, and the state's shareholding in mixed and public companies, in the context of a policy of opening up the economy to national and international capital.[65]
- The LAB also empowers the president to negotiate the assets and liabilities of the republic to generate income, which, in plain language, is an open-ended authorization to liquidate the republic's assets through a process of privatization and renegotiation of financial liabilities. All of this, without being subject to legal and constitutional controls.[66]
- The LAB establishes exceptional contracting mechanisms, a regime of confidentiality for all economic decisions of the executive, and submits disputes with foreign investors to foreign courts. All of this violates express provisions of the constitution, annuls the National Assembly's oversight functions, and ends up, effectively, abolishing the rule of law in Venezuela.[67]
- The Regionalization Law (decree-law of 2014) and the Special Economic Zones Law (draft of 2021) aim at a reorganization of the territory of the republic, outside the territorial division enshrined in the constitution. This is characterized by "maquila zones" and extractivist enclaves, typical of neoliberal "savage" capitalism, which involves the suppression of taxes and the absence of labor and environmental regulations.

- The Law Against Hatred of 2017 established penalties that can include twenty years in jail, media shutdown, and fines to companies and electronic media. It has served to imprison dozens of opposition activists for merely criticizing the actions of the government.[68]
- Finally, there has been an indefinite suspension of all trade union elections, nonrecognition of the majority of workers' federations, and the use of small trade union organizations sympathetic to the government to simulate a nonexistent "workers' democracy."

Conclusion

Despite many major mistakes made in his economic policy, the Chávez government made significant attempts to transcend neoliberalism and promote a productive economy, based on economic independence and popular participation. During the first decade of the twenty-first century, government policies enacted in Venezuela sought to leave behind oil rentierism and move toward a socialist economy.

After Chávez's death in 2013, neoliberalism and authoritarianism returned under the government of Maduro. Economist Pasqualina Curcio, a prominent supporter of Maduro's government, recognizes how the distribution of gross domestic product (GDP) has changed regressively between 2014 and 2017.[69] Using a didactic example, Curcio explains that in 2014 "the cake of the Venezuelan economy" was divided into sixteen, distributed in portions of seven for the bourgeoisie, seven for wage earners, and two for the state.[70] In 2017, with a cake one-third smaller than in 2014 (according to the Central Bank of Venezuela, the economy shrank 34 percent between 2014 and 2017), the distribution was ten portions for the bourgeoisie, five for the wage earners, and one for the state. In terms of prices and wages, between 2014 and 2017 prices increased by 10.013 percent and wages by only 6.436 percent.[71] Curcio herself recognizes that this distributional regression of GDP was further accentuated between 2017 and 2023.

Some direct consequences of this neoliberal regression are detailed in a recent Caritas study, "Child Nutrition and Food Security," of April 2020, which found that severe malnutrition in children under five years of age grew by 5.78 percent in just six months, from 11.5 percent in November 2019 to 17.3 percent in April 2020. In the same period, the number of households with access to state-subsidized food through the CLAP boxes decreased by almost a third, from 70 percent to 41 percent, while the number of people suffering from food insecurity grew from 32.2 percent to 40 percent, of which 21 percent suffer from severe food insecurity.[72]

The self-described anti-imperialist character of Maduro's government has aligned itself with the Eastern bloc, made up mainly of China and Russia.[73] However, it has simultaneously executed a neoliberal plan of privatizations, labor flexibilization, and political repression against its own people. Despite this, the Maduro administration is seen as suspect by the governments of the United States (and its allies in the European Union), which has interfered in the internal affairs of Venezuela. This interference explicitly seeks the removal of Maduro from power and the assumption of a political leadership docile to the interests of the Western powers.

In reality, Maduro's government has similarities to the populist regimes of the twentieth century in Latin America due to the predominance of an extremely radical demagogic discourse that is not inconsistent with an authoritarian and neoliberal bent, but with an orientation to the people and in the interests of national development. A complex and contradictory reality, which shows how the interests of big multinational capital have no ideological boundaries and how the neoliberal economic program can be implemented by governments that formally declare themselves to be enemies of this same neoliberalism.

CHAPTER FOUR

The Venezuelan Workers' Movement During the Bolivarian Process

Roberto López Sánchez

This analysis aims to examine the trajectory of the workers' movement in Venezuela over the span of approximately twenty-five years, encompassing the political era referred to as the "Bolivarian Revolution." Within this time frame, there were notable advancements in labor legislation and a resurgence of the labor movement that played a pivotal role in the transformative processes that characterized the initial decade of the twenty-first century. However, this period has also seen a regression toward neoliberal policies reminiscent of the 1990s. In response, the workers' movement, which became disoriented and fragmented due to significant shifts in the "revolution's" political and economic agenda, has recently initiated a process of reorganization and renewed struggle. Its focus centers on demanding the preservation of labor rights and an end to repressive measures against the workers' movement.

The Workers' Movement at the Moment of the Electoral Triumph of Chávez

At the time of Hugo Chávez's electoral victory in December 1998, the workers' movement in Venezuela was profoundly debilitated due to the cumulative impact of four decades of class collaborationist social democratic leadership by the Democratic Action party, which held sway over the country's largest labor union, the Confederation of Workers of Venezuela (CTV). This leadership adhered to class accommodation as a guiding principle. However, in the preceding decade, this approach had translated into endorsing the neoliberal economic policies of the Carlos Andrés Pérez (1989–93) and Rafael Caldera (1994–99) administrations.

Despite Chávez's electoral campaign gaining support from small labor groups with class-oriented agendas that had managed to persist in isolation within the nation, the majority of federations and unions remained under the influence of the CTV. This union body had become highly bureaucratized and had lost credibility among the working class. With no alternative political force or union available, "the existing Venezuelan labor movement in 1998 found itself completely subjected to neoliberal policies, with no capacity to resist, and facing political and organizational fragility that relegated it to secondary roles within the prevailing political landscape in Venezuela."[1] This was the state of the labor movement in Venezuela at the start of the Chávez administration in February 1999.

Labor Rights Consecrated in the Constitution of the Bolivarian Republic of Venezuela and the LOTTT

One main characteristic of Hugo Chávez's period of government was the conquest of labor rights enshrined in the constitution and laws. First in the Constituent Assembly of 1999 and later in the Organic Law of Labor, Work and Workers (LOTTT), approved in 2012.[2]

The ratification of the new constitution on December 15, 1999, introduced a series of substantial advancements in labor rights, fundamentally altering the neoliberal trajectory that the Venezuelan state had adhered to in the final decade of the twentieth century. These accomplishments emerged from the personal initiatives of certain constituents rather than being part of a preestablished political agenda within the Chavismo leadership.

The labor rights incorporated into the Bolivarian Constitution of 1999 were primarily rooted in an expanded interpretation of the welfare state concept, which originated in the twentieth century within liberal democracies across Europe and the United States. Some of these rights had already been present in the constitutions of 1961 and 1947. The distinguishing factor is that these rights were ratified during a historical juncture wherein globalized capitalism no longer defended or promoted these worker-centric achievements. Instead, the prevailing neoliberal model prevailed, marked by the neglect and constriction of these very rights.

Among the rights constitutionally enshrined in 1999 that have a direct connection to the sphere of work are the following:*

- The right of every citizen to social security as a public service, and the obligation of the state to guarantee it (Article 86).
- The right to work and the responsibility of the state to promote and guarantee employment (Article 87).
- The equality and equity of men and women in the exercise of the right to work, and the recognition of household work as an economic activity that creates added value and produces wealth and social well-being. The right of homemakers to social security (Article 88).[3]
- The progressivity of labor rights and their inalienable nature (Article 89).[4]
- The reduction of the workweek from 48 to 44 hours (Article 90).[5]
- The responsibility of the state to set the minimum wage and to adjust it each year according to the cost of the basic food basket (Article 91).
- The right of workers to be paid for seniority (Article 92).

* These are summations of articles in the Constitution of the Bolivarian Republic of Venezuela.

- The guarantee of stability at work (Article 93).
- The right of workers to form unions and their autonomy with respect to employers and the state (Article 95).
- Union democracy understood through the election and replacement of union leaders by universal, direct, and secret suffrage (Article 95).
- The right to collective bargaining (Article 96).[6]
- The right to strike (Article 97).

While the formal inclusion of these rights in the constitution did not automatically translate into their practical implementation, it is evident from a historical and political standpoint that these achievements established during the Constituent Assembly served to bolster the determination of Venezuelan laborers. These gains notably augmented their rights and their demographic representation, as exemplified by the inclusion of homemakers within the workforce.

It is crucial to underscore the progressive nature of these rights entrenched in the constitution. They were reaffirmed after over two decades of bold implementation of neoliberal policies across Latin America, which notably disregarded historical labor achievements. This reaffirmation occurred just two years after the second term of Rafael Caldera's presidency (1994–99), during which the Labor Law of 1997 was amended to introduce provisions that openly contradicted the interests of the working class. These provisions included the removal of retroactive calculations for severance pay and the elimination of protections against unjustified dismissals.

However, the creation of a new Organic Labor Law (LOT), which was mandated by the constitution to be developed within a year after the installation of the new National Assembly (as stated in the fourth transitory provision of the Bolivarian Constitution), faced delays for the subsequent thirteen years. It was not until 2012 that a new LOT was finally approved through the Enabling Law.

The adoption of a new Organic Labor Law in May 2012 not only reinstated the rights violated by the regime preceding the Bolivarian process but also introduced and enhanced new labor and political demands. This law received overwhelming support, as evidenced by the participation of thousands of workers in the May 1, 2012, demonstrations. This significant moment marked the emergence of Venezuelan workers as central figures within the country's political landscape.

The new LOTTT was a response from the Bolivarian government to a continuous process of worker leadership, which had developed in response to the employer oil strike orchestrated by Fedecámaras and the Confederation of Workers of Venezuela (CTV) in 2002–3.[7] This strike prompted workers to mobilize, leading to the exploration of novel production scenarios by reactivating halted companies and advocating for the nationalization or renationalization of privately owned firms. This movement also fostered innovative forms of organizing productive activities through workers' councils and exerting workers' control. These proposals resonated with the Bolivarian government and gradually evolved into official state policies.

In the realm of economic demands inherent to negotiations between wage labor and capital, the Bolivarian Revolution expanded rights and achieved milestones unprecedented in the country's political history. These initiatives began with the reinstatement of benefits that had been lost by workers in the 1997 LOT reform, specifically the calculation of seniority benefits based on the last salary and the provision for double compensation in cases of unjustified dismissal. Simultaneously, the new LOTTT extended other rights, such as the following:

- Mandatory two-year job protection for both parents after childbirth.
- Prenatal and postnatal leave: six weeks before delivery and twenty weeks after childbirth.
- Establishment of nurseries for children aged three months to six years. Costs covered by employers.
- Adoption of a five-day workweek with two consecutive paid days off. Standard workday of eight hours and workweek of forty hours (replacing the previous forty-four-hour workweek and single official rest day).
- Introduction of new public holidays: Monday and Tuesday of carnival and December 24 and 31.

- Vacation bonus: fifteen days of regular salary plus an additional day for each year of service, up to thirty days (replacing the previous seven days of salary, up to twenty-one days).
- Doubling of year-end bonus to thirty days (formerly fifteen days).
- Extension of the statute of limitations for social benefit claims to ten years (previously one year). For other labor claims, the limitation period is extended to five years (formerly one year).
- Prohibition of outsourcing. Within a maximum of three years, employers must transition by incorporating outsourced workers into the regular payroll (this transition period concluded on May 7, 2015).

The definition stated in Article 25 of the LOTTT, which states that "[t]he social labor process aims to overcome the forms of capitalist exploitation," represented a groundbreaking aspect that went beyond the scope of all previous Venezuelan labor legislation, which in the past had been limited to regulation of the forms of exploitation of salaried labor by capital.

These aspects encompass a range of restorative elements, some with political implications and others pertaining to proposals for socioeconomic transformation. Collectively, these elements marked significant historical progress in comparison with the achievements Venezuelan workers had pursued since the inception of their earliest forms of organization at the start of the twentieth century.

Crisis and the Decline of CTV's Hegemonic Position

The long-standing hegemony of the Confederation of Venezuelan Workers (CTV) was completely upended during the initial decade of the Bolivarian movement. Following its participation in the 2002 coup attempt and the employer-led strike at the close of 2002, the CTV experienced a precipitous decline. CTV-affiliated unions witnessed a mass departure of workers, leading to a significant migration toward the new Bolivarian unions that emerged during the initial years of Chávez's presidency. This transition was not orchestrated by Chavismo; rather, it evolved spontaneously as workers opted to disengage from their long-standing unions and federations, opting instead to create fresh unions, often embracing the Bolivarian ideology through the inclusion of the term *Bolivarian* in their names.

Between 2003 and 2004 alone, the number of unions officially recognized by the Ministry of Labor grew from 2,974 to approximately 4,000. By 2012, the CTV had lost a staggering 90 percent of the workers who had been affiliated with it in 1998, as confirmed by Daniel Santolo, the president of the CTV's Permanent Electoral Commission and a member of the Causa R party.[8]

Over time, the CTV dwindled into what some of its own leaders described as a "hollow shell." The attendance at the May 1, 2012, labor marches starkly demonstrated this phenomenon. While the march organized by the new "official" Bolivarian Socialist Central of Workers (CBST) drew around four hundred thousand participants in Caracas, the CTV's march in another part of the city garnered no more than a thousand workers. Similarly, a third march, organized by various factions of the Venezuelan National Workers' Union (UNETE), also saw minimal attendance. The CBST march's robust turnout occurred despite prevailing discontent among workers and their organizations due to the discrepancies between the assertive, worker-oriented rhetoric of Chávez and his main government representatives and the opposing actions observed within state institutions and even the labor ministry itself. This situation reflected the predominance of the working masses' aspirations for change over their critical evaluations, at least for that period.

The Birth of UNETE and CBST

Following the 2002–3 oil strike, the National Union of Workers (UNETE) was founded in Caracas, a trade union federation whose birth signaled the end of the CTV era. In a national assembly of workers held in Caracas on April 5, 2003, the constitution of UNETE was approved. This assembly designated a horizontal National Committee consisting of twenty-one members representing unions from key regions. It led to the creation of a constitutive act and a statute body. The mandate of the national committee was to establish the national and regional structures of the new labor federation.

On August 1 and 2 of 2003, the first UNETE Congress was convened, where principles were declared, a code of ethics for trade unions was adopted, a struggle platform was outlined, and an agreement on the country's situation was reached. Regional sections of UNETE were formed across the nation, and national sectors were structured. During this period, discussions also focused on the most significant collective agreements in the country.

From 2003 to 2011, UNETE represented the Venezuelan workers' movement on the international stage, as well as in the International Labor Organization. However, differences among the Bolivarian factions within UNETE eventually led to the departure of the Bolivarian Socialist Workers Federation (FSBT) in 2006. The underlying reason for this schism was quite simple: the FSBT was the trend most closely associated with Chávez, through its founder, Maduro, but it was a minority within UNETE. They destroyed what they could not control.

At the II UNITE Congress in May 2006, the FSBT barely had 10 percent of the national delegates, in contrast to 60 percent of the C-CURA (Trotskyist) tendency, 20 percent of the CTR tendency led by Marcela Máspero, and 10 percent from the other minority tendencies.[9] This didn't stop the FSBT from further fracturing the movement by establishing a parallel workers' union, the Bolivarian Socialist Central of Workers (CBST). With the assistance and full support of President Hugo Chávez and the appointment of the oil leader Will Rangel as president of the new federation, the CBST brought together nearly all national-level union federations aligned with Bolivarianism. This marked the definitive shift of influence from UNETE to the newly formed CBST. The birth of CBST displaced UNETE from the privileged position it occupied as the primary workers' union in the country (the influence of UNETE gradually crumbled between 2006 and 2011).

Around mid-2013, the unions associated with UNETE, aligned with the Cruz Villegas Trade Union Current (affiliated with the Communist Party of Venezuela), encountered conflicts with the CTR Current and also opted to join the CBST. As a result, UNETE's influence was further diminished, leaving it primarily with the Máspero faction, and it has persisted as a significantly marginalized workers' union with limited mobilization capabilities.

Within the CBST, diverse political currents emerged, characterized by significant disparities in their perspectives on the nature of the workers' movement and the methods of organization and activism. The dominance of the FSBT within the official union has been maintained through undemocratic practices, wherein political stances are imposed without consulting the worker base. This dynamic has led to fractures and the departure of federations, unions, and dissatisfied leaders who disagree with the absence of union democracy within the CBST.

At the time of writing the CBST had not yet conducted elections, and its leadership remains unchanged from the time of its establishment as a central entity in 2011.

Combativity Is Renewed in the Labor Movement During the Chávez Period

A significant transformation within the Venezuelan workers' movement emerged as it engaged extensively in protests and confrontations against the enduring neoliberal policies under Chávez's administration. A noteworthy instance was the spirited mobilization of SIDOR workers aimed at regaining control of the company, which had been privatized during the 1990s as part of the neoliberal measures enacted by Carlos Andrés Pérez and Rafael Caldera.[10] Following years of persistent and intense clashes, the Chávez government ultimately yielded to the demand for the renationalization of SIDOR in 2008. This decision was made despite the international complexities arising from preexisting economic agreements between the Bolivarian government and Argentina.[11]

The nationalization marked a substantial victory for the workers, setting the stage for the subsequent workers' control process encompassing all key companies in Guayana, known as the Guayana Socialist Plan, which was approved in 2009.[12]

Another significant instance occurred with the formal enactment of the new labor law, the Organic Law of Work and Workers (LOTTT), in May 2012. It is worth highlighting that from 2009 to 2011, a series of large-scale worker mobilizations took place, urging the government to adopt the new law. These marches were primarily organized by UNETE and proponents of workers' control. Despite the government's prolonged delay in passing this labor law for over a decade, it eventually yielded and reversed all the neoliberal measures previously introduced by Caldera in his 1997 reform of the LOT.

Throughout the Bolivarian process, the Venezuelan workers' movement exhibited signs of revival, a sharp contrast with the previous era, when the workers' movement of the 1990s struggled to mount effective protests against neoliberal labor reforms.

Prevention Delegates, Workers' Control, and Workers' Councils

During Hugo Chávez's administration, two novel forms of workers' movement organization emerged: Prevention Delegates and workers' councils. The concept of Prevention Delegates was introduced through the reform of LOPCYMAT in 2005, while the idea of workers' councils was incorporated into the new labor law of May 2012 (LOTTT).*

The concept of workers' control gained traction during the oil industry strike of 2002–3. In response to the shutdown of numerous companies and their abandonment by employers, the labor movement championed slogans like "factory stopped, factory occupied" and "control of productive activity by workers," which started to develop organically as workers occupied companies that had halted operations. Instances like the occupation of Venepal (Carabobo), Venezolana de Válvulas (Los Teques), Textiles Fénix (Guárico), and Perfumes Cristine-Carol (Caracas) exemplified this. It was not until President Chávez's 2004 expropriation of Venepal that workers' control was officially endorsed as a state policy. However, it was the 2008 renationalization of SIDOR that solidified workers' control as a central theme in the Guayana Socialist Plan, introduced in 2009.[13]

---

* LOPCYMAT is the Organic Law on Prevention, Working Conditions, and Environment. This law, enacted in 2005, establishes the legal framework for workplace safety and health and the general welfare of workers.

The objective of this Socialist Workers' Control policy was to empower workers for participatory democracy both inside and outside the workplace. Workers' councils were proposed as an organizational instrument to break away from the capitalist segmentation of workers into various categories based on their roles, replacing it with direct democracy that united revolutionary activists for discussions and political actions.[14]

According to Carlos Carcione, the experiment of workers' control (2003–10) represented an immense endeavor in the workers' struggle to replace the current bourgeois state with a transitional state leading to socialism. This struggle aimed to create a fundamentally different political system, eliminating private ownership of production means, capitalist production relationships, and dismantling the old bourgeois state to forge a new transitional state toward socialism.[15]

Although the workers' councils only gained legal recognition in May 2012, they started to emerge in 2003 as groups of workers sought to maintain control over companies that had been halted during the 2002–3 strike, or those that had been abandoned by employers and were idle. Subsequently, the promotion of workers' councils came from the state itself, facilitated by the Ministry of Labor and other ministries connected to the management of recovered factories, although without following a single coherent policy. The 2012 LOTTT stipulated the drafting of a special law for workers' councils, which was ultimately approved in January 2018 under the revised title Law of Productive Workers' Councils.[16]

This 2018 law on Workers' Productive Councils (CPT) significantly altered the objectives under which the so-called workers' control initially emerged following the defeat of the employer-labor coup strike of December 2002–January 2003. The law did not conceive of the CPTs as an organization representing all the workers of a factory or company but instead limited them to groups of three, five, or at most seven people. This marked a shift from the assembly-based practice that had been implemented in numerous companies, such as SIDOR, Alcasa, Venepal, and Venezolana de Válvulas, to a model where a very small group of individuals, designated in a "workers' assembly," assumed functions that were initially intended to be the domain of the workers' assembly itself. Notably, in companies like SIDOR and Alcasa, workers' assemblies inspired by workers' control were responsible for appointing workers who took on the management of these large state-owned enterprises during 2008–09.

Under the 2018 law, the functions of the CPTs were reduced to "monitoring production processes," "informing the employer of proposed recommendations," and "reporting to the relevant authorities" any "actions contrary to the Venezuelan economic system." From assembly-based bodies of workers' control, the CPTs were transformed into small oversight committees limited to making recommendations and reports to employers and state entities—functions that could easily be, and historically have been, carried out by existing union organizations.

Regarding Prevention Delegates and CSSLs, their promotion has been overseen by INPSASEL (National Institute for Prevention, Health, and Safety at Work), an institute under the Ministry of Labor. These concepts have been adopted across various companies and public and private institutions, making them, for a period, nearly as widespread as unions themselves.

The Prevention Delegates were elected through the Ministry of Labor during a period spanning roughly from 2003 to 2010. During this time, INPSASEL contributed to strengthening worker organization in companies where unions did not exist or where union activity was minimal. In large companies like Pequiven (Petrochemical) in the state of Zulia, up to ninety prevention delegates were elected. Prevention Delegates and CSSLs were also elected in state-owned companies with strong union organizations. In these cases, the approach taken by both the Ministry of Labor and class-conscious workers' movements aimed to promote complementarity between unions and Prevention Delegates. However, in many state-owned and private companies, contradictions arose between union leaderships and the occupational safety and health committees.

Under Nicolás Maduro's administration, the Ministry of Labor gave little continuity to the promotion of Prevention Delegates, likely because they were democratically elected in assemblies by shift and work area within companies. These delegates represented a collective of workers with autonomy, supported by the powers granted to them under the still-valid LOPCYMAT, making them difficult for state bureaucracy to control. Today, Prevention Delegates and CSSLs are severely weakened and nearly nonexistent.

The hegemony within the CBST by political factions that did not uphold the principle of union autonomy (prioritizing independence from the state, employers, and political parties), and instead advocated for labor organizations' alignment with the state and ruling party, had a detrimental impact on the future of the workers' movement. This trend posed a risk of steering the movement toward bureaucratic pathways reminiscent of the old CTV's experience.

By and large, as of 2013, similar negative patterns and bureaucratic practices that were present in the former CTV persisted within the new CBST framework. Notably, there was a complete forfeiture of autonomy and a marked submission to the directives of the executive power. The rhetoric employed by key CBST leaders closely resembled the discourse of officials in managerial roles within both companies and state institutions.

The Turn Toward Maduro's Neoliberalism and the Accommodation of the CBST to This New Neoliberal Route of the "Revolution"

Although Maduro, who assumed leadership of the "revolution" following Chávez's passing, hails from the labor sector and has received unanimous backing from the entire leadership of the official CBST, his governance approach has, contrary to the interests of the working class, gradually adopted a neoliberal economic agenda. This was coupled with an antiunion strategy aimed at curtailing labor rights and suppressing labor leaders who have opposed these strategies.[17]

Prominent among the primary labor flexibility measures implemented by the Maduro administration are the following:

- Memorandum 2792 issued by the Ministry of Labor in 2018, which, using economic sanctions imposed by the United States and Western European countries on Venezuela as an excuse, disregarded all ongoing collective bargaining agreements.[18]

- The "Onapre instructions" introduced in 2022, which prevented the salary increase decreed by the government in March of that year from influencing the salary structures of the public administration as outlined in recently signed collective contracts with the government by CBST.[19]
- The flattening of public administration salary scales, minimizing salary discrepancies between different positions resulting in salary reductions of up to 96 percent compared with 2007. This approach disregards factors like seniority, professional and technical training, levels of responsibility, and worker meritocracy.[20]
- The replacement of salary increases in the salary bonus policy with nontaxable benefits, such as food bonuses and other allowances, which are intended to cover social benefits, vacation pay, and end-of-year bonuses. Since March 2022, the government has maintained a minimum wage of 130 bolivars per month, which was equivalent to US$30 at its approval but has now dwindled to less than US$3 per month as of December of 2024, due to an inflation rate of over 400 percent during this period.[21]

Among the neoliberal economic policies implemented by the Maduro government in the last decade, the following are particularly notable:

- The establishment of Special Economic Zones, which constitute areas of economic activity where labor rights, environmental regulations, and taxation are not enforced. The most prominent example is the Orinoco Mining Arc, established in 2016 and covering 12 percent of the national territory. Its approval and operation have disregarded multiple provisions of the national constitution.[22]
- The adoption of a free-floating currency exchange rate (currency devaluation), deregulation of prices for essential goods (previously subject to regulation), and the unrestricted import of traditionally domestically produced items (favoring an import-oriented business class connected to the government while negatively affecting local producers).
- The retention of VAT (valued-added tax) as a regressive tax ultimately paid by the working population. The privatization of

various state-owned enterprises, including some that had been nationalized during the Chávez era.[23]

Maduro has also implemented repressive policies aimed at unions and labor leaders that have confronted the administration's neoliberal turn, including the following:

- Following Chávez's passing in 2013, the government has utilized Supreme Court rulings to obstruct union elections within major federations and companies, including the Oil Federation (FUTPV) and SUTISS, the SIDOR union.
- Recent court verdicts resulting in the sentencing of six labor movement activists to sixteen years in prison have sent a strong repressive message, aiming to quell the widespread labor protests that have shaken Venezuelan cities over the past year.[24]
- The detention of Leonardo Azócar and Daniel Romero, two leaders from the SIDOR union, by military intelligence for their roles in spearheading labor protests within the steel company since early 2023, demonstrates another crackdown on labor activism.[25] In the Bolívar state, military counterintelligence has also arrested Bladimir Tremaria, president of the United Front of Socialist Workers of Bolívar state (FUTSEB) and a construction sector worker, because of his involvement in organizing labor protests demanding improved wages and working conditions.[26]
- In January 2024, Víctor Venegas, president of the Fenatev teachers' union, was arrested in the state of Barinas. Until March 2024, Professor Venegas remained detained, accused of allegedly participating in a conspiracy to overthrow the government.[27] Venegas's arrest occurred in the same week in which massive teacher demonstrations took place in Barinas and other states in the country. In March, Professor Venegas was released, with precautionary measures, which included unspecified legal conditions and restrictions.[28]

Despite all the labor flexibility measures enforced by the Maduro administration and the use of repressive actions by law enforcement agencies against prominent labor figures (including the labeling of their activities as "terrorist" and the utilization of antiterrorism courts for their trials), the state-endorsed workers' union, CBST, endorsed these government strategies. The CBST cite the impact of the sanctions imposed by the United States to justify their support for antiworker policies.[29]

Workers Organize and Fight Against the Neoliberal Policies of Maduro

On March 18, 2023, a gathering of 170 delegates and representatives from unions, federations, and workers' movements across seventeen states in Venezuela took place in Caracas, resulting in the establishment of the National Committee for Workers in Struggle (CNC-TL).[30] The primary objective of this committee is to unite the various regional mobilizations and struggles into a unified effort aimed at reclaiming labor, social, economic, and civil rights that have been undermined by Maduro's neoliberal government.[31]

The CNC-TL represents a nationwide endeavor to consolidate the widespread protests led by Venezuelan workers in the year preceding its foundation. These protests are primarily centered around the demand for a decent wage, as stipulated in Article 91 of the constitution. Currently, the minimum wage in Venezuela is less than US$5 per month, making it one of the lowest wages in Latin America and the world. The CNC-TL has rapidly expanded its presence to encompass all states within Venezuela and is in the process of strengthening its organizational structure in major cities across the country, amidst ongoing mobilizations and efforts for better wages, adherence to labor laws, and opposition to government repression.

In the backdrop of extensive corruption at the upper echelons of public administration, acknowledged even by the government itself through numerous judicial arrests of ministers, presidents of public companies, deputies, and military officials, Maduro has used the economic sanctions imposed by the United States and the European Union against Venezuela to justify his neoliberal agenda, specifically his policy of eroding wages.

While acknowledging that these sanctions represent unwarranted interference by foreign powers in Venezuela's internal affairs, workers also assert that these measures do not primarily affect the ruling elite but directly impact the Venezuelan populace. The CNC-TL contends that these sanctions are not the core cause of the "flexibilization" of labor relations implemented by the Maduro government. Rather, the crisis in Venezuela's oil industry is largely attributed to widespread corruption within the upper echelons of government, as evidenced by the legal proceedings against numerous PDVSA directors over recent years.

In the present state of affairs in Venezuela, salaried employment has reached levels akin to practical slavery, as workers are unable to earn compensation sufficient to cover even the basic subsistence needs of themselves and their families. As of August 2023, a family requires 118 times the minimum wage to cover essential food expenses. Maduro's labor strategy, characterized by wage slavery, has triggered a significant exodus of young individuals and skilled workers, who, along with their families, are fleeing the country in pursuit of improved labor conditions. The exodus has exceeded seven million Venezuelans, as they perceive that the country's current wages and working circumstances make survival unattainable.

In light of this grave and harsh reality, the establishment of the CNC-TL marks a progressive stride in bolstering the labor movements that have been gaining momentum across the entire country since 2022. In the short term, the CNC-TL has proposed the initiation of a National Workers' Congress, aiming to enhance organization and discourse within the Venezuelan labor movement. This initiative is geared toward defining a comprehensive agenda of struggles aimed at confronting an unyielding government. Despite accumulating substantial foreign currency revenue from the exploitation of resources like oil, gold, coltan, bauxite, coal, lithium, and diamonds—revenues often shielded from public knowledge through unconstitutional measures such as the so-called Anti-Blockade Law, which effectively suspends the provisions of the constitution and grants extra-constitutional authority to the executive branch for steering the economy—the government remains resistant to acknowledging the necessity of fair wages and decent labor conditions for the Venezuelan population. Instead, it responds with the suppression of numerous labor mobilizations spanning the entire country.

Conclusion

During Hugo Chávez's presidency (1999–2012), the Venezuelan workers' movement underwent a transformative phase marked by organization, mobilization, activism, and theoretical reflection. This period highlighted the determination of segments of the working class to embark on a journey toward substantial political, economic, social, and cultural changes. These efforts aimed to establish a novel socialist productive model that would eradicate the exploitation of labor by capital and establish the grounds for genuine social justice.

However, this landscape of transformations was abruptly altered with the adoption of neoliberal policies by the government of Nicolás Maduro. The labor gains achieved during the Chávez era were swiftly eroded under Maduro's leadership. Simultaneously, the actions of CBST leaders during the recent economic crisis (2013–23), which included attempts to quell worker protests and endorse neoliberal labor strategies such as the salary bonus policy, along with repression against labor demonstrations, have caused their legitimacy as worker representatives to diminish.

Although there are positive aspects to be acknowledged regarding the historical progress of the workers' movement under Chávez's tenure, the limited organizational and theoretical-political solidification of this movement, coupled with the PSUV leadership's pivot toward neoliberalism over the past decade, has hindered the preservation of the significant labor achievements made during that period. Furthermore, it has impeded the advancement of workers' organizations aligned with the principles of participatory democracy and anticapitalist struggle that were initially established during the Chavista era.

In the present year of 2024, the struggle of the Venezuelan working class parallels the global fight of all workers against the escalated exploitation imposed by neoliberalism, even when it masquerades as a "pro-worker and socialist government."

PART 2

Crisis in Venezuela

CHAPTER FIVE

US Sanctions as a Factor Exacerbating the Crisis and Stagnation of the Venezuelan Economy

Omar Vázquez Heredia

The Venezuelan economy entered recession in 2014 and by 2021 had suffered a contraction of 75 percent of its gross domestic product (GDP).[1] Subsequently, there was a modest increase in Venezuela's GDP, with growth rates reaching 12 percent in 2022 and 3 percent in 2023.[2] The economic situation in Venezuela has sparked a significant debate both domestically and internationally. The interpretations on offer often juxtapose or intertwine a national economic crisis with the economic sanctions imposed by the United States.

The narrative of Nicolás Maduro's government attributes the decline and collapse of Venezuela's GDP to two external factors: the fluctuation in oil prices and the US economic sanctions, called "unilateral coercive measures" and described as an economic blockade.

The conservative faction of the opposition, meanwhile, contends that the GDP contraction resulted solely from the economic crisis induced by the policies of Hugo Chávez and Nicolás Maduro: "Our examination reveals insufficient evidence to attribute responsibility to [the sanctions] for the exacerbation of the socio-economic crisis."[3]

Moderate oppositionists suggest that the initial decline in Venezuela's GDP can be attributed to the domestic economic crisis from 2014 to 2016, stemming from an external shock caused by plummeting oil prices. However, this perspective contends that the ongoing deterioration of the Venezuelan economy since 2017 could have been prevented if not for the imposition of US economic sanctions: "We should accept that the probable outcome for the Venezuelan economy in the period after 2016, in the absence of sanctions, would have likely involved rises in oil revenues, economic recovery, and the improvement of socioeconomic indicators."[4]

A different sector of the opposition offers another view, highlighting that amid the Venezuelan economic crisis starting in 2014, the consequences of US economic sanctions yielded contradictory outcomes: On one hand, they exacerbated the reduction in oil extraction, while on the other hand, they led to an augmentation in the supply of goods. This latter effect arose because the sanctions compelled the Maduro administration to implement a shift in its governmental policies, including the removal of price and exchange controls. This perspective argues: "It is possible to argue that the shift in the government's policy direction, ultimately resulting in the easing of control measures, was also a direct result of the heightened financial sanctions against Petroleum of Venezuela (PDVSA). In this scenario, the increased external availability of food and medicine would be regarded as a repercussion of the sanctions policy, albeit indirectly."[5]

In distinction from these other analyses, the Marxist opposition sectors suggest that the economic downturn began in 2014 as a consequence of unproductive consumption of oil revenue and the accumulation of debt by the Venezuelan government during the Chávez administration. In this view, however, this crisis was exacerbated by the economic sanctions imposed by the United States, which also hinder any prospects of national economic recovery.[6] Furthermore, "sanctions significantly impede economic recovery, prolonging stagnation within the country."[7]

In our analysis, we align with this perspective. As we will explain in detail, we argue that the decline in Venezuela's GDP were initiated in

2014, stemming from the governmental policies implemented by the Maduro administration in response to the breakdown of the national accumulation process. These policies included capital accumulation and the stockpiling of resources through a significant increase in imports. However, as we will also demonstrate, this economic downturn was exacerbated by the detrimental impact of US economic sanctions. The Maduro government responded to these sanctions by implementing a series of state policies that, particularly concerning the working class, have been regressive. These policies have perpetuated the decline in real wages and undermined labor rights through the elimination of salary bonuses.

Economic Crisis in the Government of Nicolás Maduro: Its Causes and Consequences

Chávez assumed the presidency of Venezuela amidst a crisis where the state's capacities to ensure a consensus-based reproduction of the prevailing order were in question. In response, Chávez initiated a process aimed at relegitimizing the state, starting with the convening and ratifying of a new national constitution in 1999, followed by the renewal of leadership within state institutions through elections or appointments of top officials in 2000.

However, this institutional restructuring alone proved insufficient for the state's relegitimization. Consequently, in 2001, Chávez took further steps by reintroducing traditional oil nationalism in Venezuela with a series of decree-laws. These included the Hydrocarbon Decree-Law, which regulated the increase of oil royalties and the formation of mixed companies in partnership with transnational oil corporations. In response to these measures, the US government under George W. Bush, along with traditional sectors of the local bourgeoisie and the majority of opposition parties and union organizations, launched a reactionary campaign. This campaign included the national strike of December 10, 2001, the coup d'état of April 11, 2002, and the national oil strike of December 2002 and January 2003.

The Chávez government managed to defeat this antigovernment offensive, with the support of a sector of military officers and the workers and popular mobilization. Later, between 2003 and 2004, Chávez took advantage of the sustained rise in oil prices and oil revenues from the increase in royalties to orchestrate a hegemonic strategy characterized, in Gramscian terms, as a passive revolution. This approach entailed certain antineoliberal reforms alongside the preservation of capitalist structures. In general terms, this strategy manifested in the intertwining of the national accumulation process and hoarding of the ruling classes and the consumption patterns of the subaltern classes. This was achieved through a vertical expansion of private and state imports, subsidized by the state apparatus using foreign currency derived from oil revenues and allocated at an overvalued exchange rate.

In this regard, according to the Central Bank of Venezuela (BCV), the total CIF (Cost, Insurance, and Freight) imports amounted to $11.2 billion in 2003, escalating to $71 billion in 2012, marking a substantial growth of 533.82 percent. In terms of CIF private imports, the figure rose from $8 billion in 2003 to $39.3 billion in 2012, representing an increase of 391.38 percent.[8] The encouragement of imports by the Chávez administration, facilitated through the allocation of foreign currency by the government at an overvalued exchange rate, deterred the expansion of productivity within Venezuela's industrial and agricultural sectors. This practice also fostered opportunities for fraudulent activities, such as overinvoicing of foreign purchases, and reinforced the dominance of Venezuela's oil industry by large importing commercial bourgeoisie.

Consequently, the Venezuelan state apparatus continued to privatize and channel oil income toward financing the accumulation and external hoarding endeavors of both established and emerging dominant classes. For instance, according to the BCV, the amount deposited by private individuals abroad stood at $24.4 billion in 1998, before Chávez assumed power, but by 2012, during his final year in office, it had surged to $151.3 billion, marking a staggering increase of 519.92 percent.[9] In summary, significant capital flight occurred during Chávez's tenure.

Initially, the Chávez government financed the steep rise in imports and capital flight primarily through the augmentation of the state's oil revenue. However, as time progressed, it became necessary to dip into part of the international reserves and incur substantial state debt. During the peak of the oil boom, international reserves peaked at $42.3 billion in 2008 but had dwindled to $29.8 billion by 2012.[10] Additionally, PDVSA's (Venezuelan state-owned oil company) total liabilities surged from $27.4 billion in 2006 to $145.9 billion in 2012, marking a significant increase of 432.11 percent.[11] Concurrently, the national government debt soared from $29.2 billion in 2006 to $110.8 billion in 2012, reflecting a notable growth of 279.43 percent.[12]

This extent of state indebtedness, coupled with the depletion of international reserves and a certain downturn in oil prices in 2013 and 2014, precipitated a collapse of the dominant approach adopted during the Chávez administration, which relied on a sustained or increasing level of imports for its continuation. Conversely, when Maduro assumed leadership in 2013 following Chávez's death and won the presidential election that year, he pursued a gradual and unilateral reduction in the allocation of foreign currency for imports. These resources were redirected toward servicing the external debt of the national government and liabilities of PDVSA. This reduction in imports resulted in a contraction in the supply of productive inputs and consumer goods, thereby triggering rising inflation rates, shortages of goods, and the onset of the economic crisis in 2014.

The onset of the economic crisis in 2014 occurred despite a relatively modest decrease of only 13.17 percent in the price of Venezuelan oil compared with its peak in 2012. In 2012, which marked the highest level of imports, the average price of Venezuelan oil reached $100.06 per barrel, declining to $96.66 and $86.88 per barrel in 2013 and 2014, respectively.[13] Therefore, the emergence of the economic crisis in 2014, characterized by a GDP decrease of -3.9 percent and an inflation rate of 62.2 percent, can be attributed to the gradual and unilateral reduction in imports.[14] Imports, which amounted to $71 billion in 2012, experienced a contraction in subsequent years, falling to $61.5 billion in 2013 and $50.7 billion in 2014.[15] Thus, by 2014, imports had already been slashed by the Maduro government by 28.63 percent compared with 2012.

The Maduro government further reduced imports unilaterally in 2015 and 2016, prioritizing the repayment of the state apparatus's external debt amid a steep decline in the price of Venezuelan oil and a decrease in oil extraction within Venezuela. This led to a continuation and exacerbation of the economic crisis in 2015 and 2016, during which GDP contracted by 6.2 percent and -17.0 percent.[16] Consequently, the value of imports plummeted to $36 billion in 2015 and $17.7 billion in 2016, while the average price of Venezuelan oil dropped to $49.49 and $40.76 per barrel in those respective years.[17] However, during this period from 2014 to 2016, the Maduro government managed to pay off 30.05 percent of PDVSA's total liabilities, which decreased from $146.6 billion in 2013 to $102.5 billion in 2016.[18] Additionally, Maduro allocated $51.11 billion between 2014 and 2016 to service the foreign debt.[19]

From 2014 to the first half of 2017, the government's payment of PDVSA's liabilities and servicing of foreign debt took place amidst a decline followed by a collapse in the price of oil. This occurred alongside a substantial unilateral reduction in the allocation of foreign currency for imports. This strategy was part of an inflationary adjustment aimed at curbing inflation by reducing the availability of goods, which in turn led to a decrease in the real wages and consumption of the Venezuelan working class, exacerbating inequality and poverty.[20] For instance, inequality between capital and labor regressed, with employee remuneration relative to the national product declining from 35.39 percent in 2012 to 23.62 percent in 2016.[21] Overall poverty, as measured by income, surged from 48 percent in 2014 to 81.8 percent in 2016.[22] The number of undernourished individuals in Venezuela rose from 1.1 million between 2010 and 2012 to 4.1 million between 2014 and 2016.[23] It's crucial to note that this decline in living conditions in Venezuela occurred prior to the imposition of US economic sanctions, as the first sanction targeting specific sectors of the economy was not applied until August 2017.

US Sanctions on the Venezuelan State and Senior Officials: Their Contexts and Characterization

There exists a vast body of academic literature examining interstate sanctions from the perspectives of international law and foreign policy analysis, which attempts to identify their legality, typology, objectives, motivations, context, effectiveness, and impacts.[24] Consequently, there is ongoing debate surrounding the categorization of interstate sanctions, with discussions revolving around terms such as selective, general, and extraterritorial, as well as the classifications proposed by the United Nations, which include individual, sectoral, and secondary sanctions.[25] For our purposes, we will distinguish between personal sanctions, which target individuals' access to economic assets and foreign territories, and economic sanctions, which aim to impact specific sectors of economies.

During Chávez's presidency, diplomatic tensions arose with the US government. Initially, these tensions stemmed from his 1999 tour of Arab member countries of OPEC and his criticisms of initiatives such as the Free Trade Area for the Americas and Plan Colombia and the military interventions in Afghanistan and Iraq. Subsequently, between 2002 and 2004, tensions escalated due to the George W. Bush administration's involvement in reactionary efforts to overthrow Chávez.[26] In 2006, amidst this backdrop, the Bush administration prohibited the sale of weapons to Venezuela, citing perceived lack of cooperation in counterterrorism efforts. Then, in September 2008, Bush imposed personal sanctions for the first time on senior Chavista officials, including Captain Ramón Rodríguez Chacín and Generals Hugo Carvajal and Henry Rangel Silva, over alleged ties to drug trafficking and money laundering.

In September 2011, Barack Obama's administration imposed personal sanctions on three high-ranking Chavista officials (Freddy Bernal, Amilcar Figueroa, and Cliver Alcalá) over alleged ties with the Revolutionary Armed Forces of Colombia (FARC), and an extraterritorial or secondary sanction was placed on PDVSA for selling gasoline to Iran.[27] Following the repression of antigovernment protests by the Maduro administration in December 2014, the US Congress passed the Law for the Defense of Human Rights and Civil Society of Venezuela, enabling personal sanctions against senior Chavista officials. Subsequently, in March 2015, Obama signed an executive order characterizing the Venezuelan state as a threat to the national security of the United States.[28]

In 2017, following the Maduro government's crackdown on antigovernment protests and the establishment of a National Constituent Assembly in August, US President Donald Trump implemented further personal sanctions against senior Chavista officials. Additionally, he imposed the first unilateral and sectoral economic sanction on the Venezuelan government through Executive Order 13808. This order prohibited the negotiation and restructuring of PDVSA and government bonds. In 2018, Trump continued his unilateral economic sanctions on the Venezuelan state apparatus. In March, through Executive Order 13827, he banned the use of digital currencies or crypto assets issued by the Maduro government.* In May, with Executive Order 13835, he

* In response to the financial sanctions imposed by the Trump administration in August 2017, Maduro's government began using cryptocurrencies and crypto assets to conduct transactions outside of the Venezuelan state's accounts within the international financial system. Within this framework, in December 2017, Maduro established the Venezuelan Superintendency of Crypto-assets and Related Activities (Supcacven) through Decree No. 3,196 to manage the Petro, a unique cryptocurrency backed and issued by a state. Later, in April 2018, Maduro created the Venezuelan Treasury of Crypto-assets as a state-owned company under the Vice Presidency of the Republic, through Decree No. 3,353.

Simultaneously, the 2017 unconsulted National Constituent Assembly issued the so-called Constituent Decree on Crypto-assets and the Sovereign Cryptocurrency Petro in April 2018. Article 9 of this decree established that "the Venezuelan State will promote, protect, and guarantee the use of cryptocurrencies as payment methods in public institutions, private companies, mixed entities, and public enterprises, both within and outside national territory." Finally, in January 2019, after Donald Trump's oil sanctions against PDVSA, the same Constituent Assembly issued a decree to create the Comprehensive Crypto-asset System, which, in Article 8, transformed Supcacven into the National Superintendency of Crypto-assets and Related Activities (Sunacrip).

In this context, Sunacrip became a central entity for collecting payments through cryptocurrencies and crypto assets for Venezuela's sanctioned oil exports. These commercial transactions, carried out through Sunacrip to bypass US oil sanctions, were conducted in total secrecy, enabling significant administrative corruption. As a result, in March 2023, Maduro's government dismissed and detained, among other senior state officials, the vice president of the Economy, Tareck El Aissami, and the president of Sunacrip, Joselit Ramírez. (Note by Omar Vázquez Heredia.)

prohibited the negotiation or purchase of bonds or financial assets of companies where the Venezuelan state holds at least 50 percent ownership. In November, through Executive Order 13850, he halted any export and import of gold and other assets and merchandise belonging to the Venezuelan government.[29]

In 2019, President Trump openly declared his intention to bring about a change in the Venezuelan government and intensified his measures against Maduro. This included imposing additional personal sanctions on senior officials both in early January and in the final days of that month, under Executive Order 13850. Moreover, he implemented a sectoral economic sanction on PDVSA through the same executive order, effectively imposing an embargo on the Venezuelan oil industry. This embargo prohibited the export of oil to the United States and the import of inputs for gasoline and diesel production from the United States.

In January 2019, Trump also recognized the self-proclaimed interim government led by Juan Guaidó through Executive Order 13857, thereby instituting a broad sanction against Maduro and his government apparatus. Later in the same year, specifically in March, Trump applied sanctions to companies such as Minerven, Bandes, and Banco de Venezuela. Additionally, in April 2019, the International Monetary Fund denied access to resources to the Maduro government due to its lack of international recognition. Furthermore, US allies, including the United Kingdom and Colombia, seized assets of the Venezuelan state, such as gold held in the Bank of England and the Monómeros company, respectively.

Later in 2020 and at the beginning of 2021, the Trump administration established regulations regarding the imposition of secondary sanctions on maritime transportation involving weapons and natural goods from sanctioned states.[30] Furthermore, it broadened personal sanctions to include senior Chavista officials, notably adding Maduro to a list of individuals wanted for drug trafficking. These personal and economic sanctions have faced scrutiny from an institutional standpoint due to their illegitimate nature. They were not authorized by the UN Security Council and violate the right to a fair defense for those subjected to them, who endure penalties without undergoing a proper judicial process.[31]

Moreover, the economic sanctions imposed by the United States on the Venezuelan government are highly condemnable as they reflect the hypocritical double standards of the United States regarding human rights violations and its interference in the internal affairs of countries whose governments are aligned with its geopolitical adversaries, namely China and Russia. The hypocrisy of American administrations is evident in their military backing of the state of Israel, despite its blatant disregard for the human rights of the Palestinian people through colonial occupation of their land and the enforcement of apartheid policies. Additionally, scholarly literature has concluded that economic sanctions are ineffective in inducing changes in authoritarian regimes and that their adverse effects are predominantly borne by the working class and other marginalized sectors of the sanctioned states.[32]

In Venezuela, spurred by the rhetoric of the conservative and liberal opposition aligned with the United States, the economic sanctions imposed between 2017 and 2019 initially fostered unfounded optimism regarding a change in government and the defeat of Maduro's policies, seemingly without requiring organized efforts from workers and grassroots movements. However, as these sanctions intensified and persisted, exacerbating the hardships faced by the working class and marginalized sectors, they have led to a sense of political disengagement among them. This is because their primary focus has shifted toward securing their daily material needs, rather than engaging in political activism.

US Economic Sanctions on the Venezuelan State and Their Consequences

The economic sanctions imposed by the United States on the Venezuelan government, enforced between 2017 and 2019 and later suspended in 2022, worsened the already dire economic crisis in Venezuela and impeded the prospects and scale of its recovery. The financial sanction implemented in August 2017 hindered any efforts to restructure the debt owed by PDVSA and the national government, effectively cutting off Venezuela's access to international credit. Consequently, the

Maduro administration was compelled to maintain a surplus in the balance of payments, amounting to approximately 4.9 percent of GDP during the period spanning 2017 to 2022, which hindered efforts to stabilize and increase imports.[33]

In addition to the financial sanctions of August 2017, the measures enacted in May 2018, which prohibited the negotiation of debts held by companies where the Venezuelan government had a stake of at least 50 percent, had a detrimental impact on PDVSA's oil extraction activities and its joint ventures with Chevron, ENI, and Total. These sanctions constrained PDVSA's ability to finance its operations in Venezuela through credit obtained from the global financial system. However, the collapse of Venezuelan oil extraction was further exacerbated by the embargo placed on PDVSA and its joint ventures following the US economic sanctions implemented in January 2019. These sanctions prohibited the export of Venezuelan oil to the United States and restricted the importation of spare parts and supplies crucial for the Venezuelan oil industry.[34]

The average oil production of Venezuela's oil industry stood at 2,880,900 barrels per day in 2011, gradually declining to 2,372,500 barrels per day by the end of 2016. However, this decline steepened in subsequent years, with averages dropping to 2,034,800 barrels per day in 2017, 1,510,200 barrels per day in 2018, 1,012,600 barrels per day in 2019, and 568,600 barrels per day in 2020.[35] Prior to the imposition of US economic sanctions, there was already a contraction in oil production, but this trend accelerated following the financial sanctions of 2017, the oil embargo of 2019, the extraterritorial control of maritime transportation of Venezuelan oil since 2020, and the quarantine measures related to the COVID-19 pandemic starting in March 2020.

This collapse in oil production in Venezuela prevented the Maduro government from increasing oil revenues, despite the rise in the price of Venezuelan oil to $47.63 and $64.47 per barrel in 2017 and 2018, respectively.[36] Later, in 2019 and 2020, because of the COVID-19 pandemic, Venezuelan oil prices dropped again to $54.04 and $28.12 per barrel, respectively.[37] Specifically, the US economic sanctions targeting the Venezuelan oil industry affected the tax and foreign exchange earnings of the Venezuelan government. The collapse in oil production, coupled with discounts applied to the price of Venezuelan oil by foreign companies purchasing it, under the threat of potential administrative measures from the United States, led to a decrease in the government's tax and foreign exchange earnings. This, in turn, affected its ability to finance imports and sustain effective domestic demand.[38]

Furthermore, the US recognition of the self-proclaimed interim government led by Guaidó in 2019 complicated Venezuela's access to resources from the international financial system. The International Monetary Fund, citing uncertainty regarding the legitimacy of the Maduro government, denied Venezuela access to $400 million in April 2019, rejected a $5 billion loan request in March 2020, and excluded Venezuela from receiving $5 billion in special drawing rights in August 2021. Similarly, the Venezuelan government was unable to access $1.8 billion held by the Bank of England for the same reason.[39]

The so-called overcompliance with the financial sanctions imposed in August 2017 also hindered the Maduro government's ability to conduct various commercial transactions through the global financial system. Enhanced scrutiny of banking operations resulted in delays or suspensions, along with increased banking fees. A notable instance occurred when Swiss bank UBS blocked four transfers from the Venezuelan government intended for purchasing COVID-19 vaccines through the Covax fund. Moreover, the trade sanctions implemented in November 2018 sometimes compelled the Venezuelan government to pay inflated prices for state imports, as it was compelled to procure goods from non-US companies that imposed premiums because of the risk of facing US administrative measures.

The US economic sanctions targeting the Venezuelan government have not only affected the state apparatus but have also directly affected private companies and individuals. This includes the suspension of accounts in US banks, delays, refusals, and increased fees on financial transactions, inability to access services from companies that have ceased operations in Venezuela, such as Adobe, Oracle, Wise, Sedo, and DirecTV, as well as the loss of business and employment opportunities due to the reputational or financial risks associated with engaging in exchange and payment operations with legal and natural persons residing in Venezuela.[40]

Consequently, these sanctions have perpetuated and exacerbated the crisis in the Venezuelan economy. GDP contracted by 15.7 percent in 2017, 19.6 percent in 2018, 28.0 percent in 2019, 30.0 percent in 2020, and 3.0 percent in 2021.[41] They also contributed to a rise in overall poverty levels, measured by income, which escalated from 81.8 percent in 2016 to 94.5 percent in 2021. Social inequality, as measured by the GINI index, also increased from 0.462 in 2016 to 0.567 in 2021.[42] Additionally, the number of undernourished individuals in Venezuela surged, reaching 7.8 million people between 2018 and 2020, representing 27.4 percent of the total population during that period.[43] Consequently, US economic sanctions emerged as a significant factor driving the massive migration of Venezuelans.

The deterioration in these socioeconomic indicators was also fueled by the regressive state policies implemented by Maduro in response to the US economic sanctions, commencing with the introduction of the Program of Recovery, Growth, and Economic Prosperity. This structural monetarist macroeconomic adjustment, initiated since August 2018, encompassed various measures, including the liberalization of the exchange rate, the repeal of foreign exchange regulations, the elimination of price controls, tariff exemptions for importers and the oil and mining sectors, gradual reduction of the money supply, increased banking reserves, the revitalization of special economic zones, and the introduction of salary bonuses. In this sense, these governmental actions represent a shift toward an "elitist bodegón capitalism," characterized by "the formation of new commercial elites and the growing empowerment of importing and extractive economic classes in alliance with state power."[44]

In terms of labor policy, the response to the US economic sanctions was embodied in Memorandum 2792, which mandated that collective and individual contracts be linked to the official minimum wage. Consequently, this led to the proliferation of supplementary labor bonuses, which had no bearing on the calculation of salary benefits such as vacations, bonuses, and social benefits. Initially adopted by private companies, the use of labor bonuses became widespread, with 91.17 percent of private enterprises utilizing them by 2023.[45] Moreover, through presidential Decree No. 4,805 in May 2023, Maduro introduced the Minimum Monthly Income, comprising a food bonus and an economic war bonus, aimed at remunerating active and retired state workers.

The approval of the Anti-Blockade Law of 2020, passed in response to US economic sanctions, has also had a significant impact. This law facilitates the privatization of state-owned companies by granting the National Executive the authority, as stated in Article 26, to modify the mechanisms governing the establishment, management, administration, operation, and state participation in certain public or mixed companies. Furthermore, Maduro's negotiations with the Biden administration and US corporations aimed at easing and suspending economic sanctions have prioritized the interests of oil companies such as Chevron. While Chevron resumed oil exports from Venezuela to the United States as a result of these negotiations, it also leveraged the opportunity to press for the collection of debts owed by the Venezuelan state.[46]

Conclusion

The first section of this chapter outlined the genesis of the crisis that began in 2014, which was rooted in the unproductive consumption of oil revenues and the state's accumulation of debt during the Chávez administration. However, the crisis reached a critical juncture when the Maduro government unilaterally curtailed imports to redirect resources toward servicing foreign debt obligations. During the period from 2014 to 2017, the left opposition actively opposed Maduro's inflationary measures, demanded an audit, and repudiated the spurious foreign debt, which was primarily incurred to facilitate capital flight and foster corruption among both established and emerging bourgeois.* The next section demonstrated how the economic sanctions imposed by the United States on the Venezuelan government since 2017 represent a

* This left opposition included a variety of left organizations and movements, including Marea Socialista and the Socialism and Liberty Party (PSL).

protracted and objectionable form of interference in Venezuela's political landscape, perpetuating the conflict between the national-populist Chavista movement and the conservative and liberal opposition factions. Lastly, the third section examined the significant role played by US economic sanctions in exacerbating the economic crisis in Venezuela, a burden that has disproportionately affected the working class and marginalized sectors due to the Maduro government's implementation of monetarist macroeconomic adjustments since August 2018.

All of which points to the urgent need to reject the reprehensible US sanctions on the Venezuelan state and demand their complete removal. Simultaneously, we must stand in opposition to the Maduro administration's implementation of tax, fiscal, and labor measures that prioritize the interests of multinational corporations and domestic capital amidst the economic crisis and stagnation of the national economy.

CHAPTER SIX

Bureaucracy and Lumpen Capitalist Management in the Maduro Government

Gonzalo Gómez

From 1999 to 2023, senior public and military officials in government positions, leading state institutions, organizations, and companies transitioned from being primarily of working class and petty bourgeois backgrounds to forming an elite class, engaged in criminal and corrupt wealth accumulation within Venezuela. This transformation led them to become a predatory class, ultimately leading to economic mismanagement and the erosion of the progressive principles and promises of the "Bolivarian Revolution." Their original social class status underwent a change, giving rise to a parasitic, rentier, and exploitative bourgeoisie, often in association with the so-called revolutionary bourgeoisie consisting of business figures and their allies. This shift explains the increasing procapitalist and antiworker policy orientation of the Maduro government and the abandonment of the ideals and accomplishments of the Bolivarian Revolution, amounting to a counterrevolutionary transformation of the whole government and the Bolivarian process. Changes some factions of the international left appear reluctant to acknowledge.

This transformation combines the amplification of certain preexisting counterrevolutionary tendencies with the bourgeois inclinations of the leadership, shaped by its dialectical, multiclass, and civic-military nature. Initially supported by the masses, this leadership wrested control of the state administration and political regime from the traditional bourgeoisie, even seizing some of their properties, only to subsequently turn against the very populace it once championed.

Our thesis asserts that while the seeds of bureaucratism and corruption were sown from the beginning, alongside the blossoming of the Bolivarian Revolution (which has since withered), a structural shift occurred. This transformation led the civil-military leadership, initially connected with the masses, to gradually evolve into an emerging bourgeois class, composed of newly wealthy capitalists. They amassed their wealth through a corrupt, mafia-style mode of accumulation, characterized by embezzlement, dispossession, capital flight, parasitism, and participation in illicit economies.

This transformation, in turn, influenced their behavior, style of governance, and social relationships with the people and led to the abandonment of "progressive" policies in favor of hybrid approaches marked by elements of neoliberalism that are decidedly antiworker and authoritarian in character.

What follows is an examination of a multitude of factors that resulted in the erosion of public assets and the public economy, as well as the deterioration of the social and political conditions of those who, during a period of relative revolutionary vigor, formed the social base of the Bolivarian process and benefited from its more progressive measures.

About the Terms *Bureaucracy*, *Lumpenbourgeoisie*, and *Lumpen Capitalist*

In discussing bureaucracy, lumpenbourgeoisie, and lumpen capitalism within Maduro's government and various stages in the Bolivarian Revolution, we will employ these terms in a sense that is partly similar but also somewhat different from the concepts put forth by Gunder Frank.[1] Frank attributes such conditions to the bourgeoisie and elites of semicolonial or neocolonial countries, which are subject to imperialism, among them being the Latin American bourgeoisie. He also discusses lumpen capitalism and lumpen development to describe the incapacity of these bourgeoisie to develop production and move beyond a model of dependence based on state revenue from raw material exports or a mere commercial form of capitalism. They struggle to implement an independent national development plan and, as a result, remain heavily reliant on neocolonial powers or align themselves with them. Chavismo aimed to achieve a second national independence, but the outcome has been quite the opposite, partially replacing some dependencies with others (such as China and Russia) or reverting to prior dependencies, often against the regime's explicit intentions.

Frank's definition does not exclude the emergence of a neo-bourgeoisie that has been taking shape since the time of Chávez, particularly during Maduro's rule, yet this neo-bourgeoisie has not fully matured and is still in the process of consolidation. Therefore, in this context, we will refer to lumpenbourgeoisie to characterize a type of bourgeoisie whose primary mode of capitalist accumulation is fundamentally rooted in the corrupt acquisition of income, involvement in criminal economies, and engagement in speculative financial activities.

This emerging neo-bourgeoisie originates from the state bureaucracy, both civil and military, and its surroundings. It has not yet established a substantial foothold in property ownership or industrial production. Furthermore, it does not directly possess significant bank capital. However, it does engage in capitalist and illicit activities involving state-controlled companies, banks, and natural resources. This group leverages its power to influence other bourgeois sectors to align with their bureaucratic interests or preferences.

The levels of corruption, embezzlement, illegal capital flight, and speculative banking are so vast that this lumpenbourgeoisie aims to construct a comprehensive national-international capitalist structure of its own. Rather than generating new wealth, it seeks to appropriate what already exists. It tends to transform state capital into private corporate capital, either through direct privatization or through businesses operating under the state's auspices. Initially, they took control of the state as a bureaucracy, and now their inclination is to privatize public assets, reflecting a new bourgeoisie that is not content with mere control but desires full ownership.

The term *bureaucracy* is closely related to the term *treasury*, which encompasses the various organizations and entities responsible for managing the state's financial resources. Fiscal resources are the revenues the state generates through taxes, fees, contributions, and other means to finance its expenses and fulfill its functions. In Venezuela, these resources are intricately tied to income from oil and the sale of other state-owned raw materials, in addition to taxes. These revenues represent the primary sources of funding for the state and its public programs and services. They should be managed in the national interest and for the benefit of the people, in accordance with the constitution and the laws of the republic. However, this is not the reality in practice. When this bureaucracy is manipulated through practices such as clientelism, nepotism, and influence peddling and by authoritarian methods, or through dispossession, among other mechanisms intertwined with corruption and the abuse of power, it evolves from a mere administrative and executive actor into a privileged class that siphons resources away from the people.

In essence, through this manipulation, the administrative social class operates as if it were the de facto owner of the state's assets. By accumulating capital in this manner, they can invest, engage in trade, acquire properties, or eventually even become indirect "co-owners" in mixed economies or in privatized companies, using figureheads in their service and capital acquired through corrupt means.

An owner, in this context, refers to someone who has something under their control and enjoys the use of that public resource (though not by right or in a legitimate and permanent manner), whether through misappropriation or financial gain. Assuming this status can lead to a reversal of previous bourgeois nationalist policies or a significant change in direction, contrary to what Chávez envisioned. It may involve engaging in transactions that favor transnational and imperialist powers, both established and emerging, in the economic and geopolitical spheres.

In his analysis of the bureaucratization of the Russian Revolution, Leon Trotsky explained the existence of a sizable ruling social stratum with a monopolistic grip on production and its outcomes, which significantly appropriated a substantial portion of these products (performing an exploitative function). This stratum was bound by shared material interests and stood in opposition to the class of producers. Trotsky went as far as to suggest that in the Soviet Union, the bureaucracy became "more than just bureaucracy," though he refrained from defining it as a bourgeois class.

Trotsky argued that "classes are defined by the place they occupy in the social economy, primarily in relation to the means of production." He also observed that the Soviet bureaucracy shared resemblances with other bureaucracies due to its role as a regulator and intermediary. Furthermore, it exploited the state apparatus to maintain the social hierarchy. He highlighted that while fascist regimes ally themselves with the bourgeoisie for common interests, including friendships and marriages, the USSR's bureaucracy assimilated bourgeois customs without having a national bourgeoisie of its own. In this sense, it is undeniable that the Soviet bureaucracy went beyond being a simple bureaucracy; it constituted the only privileged and dominant social stratum within Soviet society.

In the case of Venezuela, there are notable differences when compared with the USSR. Unlike the Soviet Union, where the bourgeoisie was effectively expropriated, in Venezuela, the bourgeoisie, as a class, was never subjected to expropriation, and the social relations of production and property have not undergone such extensive changes. Instead, what the bureaucracy in Venezuela has done is attempt to reap the benefits of certain state-owned assets and even directly appropriate them, as seen in the actions of senior military officers who acquired expropriated lands previously allocated to peasant communities.

From a political perspective, while a significant portion of the bourgeoisie in Venezuela has opposed the bureaucracy, often with varying degrees of resistance, the self-proclaimed "Chavista" bureaucracy continues to coexist with the national bourgeoisie within a capitalist economy and state. In some cases, it partners with or becomes assimilated into certain sectors of the bourgeoisie. However, the bureaucracy stands as a relatively independent social stratum apart from the bulk of the bourgeoisie, despite controlling the bourgeois state. Their aim is not to govern based on proletarian interests but rather to replace or compete with the bourgeoisie for a share of state resources and income.

The Dynamics of the Bolivarian Leadership

While serving as vice president, Maduro assumed responsibilities in Chávez's government for several months in 2012, during Chávez's illness and treatment in Cuba. Maduro's initial term as interim president began on March 8, 2013, following Chávez's passing, and he was officially confirmed as the constitutional president on April 19 after narrowly winning a presidential election.

Initially, Maduro appeared to be continuing the policies initiated by his predecessor, even in the face of escalating economic challenges and alleged acts of economic sabotage often referred to as the "economic war." However, over time, his administration began to adopt a blend of economic policies, which included elements typical of neoliberal adjustments, coupled with an increasingly evident authoritarian shift. Despite these changes, state intervention remained marked, while imperialist pressures intensified, ultimately leading Venezuela into one of its most severe and protracted crises.

Between 2014 and 2017, as well as in 2019, there were political situations that threatened presidential power. Concurrently, economic measures were implemented that contributed to a decline in the general living conditions, particularly for workers and those with lower incomes. This period witnessed intense antigovernment protests, particularly from the middle class, youth, and university students, influenced by the more conservative factions of the opposition. It was also marked by conspiratorial movements within the bourgeois opposition, Venezuela's largest-ever national power blackout, hyperinflation, significant currency devaluations, a sharp drop in oil prices in 2015, and the deterioration of PDVSA's production capacity. International economic sanctions imposed by the United States further compounded Venezuela's challenges, resulting in hindrances and damages to trade.

Workers' wages were effectively reduced to near zero in terms of covering the cost of the food basket and the basic basket, despite constitutional guidelines. This tumultuous period triggered a humanitarian crisis of migration and survival unprecedented in many decades, with over seven million displaced people. The situation was further aggravated by the outbreak of the COVID-19 pandemic in 2020.

Throughout most of the Chávez era, Venezuela enjoyed significant economic resources and financial stability, fueled by high oil prices. This period of prosperity led to distribution policies that markedly improved nearly all indicators of quality of life. Nonetheless, instances of corruption were exposed, although their impact was less conspicuous due to the availability of substantial income. In the final two years of Chávez's rule and up to his passing, the country was already experiencing economic decline.

Starting in 2013, increased awareness and understanding emerged regarding the extensive misappropriation of state resources and public funds. This revelation came to light when former finance minister and former president of the Central Bank of Venezuela (BCV), Edmée Betancourt, in 2013, and Chávez's former minister of Planning and Finance, Jorge Giordani, in 2014, independently disclosed substantial losses or capital flight totaling at least $20 billion from national assets.[2] These financial irregularities occurred within the foreign exchange allocation system during 2012 and 2013.

Subsequent investigations initiated by collective and citizen efforts provided further evidence of ongoing misappropriation and illicit capital flight affecting the country. Notably, the Punta de Lanza Social Battle Movement, led by L. E. Gavazut Bianco, published a report on March 24, 2014, titled "Suitcase Dollars, Foreign Companies, and the Socialist Economic Model."[3] This analysis drew upon statistics from the CADIVI database for the years 2004 to 2012, revealing significant concentrations and highly unequal distributions of foreign currency allocations to companies during the exchange control period. The report also raised concerns of alleged fraudulent practices and overinvoicing in imports, or the lack thereof, using these allocated funds.

Gavazut's report referenced statements made by the then minister of the Interior, Justice, and Peace, Miguel Rodríguez Torres (who was subsequently imprisoned and exiled) in December 2013. Rodríguez Torres asserted that investigations up to that point had revealed that "shell companies" received approximately 40 percent of official dollars in 2012. He further disclosed that complicit officials were under investigation.[4] Shell companies are fictitious or fraudulent entities that purport to be "legal," created to carry out and conceal illegal and corrupt activities. Such companies often exist only on paper or in falsified documents, without any real business operations, corporate history, employees, or physical assets in a specific location. They hide the identities of the ultimate beneficiaries and key figures behind the corruption and are used to move money clandestinely. They are typically registered in so-called tax havens, or territories with very flexible or permissive regulations that enable opacity in their operations. Large private companies were also found to have secured substantial sums of foreign currency.

Concurrently, Jesús Montilla, the vice president of the Permanent Comptroller Commission of the National Assembly, stated that the crimes encompassed "fraudulent imports," with involvement from both public officials and private individuals. Minister Rodríguez Torres noted that many dollars had been removed from the country without corresponding imports, or only half of the expected goods had been brought in, and there were instances of "over invoicing."

A study by the Marea Socialista research team, *Embezzlement of the Nation*, published in September 2014, indicated that the amount of misappropriation and criminal capital flight between 1998 and 2013 could exceed $259 billion, with the highest peaks occurring in 2008 and 2011.[5]

Another investigation found a "missing without record" of over $216 billion in PDVSA accounts, as presented by a political organization in December 2015. This covered the period between 1998 and 2014 and revealed discrepancies in PDVSA's financial records due to the substantial volume mentioned. This was corroborated by a study conducted by Carlos Carcione, a member of CER-Latinoamericana and a member of the National Political Team of Marea Socialista at that time.[6] Carcione's work, titled *Corruption in PDVSA: Just the Tip of an Iceberg*, from May 9, 2017, highlighted a significant difference between the income and allocations of dollars generated by PDVSA, amounting to $216 billion. This disparity could be considered a shortfall, an example of illicit accumulation, or, at best, a recording error that needed clarification. Despite these studies being made publicly available and presented to government authorities, the Public Ministry, and the Comptroller General of the Republic, there was no official clarification or response. Marea Socialista sought the opportunity to address the National Assembly, which had both opposition and progovernment members on its board.[7]

The report on embezzlement and capital flight reveals that "over the entire period examined, a process of mafia-style capital accumulation unfolded, resulting in a net flight of over $259 billion between 1998 and 2013." When combined with the missing $216 billion observed in PDVSA, the total exceeds approximately $475 billion.

To provide a point of reference for the significance of this foreign currency gap, it is noted that this amount could have been sufficient to construct over ten million homes, considering the government's reported construction costs. These calculations relied on data from official sources, such as the Ministry of Finance, the Central Bank of Venezuela, PDVSA, INE, and others.

Subsequent cases known through 2023 have exceeded $500 billion, which is several times higher than the country's external debt, a decade's worth of budgets, or the combined volume of all imports within a given year. Given the persistence of corruption and the failure to recover embezzled resources, it is presumed that the amount of misappropriation has continued to grow.

It was recognized that the scale and impact of the harm caused or permitted by the bureaucracy overseeing assets, businesses, and state funds, in conjunction with both new and existing capitalist sectors, was undermining the Bolivarian Revolution's goals of social and political transformation. It also became evident that the country's challenges could not be solely attributed to the "economic war" waged by the bourgeoisie and imperialism, international sanctions, or the blockade, as the government often claimed, even though these factors did play a significant role. Thus, there was a pressing need to scrutinize and reevaluate what had altered the expected trajectory of the Bolivarian Revolution and contributed to the substantial setback in its most significant social achievements.

Therefore, it is imperative to conduct ongoing monitoring and assessment to scrutinize the factors that altered the anticipated trajectory of the Bolivarian Revolution, resulting in a severe regression of its most significant social accomplishments. This regression encompassed the complete elimination of "democratic and participatory involvement" as well as the suppression of any genuine manifestation of "people's power."

Consequently, the once-promising ideals of achieving a "second independence" and fostering "integration" and Latin American liberation, which Venezuela had vigorously championed, dissipated. Instead, these ideals gave way to a process of assimilation into capitalism and bourgeois values, a stark contrast with the essence of the "Bolivarian Revolution" embodied by Chávez's associates and successors.

The explanation for this transformation can be traced back to the central player that wielded significant influence in the Venezuelan political superstructure and interfered with the economic framework: the bureaucracy, constituted by the military and the United Socialist Party of Venezuela (PSUV), coupled with widespread corrupt practices.

In an article I wrote in 2008 evaluating the revolutionary process, I argued that the imperialist strategy aimed not only to dismantle Chavismo but also to sustain the functionality of capitalism.[8] This occurred despite the inherent contradictions with imperial geopolitical interests, resulting in a form of assimilation.

The current situation in Venezuela, under the leadership of Maduro, is marked by a combination of preexisting elements from the period before Chávez's passing and newly emerging factors. It is undeniable that during Maduro's tenure, particularly following the conclusion of the 2013–19 presidential term, there has been an ongoing regression and erosion of the social and democratic achievements that the Venezuelan populace had acquired through the Bolivarian Revolution. This retrogression has occurred concurrently with the exacerbation of preexisting issues and the intensification of economic hardships, whether stemming from internal or external factors.

In Venezuela, a unique class coalition had been in power, held together primarily by Chávez's strong leadership. This coalition consisted of military figures with predominantly humble origins, as well as segments from the lower-middle class, popular sectors, and the working class. Over time, there was a growing bureaucratic influence, characterized by an escalating trend of bureaucratization, the utilization of state resources, the appropriation of state privileges, the dispossession of certain sections of the traditional bourgeoisie (those who thrived during the Fourth Republic), a surge in corruption, capital flight, and involvement in private international enterprises profiting from state resources.

Additionally, there were relatively feeble bourgeois factions that initially supported the Chávez government, some of which eventually disassociated themselves and even participated in the 2002 coup d'état. These factions included segments of the medium-sized business community, some of whom had connections with major capital. Notable figures like Luis Miquilena, a former close associate of Chávez who distanced himself in 2001, and Alfredo Peña (associated with *El Nacional* newspaper, the first mayor of the Metropolitan District of Caracas, and a former minister in the Secretariat of the Presidency) represented this group. However, they did not achieve significant prominence within the government.

The most influential faction within the Chávez government was the so-called military party, stemming from the Bolivarian uprisings of 1992. The second tier was composed of former members of leftist groups or guerrilla movements, associated with the popular movement, and included future leaders of the PSUV union bureaucracy who would assume political and governmental roles.

Subsequently, the phenomenon of "bolibourgeoisie" emerged, composed of businesspersons who were not government officials but who leveraged opportunities facilitated by the state or held directorial positions in shell companies formed around illicit or dubious dealings. These arrangements often involved close collaboration with state bureaucracy or the leadership of the official party.

The transformation of both the state leadership and the governing party (PSUV), alongside the mounting influence of the military sector, correlated with changes in how they engaged with the working-class sectors and their communities on a sociopolitical level. This shift entailed a transition from a form of "democratic assistanceism," which could be considered progressive and is often criticized as "populist" by the political right, to a clientelist-authoritarian subordination of the social base of Chavismo. This subordination served the interests of the bureaucracy, the proto-bourgeoisie associated with the PSUV, or its periphery, as well as the military establishment.

This subordination was also embedded within a corrupt system, ensnaring many officials and workers who, in exchange for their cooperation, secured employment, sought favors, retained their positions, or obtained supplementary benefits to augment their meager salaries. The cooperation often encompassed complicity in illicit activities, such as overcharging service users, receiving payments for both legal and illegal procedures, misappropriating and selling state assets, demanding illegal tolls at police or military checkpoints, and participating in smuggling operations orchestrated by authorities. This pattern was notably conspicuous in the judicial system, featuring extortion, blackmail, the sale of legal processes, verdicts, and other actions favoring or opposing certain individuals, sometimes in association with criminal syndicates.

This shift was reflected in the transition from what was labeled as "populism" under Chávez to the antiworker policies and economic adjustment "packages" enforced during the Maduro presidency. The most pronounced alterations occurred between 2013 and 2017 and were subsequently intensified and refined from 2017 to 2023.

While we have already noted that the Bolivarian Revolution inherently carried bureaucratic elements from its inception, it is essential to acknowledge that during Chávez's leadership, a socially and politically progressive momentum prevailed, despite other inherent contradictions and areas open to critique. Periods of both advancement and regression characterized the efforts to foster worker and popular participation and leadership. Nevertheless, all these endeavors and progressive reforms consistently unfolded under conditions meticulously controlled and restricted by state power or the PSUV party. The process was persistently marred by regressive interventions that halted or dismantled the strides made in popular empowerment initiatives.

What had initially been a leadership primarily composed of individuals from working-class and humble backgrounds, involving rebellious intermediate layers of the armed forces as well as civil segments from working-class or lower-middle-class backgrounds, underwent a transformation into a dominant social class and an emerging bourgeoisie.

This transformation was closely tied to a new class of capitalists, characterized as a neo-bourgeoisie distinct from the traditional or conventional bourgeoisie. This new class was founded on the management of pivotal roles within the state apparatus, the administration of large public or nationalized companies, political leadership, the management of national revenue, and the participation in illicit business ventures.

Reflecting this shift, the concept of the "revolutionary bourgeoisie" began to emerge, underpinning the notion that it needed to be cultivated to "prepare the conditions for the capitalist system" and, eventually, to pave the way for "socialism." Prominent figures like the retired military officer and minister of Agriculture and Lands, Wilmar Castro Soteldo, expressed this idea explicitly.[9] Castro Soteldo openly advocated for fostering this revolutionary bourgeoisie to achieve the "recovery" and "liberation" of the country, emphasizing the allocation of resources, land, and lucrative contracts to government officials and associates who had become part of the so-called progressive bourgeoisie. In his view, this "anti-imperialist" group represented a "perfect alliance" and even characterized it as a "magic formula" to break free from dependency and attain self-sufficiency. These ideas, he maintained, formed the basis of Maduro's economic policies.

Furthermore, a narrative praising the "Chinese model" of "socialism" intertwined with capitalism began to gain traction as the direction toward which Venezuela should aim.

Bureaucratization and Lumpen Capitalist Degeneration: A Destructive Factor in the Bolivarian Revolution and Its Initial Gains

In Venezuela, a political-military bureaucracy has developed that, through corrupt, antiworker, authoritarian control and the systematic exploitation of state resources, along with the dispossession of certain segments of the traditional bourgeoisie, has established a mode of accumulation and rent distribution. However, this new capitalist sector is in competition with the traditional or conventional bourgeoisie, even though it hypocritically embraces the ideological tenets of the Bolivarian Revolution that it has ultimately betrayed.

Since this neo-bourgeoisie's capitalist gains are derived from corruption, misappropriation, commissions, nonexecuted infrastructure projects, and illicit economic activities such as smuggling, theft and trafficking of goods, machinery, and even narcotics or from speculative financial and currency operations (all of which are illicit), it has yet to establish a solid foundation in productive investments. This reluctance to prioritize productive investments is due to its focus on corrupt practices, misappropriation, and looting as primary profit sources.

Consequently, this emerging class is beginning to invest in businesses where it can leverage its connections with the state apparatus, notably in establishments referred to as *bodegónes*. These stores sell imported products at exorbitant, dollar-denominated prices, making them inaccessible to the majority of the population while catering to the wealthy elite, within which these newly affluent individuals are gaining prominence.

This neo-bourgeoisie wields the power of the state but lacks the economic weight in productive ventures and market influence associated with the classic bourgeoisie that it politically displaced. Although it has amassed resources through theft and money laundering (particularly in offshore tax havens), it could be more accurately described as a lumpenbourgeoisie. This term is used because it exhibits characteristics reminiscent of mafia behavior, and, despite attempts to conceal its ill-gotten wealth, it is more inclined toward reckless extravagance than responsible estate management. Consequently, this behavior has contributed to the destruction of the national productive infrastructure in the country.

A report published in November 2022 by *Armando.info* and the *Miami Herald* unveiled that numerous high-ranking government and military officials appeared to be owners of businesses in Florida.[10] The report was compiled using data from 3,050 editions of the Venezuelan state's *Official Gazette*, cross-referencing the information of over 128,082 Venezuelan officials who held public positions between 2007 and June 2022 for free appointment and removal. The data was compared with records from the Florida Division of Corporations.[11] The findings revealed 724 senior officials from the governments of Chávez and Maduro, as well as approximately 232 officers from the Venezuelan Armed Forces and former officials from the Ministry of Defense, whose names coincided with the owners of companies registered in Florida.

These individuals are cited as members of a list of business owners in Florida, some of whom transitioned from holding management positions in public agencies to directly contracting with the Venezuelan state or becoming owners of private companies abroad. A number of these officials were implicated in investigations involving corruption and high-value projects that were never completed.

In summary, the transition from being state officials or occupying high government positions, whether in the Bolivarian National Armed Forces or within government bureaucracy, has resulted in certain individuals leading parallel lives as entrepreneurs and business owners abroad, including, rather paradoxically, in the United States, despite their anti-imperialist rhetoric. These figures have transcended their roles as mere bureaucrats in positions of privilege and have become new entrepreneurs, birthed from a culture of corruption and self-enrichment.

Economic Management Linked to Corruption, Embezzlement, and Illicit Economies: The Driving Force Behind the Counterrevolutionary Transformation, the Shift Toward Capital Assimilation, and the Reactionary Change in the Behavior of the "Bolivarian" Leadership

A significant portion of the ongoing economic and social hardships in Venezuela can be attributed to persistent large-scale embezzlement and corruption, as previously discussed. This practice has become the primary modus operandi and underlying objective of the current ruling elite within the country's capitalist, dependent, and rentier economic system. This is closely intertwined with pervasive "mismanagement," often inseparable from corruption, which taints the governance of all things public. It is practiced in collaboration with the national and transnational private sectors, effectively entangling the entire production system and the social relations associated with it.

The brunt of Venezuela's crisis falls disproportionately on the working class and popular segments of society. The country's dire wage situation, produced by soaring costs and criminal sanctions, can be aptly characterized as a "zero salary," as Venezuela's minimum wage has languished below $5 per month for several years. Such an income fails to cover a single day's worth of meals for a family and renders commuting to work more expensive than the actual earnings. Government-supplied salary bonuses do little to offset this discrepancy. Working for this meager wage is tantamount to unpaid labor and can be likened to semi-indentured servitude. This results in a labor cost for both private employers and the state that could effectively be labeled as "zero cost," as the majority of labor is converted into surplus value.

A corollary of this situation is the reduction in domestic consumption, which further contributes to a depressed economy. However, those capitalists producing for export or catering to a smaller, affluent domestic market with dollar-denominated high-priced goods benefit from this scenario.

The state bureaucracy exhibits a distinct indifference to these consequences since its primary aim is to exploit the public sector in the most predatory and expeditious manner, even if it means annihilating the economy. The almost cost-free labor force remains ensnared in clientelistic dependencies and as a coerced mechanism of corruption. This arrangement cultivates a captive electorate and a "mass" that can be mobilized forcefully in support of the government, in addition to acting as a deterrent to the struggles of other population segments. When these measures prove inadequate, repression is deployed. Consequently, corruption in Venezuela is among the highest globally and is "prevalent at all levels of the Venezuelan social scale."[12]

The government's so-called anticorruption campaign is essentially an expression of internal mafia disputes and, simultaneously, a public relations exercise aimed at presenting a façade of reform.* It is part

---

* This "anticorruption" campaign refers to the Maduro government's recent initiatives aimed at addressing corruption. For example, it has launched investigations at opposition figures (of the left and right), accusing them of "treason." Critics argue that these actions are less about genuine anticorruption measures and more about consolidating power and suppressing dissent.

of the government's internal adjustments and realignments, which are also evident in the geopolitical context. This is all part of the government's efforts to assimilate into the capitalist system, albeit with the lingering use of the language and symbols from the early Chavismo era.

The combination of embezzlement, economic sanctions, and simultaneous decline in global crude oil prices contributed to the weakening of Venezuela's rentier oil economy. This decline was accompanied by a notable shift toward extractive industries like mining. The government has pinned its hopes on a partial recovery in hydrocarbon production and sales by easing sanctions and reengaging with transnational oil companies, as well as entering into agreements with nontraditional investors, such as the Chinese, Russians, Iranians, Turks, and Belarusians. Nevertheless, the rentier oil economy has been eroded, dismantled, or replaced by the lumpen capitalist economy led by the ruling bureaucracy and lumpenbourgeoisie.

Venezuela has been plagued by recurring corruption scandals. Notably, since 2017, several major cases have come to light, including the overpriced vehicle acquisitions by PDVSA, the issues surrounding the José Antonio Anzoátegui TAECJAA Complex, the alleged misuse of resources associated with former minister and ex-president of PDVSA, Rafael Ramírez, and the Cuferca case.[13]

According to Transparencia Venezuela, more than $42 billion of Venezuelan public assets have been compromised in a total of 127 cases involving alleged corruption or irregular management of resources by PDVSA. This does not include other multi-billion-dollar "giant cases" implicating more individuals working within the state and fugitives from US authorities.[14] Moreover, data from the same source indicates that courts in over twenty-two countries have initiated 116 cases related to Venezuelan corruption, with over $64 billion at stake.[15] Numerous other corruption cases involve the irregular and unrecorded transfer of state companies or assets to private individuals, both within Venezuela and abroad. These actions result in the loss of significant annual revenues worth millions of dollars, benefiting select individuals.

As indicated in the statement "Marea Socialista Against Corruption: Our Grievances, Demands, and Proposals for Struggle," there is evidence suggesting that illicit economies in Venezuela account for more than 21 percent of the gross domestic product (GDP), amounting to approximately $9.4 billion per year.[16] This data reinforces our claim that these illicit activities constitute a significant component of the means of appropriation used by the bureaucracy and the capital sectors associated with or stemming from it. The primary forms of illicit activities include drug trafficking, smuggling of gasoline and gold, extortion in ports, fraudulent currency exchange practices, kickbacks, illegal gambling, and financial speculation.

Additional sources have reported even higher percentages for Venezuela. For example, a report by Global Financial Integrity covering the period from 2008 to 2017 revealed that the global average for illicit financial flows related to international trade in 2014 was 18 percent of the total trade. Venezuela was among the countries with the highest percentage, registering at 56 percent, equivalent to approximately $70 billion. This figure and percentage exceed those of Afghanistan. According to the report's estimates, "more than $33 billion of illicit capital left Venezuela in 2008 alone. This translates to nearly ten percent of the country's entire Gross Domestic Product, representing all the goods and services produced by Venezuelans in that year, which left the country and disappeared."[17]

In a global study conducted in 2018 by the Transnational Alliance to Combat Illicit Trade, which assessed eighty-four countries, Venezuela received a score that ranked it eightieth among nations evaluated. It was surpassed in its low score only by Syria, Yemen, Libya, and Iraq, all of which were or are at war. In the Global Illicit Trade Environment Index, Venezuela found itself among the last five countries evaluated and was at the bottom of the list among the nineteen countries examined in Latin America.[18]

The Global Illicit Trade Environment Index comprises four categories: (1) "government policy" assesses the presence of policies and legal approaches for monitoring and preventing illicit trade; (2) "supply and demand" gauges the domestic environment that either promotes or discourages the supply and demand of illicit goods; (3) "transparency and trade" measures the level of transparency within an economy regarding illicit trade and the effectiveness of governance over its free zones and transshipments; and (4) "customs environment" evaluates how efficiently an economy's customs service fulfills its dual mandate of facilitating legal trade while preventing illicit trade.

Venezuela's performance in these categories indicates severe shortcomings. In the "supply and demand" category, the country ranked eighty-third, second to last, suggesting a significant incentive for illicit trade. In the "customs environment" category, Venezuela secured the eighty-first position, with only three countries scoring lower. In the other two categories, although Venezuela did not rank among the ten countries with the worst results globally, it still obtained low scores.

Studies conducted by Transparency International Venezuela and Ecoanalítico revealed that the criminal economies involved in gold, drug, and fuel trading, facilitated by corruption within the state, accounted for an estimated 21.74 percent of Venezuela's GDP in 2021.[19] Analysts argue that these illicit or criminal economies now carry more weight than many other economic sectors, even surpassing the oil sector during its most challenging periods, considering the significant decline it has undergone in recent years. The illicit trade in gold and other minerals represents one of the primary channels for corruption and illicit economies within the Orinoco Mining Arc. Video evidence has surfaced showing individuals associated with corrupt networks holding gold bars in their possession. A self-assessment conducted by Transparency Venezuela in 2022 highlighted that

> with illicit economies, under the protection of corruption, the organization set a precedent by identifying a relationship of interdependence between illicit economies and the criminal bureaucracy established in Venezuela. The work included an analysis of drug trafficking activities, fuel smuggling, illegal gold trafficking, scrap metal smuggling, and corruption in ports and airports. In addition, aspects related to some of the most important criminal groups, their main illicit activities, their areas of influence, the approximate number of their members, and their alleged links with power were outlined. The first confirmation, from the investigation, is that we are dealing with organizations that have managed to weave important national and international networks thanks to the

> support of a group of corrupt public officials who coexist, support, and promote these actions to obtain personal benefits.[20]

The researchers at the outset discuss the considerable challenge of differentiating between the legal activities and benefits that the state derives from taxes, royalties, sales, and production and the activities and benefits that corrupt officials gain. This challenge is exacerbated not only by the inherent opacity of the Venezuelan state but also by the fine line that blurs these operations, the frequent shift of participants across various spheres of power, and the involvement of various national and international actors.[21]

One of the most noteworthy conclusions is that organized crime in Venezuela has entered a "symbiotic phase," as per the classification by Edwin Stier and Peter Richards, as adapted by Edgar Gutiérrez. In this phase, "the interdependence of organized crime with the political and economic system has reached a point where the boundaries become indistinct, and the actors function as a unified political-bureaucratic-economic-criminal entity. This represents the highest risk phase for democracy since the organization appropriates the symbols of liberal democracy within the context of electoral legitimacy and social acceptance, including those that can be conferred upon it by traditional and emerging allied economic elites."[22]

The majority of corruption cases in Venezuela have their origins in the state-owned PDVSA, which has traditionally been the source of over 90 percent of the country's foreign exchange earnings, at least until 2016. The investigation reports encompass practices that cater to maintaining the existing political bias in power, involving the use of monetary resources, vehicles or aircraft, as well as facilities and logistical support (misappropriation of resources).

In various instances between 2017 and 2018, the US Department of the Treasury imposed sanctions on numerous Venezuelan government officials, accusing them of involvement in a corruption scheme connected to the state oil company PDVSA and money laundering operations facilitated by bribery and corruption. Such cases have continued to surface regularly.

Another study conducted by Transparencia Venezuela in 2023 titled *Illicit Economies: Under the Cloak of Impunity* is instructive. This report found, based on an analysis of Venezuelan institutions, that Venezuela is a conducive environment for the development of complex criminal networks. It illustrates how the growth of illicit activities has been sustained and, simultaneously, has led to varying degrees of corruption.[23]

Therefore, to witness a substantial number of cases involving high-level corruption associated with illicit economies, an extensive network must have been intricately constructed. This network enables and eases all manner of unlawful transactions, with the active complicity and participation of various bureaucratic sectors that benefit from these activities. This includes institutional actors functioning across multiple domains and levels, such as the judiciary, taxation, customs, border control, law enforcement, military, and auditing. Effectively, the entire state machinery operates in the service of corruption and illicit economies, serving as primary sources of income for the prevailing elites deeply entrenched within the societal base. This setup is crucial for the perpetuation of the system.

In regard to corruption in Venezuela and the investments of capital in foreign companies, tax havens, the United States (particularly Miami), Central America and European banks, real estate in Spain, and businesses registered in countries within the Arabian Peninsula, there is a wealth of material available in specialized economic, financial, and political publications.[24]

According to the Pandora Papers, Venezuela ranks as the country with the seventh-highest number of individuals who own companies in tax havens. More than 1,200 Venezuelans have been identified as having offshore companies. Among the owners of these companies are former officials, business figures, and individuals linked to corruption cases in Venezuela. Notably, the data does not currently include the highest-ranking members of the Venezuelan executive branch or senior personnel within the PSUV.[25]

However, the information is most compelling when it helps us understand what we have been emphasizing regarding the formation of an emerging socioeconomic class within Venezuela. This class is characterized by a corrupt and mafia-like pattern of wealth accumulation and is built upon the foundations of the prevailing political power. It is a bureaucratic-lumpenbourgeois class that originated from the state bureaucracy, the official political establishment connected to the PSUV, the military, and the so-called bolibourgeoisie that conducts business transactions with the state. These actors are responsible for the embezzlement and large-scale dispossession experienced by the Venezuelan nation and its working class.

The government of this class manages the state apparatus, shapes international geopolitical relations (realignment with emerging imperial powers, alongside the BRICS group), formulates internal policies, and establishes specific modes of production relationships with the Venezuelan working class. All of these factors are intricately tied to the pattern of accumulation outlined previously. The government sustains this pattern through authoritarianism, simulated democracy, and social control measures designed to contain and subdue the populace.

The traditional bourgeoisie, which was ousted from political power and the management of the state, lost control over national income and, to some extent, relinquished a portion of its properties, means of production, businesses, and communication resources. In its place, a transformed bureaucracy with lumpen characteristics emerged as the new dominant bourgeoisie. This bourgeoisie was fundamentally shaped by corruption, illicit economies, and plunder, even at the expense of other bourgeois sectors. Additionally, it subjected the working class to superexploitation.

With the ascent of this new class, the traditional Venezuelan bourgeoisie was compelled to adapt its strategies because it also seeks to continue benefiting from a transformation that no government with a neoliberal agenda had managed to accomplish: the conversion of the working class into almost cost-free labor, devoid of the capacity to resist, and contributing to a "zero" labor cost that boosts their profits, despite the economic crisis. This strategy underpins the moderation and "dialogue" pursued by a significant segment of the employers' political parties and leaders. They now opt to engage in the political process, abandoning or deprioritizing direct confrontation tactics with a coup or pro-interventionist agenda. This shift explains, in part, why they moved away from the experiment of Guaidó's parallel government and now aim for cohabitation, competing for positions of power in upcoming elections, which naturally correspond to business opportunities.

Bureaucratic Administration—Possession and Privatization: The Possession and Management of the State's Means of Production by the Administration, Along with the Institutional Monopoly That Serves as a Channel for Embezzlement of Financial Assets, Contribute to the Transformation of the Administrative Bureaucracy or Its Intermediaries into Private Proprietors

What is stolen through corrupt practices and illegal economies exits the country and often undergoes a transformation into assets like goods, land, and companies. These acquisitions are typically funded with the proceeds from the misappropriation of resources, including luxury goods. The act of personal gain through corrupt accumulation and transactions, such as privatizations and the granting of state concessions to private administrators, contributes to the evolution of the bureaucracy into a bourgeoisie.

When discussing privatization, it's important to note that it encompasses not only the partial or complete transfer of state-owned enterprises to the private sector but also practices like awarding operational concessions. Additionally, resources acquired from the state can be diverted into various forms of private investments, exemplified by businesses like the *bodegónes* that have emerged in Venezuela in recent years.

Drawing comparisons between the Chávez era and the current Maduro administration, with some limited instances of "workers' control" along the way, we observe how bureaucratic management is gradually turning into a form of capitalist ownership. Through the misappropriation of public assets, capital flight, financial speculation, and similar activities, the bureaucracy pilfers or disassembles state-owned entities and assets, creating opportunities for privatization, personal profit, and even partnerships with other bourgeois sectors, including imperialist capital.

This is, in part, the role that the new "bodegónes economy" plays. It represents one facet of President Maduro's economic liberalization measures in recent years. The alleged capital acquired illicitly or with the tacit support of the state bureaucracy appears to have found a home in businesses like the bodegónes. The bodegónes have been facilitated by shifts in economic policies, whether legislative or de facto, including unofficial dollarization and tariff exemptions, enabling the direct import of goods despite international sanctions and other purported impediments. This approach has helped alleviate supply shortages for many items, albeit at prices denominated in dollars at the "parallel" exchange rate or directly in dollars.

The recently established bodegónes in Venezuela cater to an exclusive market accessible only to individuals who earn their income in dollars, receive significantly higher salaries than the majority, receive substantial remittances from abroad, or have capital and investments located outside the country. In contrast to Maduro's administration, Chávez's policies during his time in power were primarily focused on ensuring affordable access to basic basket products. This was achieved through initiatives like Mission Mercal and Abastos Bicentenario, both of which were dependent on the state.[26] While these programs did suffer from financial mismanagement and instances of corruption, they largely benefited the general public by maintaining an abundance of essential products, even though money was often squandered. However, in the current crisis, the burden of economic adjustment has fallen disproportionately on the impoverished segments of the population.

Government officials acknowledge that there are hundreds of these bodegónes, although there are no figures that reflect their weight in the economy. Given the exorbitant prices charged in dollars, it is presumed that these establishments cater to a very select, privileged portion of the population, and they may also be used for money laundering purposes. This phenomenon extends to other luxury venues, including restaurants, nightclubs, casinos, and real estate.

A study conducted in collaboration with the Center for Workers' Research and Training, as reported on the BBC under the title "Venezuela Is Not a Socialist Country. It Is a Country with a Capitalist Economy of Bodegones," characterizes this type of business as representative of "elitist capitalism." It asserts that these establishments epitomize a de facto "anarchic dollarization" and exemplify the new disparities in the country.[27]

Numerous instances illustrate that the Maduro government has pursued a policy of privatization and entered into alliances with private capital in various sectors, including retail, construction, agri-food, services, mining, and even the oil industry. Private participation in mixed companies has expanded, and the operation and management of these entities have begun to shift to private partners. Debt-for-privatization offers have also been put on the table.[28] The assets transitioning into private hands are quite diverse.

This transition partially stems from the government's efforts to attract private capital to Venezuela as a means to counteract international sanctions. Given that sanctions obstruct the flow of such capital, economic agreements, especially with North American and European investors, are often facilitated through political negotiations. Furthermore, attracting foreign capital to the country can serve as a way to legitimize and reintroduce capital that was previously acquired through embezzlement.

One of the measures aimed at facilitating this capital influx is the so-called Anti-Blockade Law, which was approved by the one-party National Constituent Assembly in 2017. The law not only aims to provide greater incentives for investors but also grants the president and the executive branch expanded powers, discretion, and confidentiality, which they had already been exercising informally in matters related to foreign investments. However, this development has raised concerns among some prominent left-wing analysts who see it as a potential threat to national sovereignty.

Rafael Ramírez, the former minister of Energy and Oil and former president of Petróleos de Venezuela (PDVSA), who is also implicated in alleged national embezzlement, has been publicly raising accusations of similar misdeeds. He asserts that forms of oil privatization have been implemented, involving the sale of PDVSA's majority stake in mixed companies and the relinquishment of control over oil operations (an action he deems unconstitutional) as well as in the realm of marketing, which, according to the Organic Law of Hydrocarbons, is designated as a state monopoly.[29]

Ramírez contends that "behind the privatization of PDVSA, there exists not only the interest of transnational corporations but also the interests of various national economic groups, both traditional and newly emerged. These groups have connections with Maduro and his network of political, military, judicial supporters, as well as economic entities associated with the opposition who have entered into a coexistence pact with the Maduro regime." He further emphasizes that "the surrender of the nation and the appropriation of its companies and resources have become fundamental tools through which Maduro consolidates support from various quarters."[30]

In reference to the joint ventures that have been sanctioned or modified during Maduro's tenure, Ramírez asserts that

> invariably, there is a member of these economic groups partnering with PDVSA. For instance, joint ventures like PetroDelta and Petrozamora have these connections. When Quevedo, a former PDVSA president under Maduro, approved the "Oil Services Contracts," he did so with the participation of fourteen national companies linked to the proxies and economic operators of the Maduro regime, out of the five that govern the country. Moreover, when the Supreme Court (TSJ) approved the transfer of the Junín 10 Block in the Orinoco Oil Belt to a Maltese shell company, it was evidently done to favor a prominent economic operator of Maduro and members of his inner circle, in alliance with capital affiliated with the conservative Spanish right.[31]

As an example, there is the recent case of Petropiar in the oil sector, now being led by directors from the American company Chevron. Employees of the joint venture have raised concerns about their deplorable working conditions and have attributed these conditions to Chevron, which now has control over the company.[32] This type of transfer has also occurred with previously expropriated or failing companies, which were subsequently placed into other private hands, whether national or foreign. This phenomenon is particularly evident in the agroindustrial and food sector, as seen in the cases of Agropatria (formerly Agroisleña) and Lácteos Los Andes.

A similar trend has emerged in the roasting industry of the Venezuelan Coffee Corporation, where private entrepreneurs have assumed managerial roles and later become co-owners or outright owners. These entities include both foreign and domestic capital, with some investments originating from countries with governments that maintain alliances with the Venezuelan leadership, such as Iran. Workers were taken by surprise when they learned that all management positions at Lácteos Los Andes would be taken over by Iranians.

One of the beneficiaries of the enterprise that was once Agroisleña (subsequently converted into the state-owned Agropatria) is Grupo Agrollano 2910 CA, owned by Syrian-Venezuelan Atef Nemer. Nemer has amassed considerable wealth since the era of the Chávez government, with extensive business holdings and investments in Venezuela, Panama, and the United States.[33] These deals are often conducted with a high degree of secrecy, and the workers are frequently excluded from the decision-making process. This starkly contrasts with earlier rhetoric surrounding "socially owned" companies and attempts at "workers' control," which were obstructed or prematurely terminated and often replaced by military administrations prior to the privatization of specific processes or entire companies.[34]

Corrupt and Illegitimate Debt and Corruption Greater Than the Debt: Sources of Nutrition for the Ruling Bureaucracy in Its Transition to Being Part of the Capitalist Class or Associated with Sectors of Capital

The matter of external debt is intricately linked to the global system's imposition on dependent, semicolonial, or neocolonial nations. However, our focus is to underscore the corrupt and illegitimate nature of debts incurred to satiate bureaucratic greed, as part of the process of transforming bureaucracy into a lumpenbourgeoisie. This corruption includes aspects like commissions, unfinished projects, inflated costs, fraudulent financial dealings, and fictitious operations. In Venezuela, the corrupt and illegitimate nature of the external public debt is evident, and it is reasonable to suspect a similar situation in the internal and private debt.

In an effort to empower workers and the public with more significant oversight, the proposal for a Public and Citizen Audit of the Debt (as well as state accounts and businesses) was championed by Marea Socialista, in collaboration with other groups and individuals at various levels. The antidebt movement in Venezuela has its origins in the protests and initiatives of the Venezuelan Network Against Debt (between 1999 and 2002) and the establishment of the Platform for Public and Citizen Audit (commencing in 2015 and lasting for several years).

Foreign debt forms one of the most potent means by which countries are ensnared within the global system of subjugation to capitalism. Frequently, these are illegitimate debts with corrupt elements due to both the circumstances of their acquisition and the way the funds were employed, often contributing to bureaucratic and corporate corruption and resulting in unfinished projects, fraudulent activities, and tax evasion. In the case of Venezuela, this issue is conspicuous and is an integral part of the capital accumulation process undergone by the upper echelons of the state bureaucracy, effectively transforming them into the lumpenbourgeoisie.

Despite the fact that Hugo Chávez inherited debt from the Fourth Republic (prior to 1998), which he criticized, he never pursued any of the options outlined in his Bolivarian Alternative Agenda, including the possibility of a partial or total moratorium. Instead, buoyed by escalating oil revenues and rising hydrocarbon prices, he opted to repay the portion of the Venezuelan debt held by the World Bank, which amounted to approximately $3 billion. This was often misconstrued as Venezuela having paid off its entire external debt, when, in fact, only a fraction had been settled.

Subsequently, new debts were incurred, albeit not from organizations like the World Bank or under IMF conditions. Venezuela's mounting external debt largely stemmed from increased public spending on development plans centered around the vision of "Venezuela Power," coupled with fluctuations in hydrocarbon prices that led to reduced oil revenues. However, poor economic management also contributed to the escalation of external debt. Numerous projects were undertaken and financed haphazardly, with inadequate supervision and oversight. Many of these initiatives were never initiated, and the allocation of resources remains unclear, while others were left incomplete, with funding having been exhausted. Evidence of this includes the abandoned infrastructure projects scattered throughout the country. There are numerous examples of such projects, often involving substantial sums of money.

One of the most prominent instances is the railway line and train project connecting Tinaco and Anaco. The financial resources (contributed by the Chinese Fund), reported to be around $7.5 billion, were said to have been received by the then–Minister of Public Works and Housing Diosdado Cabello, who made this announcement in a public speech in the presence of Chávez. Regrettably, this project was never completed—only the initial phases were carried out—and the project has since been at a standstill. The whereabouts of such a substantial sum remain unknown, and no one has been held accountable for it.[35] Cabello had declared that this railway system would commence in 2009 and be completed within forty months (by 2012). To date (in 2023), it has not even reached halfway toward completion.

Hence, it can be affirmed that debts resulting from unfinished projects, as exemplified in the aforementioned case, have not been in any way advantageous for the nation and its citizens. Venezuela's external debt spiraled out of control and became unmanageable within the context of the prolonged crisis that has characterized the country over the last decade. However, the failure to make payments on certain portions of the debt, particularly bonds, did not alleviate the problems faced by Venezuelans. On the contrary, the government resorted to further reductions in public expenditure, either to service the remaining debt or for other purposes.

Throughout the Maduro administration, Venezuela defaulted on its foreign debt on multiple occasions. In 2017, partial default occurred due to non-payment of interest on sovereign bonds, followed by total default in 2018. Economic sanctions and financial blockades hampered Venezuela's capacity to meet its debt obligations and constrained its ability to secure further financing. In addition, some of the republic's assets and funds held abroad were seized or frozen or were not returned to the country as a result of legal disputes brought by foreign companies and investors seeking compensation for expropriations.

It should be noted that there is suspicion that among the bondholders of the country; there were officials from the bureaucracy who engaged in investments in dual-denominated bonds (acquired in bolivars but yielding dollars) or acquired foreign currency through irregular means and subsequently engaged in money laundering through such transactions. Nevertheless, the majority of Venezuela's debt is bilateral, primarily with states like China and Russia, in exchange for oil.

The Venezuelan state ceased to provide official figures on foreign debt during Maduro's administration. However, estimates from various sources suggest that Venezuela's public external debt stood at approximately $165 billion by the end of 2020, equivalent to over 284 percent of the nation's GDP, amidst the protracted economic crisis it has been enduring.[36] The debt-to-GDP ratio escalated after 2012, following the passing of Chávez, despite a substantial reduction in public spending on essential services and salaries. This has resulted in a debt that is practically unpayable in the current economic conditions of Venezuela and its populace, even without considering the substantial embezzlement of funds over the past two decades.

The extent of corruption in this context has been of such magnitude that even in a single case partially revealed within PDVSA in 2023, associated with former minister Tareck El Aissami and the National Superintendence of Cryptocurrencies (SUNACRIP), estimates suggest that $23 to $30 billion have been embezzled from the Venezuelan state, according to sources from the National Assembly.[37] This figure accounts for just over a fifth of the total debt, without taking into account the larger sum pilfered from the nation over the past two decades.

The embezzlement, the illicit capital flight, and the financial deficits discovered within the PDVSA's coffers, as previously mentioned, have been estimated to exceed $500 billion. This staggering figure is more than three times the country's external debt, as noted in studies and statements previously mentioned by Marea Socialista (*Embezzlement to the Nation*).[38] It is crucial to emphasize this corrupt component of the external debt amount.

When we consider that many of the infrastructure projects initiated by the Venezuelan government were funded through credits that led to external debt and then examine the number of projects that remain unfinished, dormant, unusable, or never even initiated, we start to grasp the enormity of this component. It also raises questions about the true allocation of resources that were ostensibly meant for these unfinished projects.

Corruption has played a pivotal and decisive role in the escalation of Venezuela's external debt. Poor economic management and corruption have contributed to the increase in public expenditure and a decrease in oil revenues, further augmenting the burden of external debt. This is a result of both the accumulation of interest and the proportional increase in debt relative to income from oil and GDP. As we have seen, the Venezuelan government used external debt-generating financing to build public infrastructure that was never completed.

The embezzlement and the debt marred by corruption have led to the intensification of policies detrimental to workers, resulting in a substantial reduction in the minimum wage and wages overall. Precarious working conditions serve as a means to reduce labor costs for both the public sector and private companies.

As of July 2023, the minimum wage stands at less than $4.25 per month, a stark contrast to the value of the family food basket, which amounts to $502.27, according to calculations from the Center for Documentation and Social Analysis of the Venezuelan Federation of Teachers, and the basic basket (comprising food, essential goods, and services), which is typically double that figure.[39] This would correspond to a range between $900 and $1,000 per month. This situation, referred to as a "zero wage" because it represents less than 1 percent of the basket's cost, essentially results in an almost "zero" labor cost, constituting a mere 0.8 percent of the cost for the food basket and less than 0.5 percent for the basic basket, both in the public and private sectors.

The shortfall in access to food, goods, and services is not alleviated by government expenditures on assistance programs, such as food parcels and CLAP products, which are delivered at the government's discretion. These programs have been frequently reported as sources of corruption and clientelism and as tools for social control. This situation is exceptional, as it means that in Venezuela, those who exchange their labor for the official minimum wage are effectively working for little to no compensation, often unable to cover even the costs of commuting to their workplaces, which are typically borne by the workers themselves.

In approximate terms, we can estimate that the total amount of embezzlement would have been sufficient to provide a minimum wage covering the basic necessities to an active workforce of fourteen million people for more than three years (the constitutionally established minimum wage), and for twice that duration if the aim was to at least meet the cost of the family food basket.

Returning to the indicators of debt suspected of being illegitimate and tainted by corruption, the list of significant public infrastructure projects left unfinished or never utilized in Venezuela since 1999 is extensive, as previously elucidated. A report from Transparencia Venezuela highlights the substantial sums of public funds invested in projects that remain incomplete or have fallen into "total abandonment." The NGO identifies at least 246 such projects in Venezuela, involving investments exceeding $316.025 billion, with 124 state entities implicated. Among the noteworthy projects are the General Rafael Urdaneta Bridge, La Cabrera Viaduct, Bridge over Lake Maracaibo, Mérida Cable Car, and the Simón Bolívar Hydroelectric Power Plant, to name a few.[40] Another illustrative example is the Tocoma Dam, intended for water usage in the lower Caroní region, which has remained half-finished and paralyzed since 2013.[41] Additionally, Transparencia Venezuela cites works related to the rehabilitation of water treatment plants, sugar complexes, petrochemical facilities, thermoelectric power plants, wind farms, official buildings, educational institutions, sports facilities, health care facilities, markets, and food processing facilities, among other areas of investment.

The failure to complete these projects signifies a derailment of an entire national development plan and the squandering or embezzlement of resources equivalent to the GDP of 2012 and even 2014, which was one of the highest in the country's history, and several times lower than the GDP observed in 2020, marked by reduced oil production and US economic sanctions.[42]

It is important to highlight that Transparency Venezuela has indicated that part of the funds allocated by the state do not align with the figures outlined in some budgets, leaving open the possibility of misappropriation of public funds.

Moreover, it is noteworthy that on January 15, 2022, the Venezuelan government announced the resumption of work on Line 5 of the Caracas Metro. These works had initially commenced during Chávez's administration in 2006 when the foundation was laid, yet more than a decade later, the first stage was still incomplete. Furthermore, the involvement of international companies, including the Brazilian firm Odebrecht, which had been embroiled in corruption cases across several Latin American countries, adds a significant dimension to the situation.

The lack of comprehensive or accessible financial information regarding these projects remains a significant hurdle. In fact, details were only available for slightly over 60 percent of them, with no information provided for the remaining 40 percent. Furthermore, concerning the allocation of the missing financial resources, opacity and a lack of transparency in financial figures persist, even in the presence of laws that have been enacted, such as the so-called Anti-Blockade Law, the Foreign Investment Law, and Special Economic Zones legislation, which permit the confidentiality of contracts, agreements, and transactions.[43]

To summarize, the Venezuelan debt is highly suspected of being illegitimate, illicit, and significantly tainted by corruption. It has, in various ways, provided sustenance for the emerging protobourgeois bureaucracy and the nascent lumpenbourgeoisie, whether through embezzlement, fraudulent transactions, the collection of commissions, or detrimental bond negotiations that have harmed the state.

Therefore, it is of paramount importance for civil society organizations to incorporate the demand for a Public and Citizen Audit of the External Debt into their plans, programmatic formulations, and preparatory efforts. This audit is a fundamental prerequisite for addressing the issue of illegitimate debt, holding those responsible for it accountable, and working toward the recovery of mishandled resources or seeking compensation.

The Public and Citizen Audit of the Debt should be closely linked to the implementation of anticorruption audits within public companies, institutions, and state funds. Such audits can lead to actions aimed at resource recovery, prosecution of corrupt individuals, and measures to compensate the national community. These actions are essential for cleansing the public administration and the economy, and they play a vital role in the restoration of public morality and the establishment of people's control over the state apparatus. Achieving this requires a democratic, anticapitalist government led by the working class.

The following are some conclusions and proposals for struggle:

- The leadership of the Bolivarian Revolution has undergone a process of bureaucratization and transformation, evolving into a lumpenbourgeoisie characterized by corrupt economic management, embezzlement, involvement in illicit economies, and a tainted external debt.
- With this shift in their class status and their transition into an integral part of the property-owning class, the social dynamics between this leadership and the working class and popular sectors have also changed.
- Driven by their new class interests, despite contradictions with their professed ideology and historical support base, the leadership has altered its policies significantly. These changes encompass economic strategies and the exercise of power, moving from a nationalist-democratic regime with Bonapartist elements (notably Chávez's strong leadership) and a progressive stance to an increasingly reactionary, authoritarian regime displaying tendencies reminiscent of neoliberal policies. These inclinations are

evident through de facto dollarization, increased precariousness, extreme labor flexibility, a growing openness to foreign capital, and measures akin to economic "adjustment" packages, more in practice than on paper. As a result, the bureaucracy turned lumpenbourgeoisie has taken a decidedly counterrevolutionary path, drifting further to the right and shedding any vestiges of progressivism.

- The antagonism continues, nonetheless, with segments of the traditional or classical opposition bourgeoisie, which were displaced from power by the Bolivarian government and, in many instances, subjected to economic dispossessions. Yet, there is a discernible trend among certain sectors of the opposition to explore economic and political negotiations, prompted by the failure of coup attempts and the ongoing assimilation of the government bureaucratic apparatus into capitalist structures. This occurs within the framework of the "carrot-and-stick" game governing imperialism's interactions with the Venezuelan leadership.
- Consequently, the national and international left must recognize that the current leadership cannot steer the course of the Bolivarian Revolution back on track. The current leadership has instead ushered in a counterrevolution that has instituted a regressive, antiworker regime. It is important to emphasize that opposing the blockade and economic sanctions should not justify providing political support to the Maduro government.
- A pivotal question that remains to be answered is why revolutions consistently succumb to bureaucratization, degenerate, and ultimately transform into their antithesis—some sooner, others later. This process predominantly involves the symbiotic relationship between the political and military bureaucracy.
- The development of policies and a program that are both anticapitalist and antibureaucratic becomes critically important to counteract the creation of new bureaucracies and to challenge both the emerging neobourgeoisie within Chavismo and the classical or traditional bourgeoisie in Venezuela.

CHAPTER SEVEN

Revolution and Counterrevolution in the Bolivarian Process

The Authoritarianism of the Government of Nicolás Maduro

Carlos Carcione

In the first decade of the twenty-first century, Latin America was infused with the hope of a new political experiment, with its most complete expression in Venezuela's Bolivarian process. After years of continental struggle and driven by an active mass movement across the region, a robust political process emerged, becoming a global reference point and extending its influence beyond Latin America. Similar phenomena appeared elsewhere, albeit with less intensity and consistency. The so-called progressive governments that rose to power and persisted in South America during this period were the political manifestations of this prior upheaval. This period saw the advancement of rights and demands that relatively improved the lives of the popular sectors, fueled by deep and ongoing rebellions. These rebellions and insurrections toppled neoliberal governments and undermined

---

Carlos Carcione passed away while writing this chapter. It was completed by Martin Carcione and Martin Poliak, using Carlos's notes and writings on the topic.

or dismantled political regimes that, while democratic or electorally focused, had conservative and imperialist tendencies.[1]

The Bolivarian process in Venezuela, led by Hugo Chávez, was the most advanced of these movements, pushing the boundaries of traditional politics by introducing new concepts and political explorations, breaking down economic and social barriers, and fostering hope. At the time (just as today's global political debates and academic research focus on the rise of the far right), discussions, studies, and media attention were centered on the new categories introduced by Bolivarianism. These included the Socialism of the Twenty-First Century, Participatory Democracy, and the Commune, among other concepts and tools aimed at confronting the capitalist system in crisis and the neoliberal offensive.

A decade after Chávez's death, the political landscape has undergone a dramatic transformation. The extreme polarization of the current world stage now places the far right, exemplified by Javier Milei in Argentina, in the position once held by Chavismo as a leading political project at the start of the century. However, it's important to note that strong processes of struggle, mobilization, and social and even military confrontations persist, highlighting the overarching world crisis of capitalism. This crisis, ongoing since 2008, has fueled the inter-imperialist dispute between the United States and China.

This significant shift in global and Latin American political dynamics requires analysis, especially considering the transition from progressive political influences to the growth and electoral prominence of the far right. Understanding this change necessitates examining how the relatively progressive policies and advances evolved, leading to governments and regimes that, despite some continuities, show a reactionary break in the key aspects that initially inspired those expectations. In essence, it involves comparing the Hugo Chávez and Nicolás Maduro periods of the Bolivarian process.

Additionally, the increasing pressure from the United States, marked by escalating sanctions and financial support to install a puppet government like Juan Guaidó's after Chávez's death, mirrors the intense inter-imperialist competition of the new global scenario. These efforts, reminiscent of the 2002 coup attempt and the oil strike of that same year, should be considered within this context. However, this analysis should not overlook the significant transformation and rupture between Chávez's and Maduro's regimes.

The Changes in Class Struggle and Its Expression in the Political Regime

As discussed throughout this book, various factors explain the shift from an advanced progressive regime within the framework of capitalism to a deeply authoritarian one. Without prioritizing these factors based on the order mentioned, we can identify the following influences: changes in international economic conditions, alterations in the class composition of the Bolivarian government, the increasing pressures from inter-imperialist disputes, the absence or extreme weakness of an alternative working-class and revolutionary leadership, and the subsequent defeat of significant mobilizations in the streets.

Many of these elements are analyzed in the different chapters of this book, so our focus will be on how these multiple factors affected the political regime, transforming it into its current state. It is important to understand that the political regime—comprising various institutions, both state and nonstate, and their organization to direct the country's future—is essentially a distorted reflection of the class struggle. This struggle is built on the ongoing conflict between the interests of different classes or class sectors and their leadership.

Given the massive embezzlement of national resources and the corrupt appropriation of extraordinary income by a small elite, a transformation occurs in the class character of the Bolivarian government. Gonzalo Gómez highlights this shift:

> As the class composition shifted from a bureaucratic caste to a property-owning class, the nature of social relations between the state's political leadership and the working class or popular sectors also changed. This shift contradicts its stated ideology and the historical social base of its support. The government increasingly drifted towards a regime that became more reactionary, authoritarian, and inclined towards neoliberal-like policies, including de facto dollarization, extreme job

> insecurity and labor flexibility, a tendency to reopen to foreign capital, and measures to typical "economic adjustment" packages.[2]

But, this economic engine of the counterrevolution not only causes a break with the popular and working support base but also creates an "imbalance" with the displaced bourgeois sectors that had largely been assimilated after their coup defeats. A new, unstable formation with internal friction is emerging within the bourgeois opposition to Madurismo.

The initial step, or impetus, for the transformations in the political regime comes from the new bolibourgeoisie, the military caste, and related sectors needing to establish a new management scheme for the country, reflecting this new reality. This involves eliminating pressures from the left, which aimed to deepen the Bolivarian process, and countering the newly formed bourgeois right, which is more directly aligned with the United States and eager to regain prominence. The first blows in this transformation were directed against the left, as seen in other historical contexts.

Thus, using the rhetoric of the right-wing threat, Maduro systematically attacked the "critical Chavismo" sectors at political, union, and institutional levels. One of the first expressions of this shift was the persecution and prohibition of Marea Socialista from participating in the electoral process. Marea Socialista, an anti-imperialist current with a long tradition of struggle and support for the Bolivarian process, had attracted a significant portion of "critical Chavismo."

In May 2015, six months after its request, the National Electoral Council (CNE) denied Marea Socialista the possibility of legalization to participate in the December legislative elections, citing the ridiculous pretext that its name "constitutes a phrase and not a name as such." Despite this abuse, and even after requesting intervention, the Supreme Court of Justice (TSJ) refused to intervene, only endorsing the CNE's decision in March 2021, six years later. Nevertheless, with support from nine already legalized electoral cards (previously recognized national and local parties), Marea Socialista managed to register its candidates in fifteen states. However, under the guise of enforcing gender parity—a measure imposed after legal deadlines—the CNE eliminated 70 percent of these candidacies, even though their lists included more women candidates than required in the quota law. It also pressured, threatened, and co-opted some of the parties that had lent Marea their support.

The persecution of Marea Socialista included sabotaging its public activities, such as power outages during events, hacking its social media accounts, and raiding its headquarters in Caracas. Along the same lines, renewal processes were suspended in unions where the bureaucracy was at risk of being defeated. For example, in January 2015, to prevent a clear defeat of the government candidate, the TSJ annulled the union elections in SIDOR just two days after the process began. Similar actions occurred with the Federation of Electrical Workers and the Federation of Oil Workers, among others. This was accompanied by the criminalization of union struggles and the imprisonment of numerous union activists and leaders.

The CNE took similar actions against the few initiatives that had managed to advance worker control or management. A clear example of this occurred in the industrial zone of Bolívar, where since 2009, an experiment in workers' control was underway as part of the Socialist Guayana Plan in steel and aluminum companies. Almost all these companies were taken over by military officials, and by mid-2015, there were no longer any signs of worker participation.

Additionally, cases of political retaliation, institutional abuse, and various forms of persecution—including physical violence and crimes against those who tried to report irregularities in the functioning of the state—multiplied. An extreme example is the forced disappearance of Alcedo Mora, an official of the secretariat of the governorate of the state of Mérida, who was about to file a corruption complaint against Petroleum of Venezuela (PDVSA).

It is important to highlight that the bureaucracy's actions were facilitated by the existence of a "single" party founded by Chávez himself, with advice and direct intervention from the Cuban leadership. "Chavismo" as a political movement was a heterogeneous force without clear organization beyond the plebeian sectors of the army. The establishment of the United Socialist Party of Venezuela (PSUV) occurred amid debates and discussions about the party's model, leading to massive membership from its inception.

The Third Congress, held July 26–28, 2014, exemplifies this shift. During the congress, the bureaucratic apparatus solidified its dominance over the large mass of workers affiliated with it. In the lead-up to the congress, Marea Socialista was prominent in voicing strong criticisms of this shift, advocating for a thorough assessment of the entire process and the party's condition and proposing a series of measures to bring about a revolutionary change in direction. They expressed these views in their PSUV document *Congress Must be Democratic to Reinvigorate the Revolution*, published on Aporrea.org and widely distributed. In the document they wrote,

> We must examine why our organizational structures were altered at the whims of the electoral commands in power, outside of party congresses, resulting in visible organizational disintegration, massive loss of militants, increased bureaucratization, dissolution of the few training and debate spaces, discouragement, decreased mobilization capacity, and lack of genuine consultation with the base. [. . .] If we have a Party-State, with leaders who elect each other while also serving as managers, ministers, and heads of public companies, how can PSUV members exert any control over the government and the state apparatus? How can policies be reviewed and corrected? With an organization filled with officials and increasingly detached from the people, the working class, and the popular vanguard, there is no way to combat bureaucratism and corruption [. . .] . The methodology designed by the Management for this congress violates the party's principles and statutory norms. It has little to do with the Defending Principle of Participatory and Protagonistic Democracy, Internal Democracy, and Equality Within the Organization. Nor does it align with the Unitary orientation that should prevail in the PSUV.[3]

By first stifling the party base, the Nicolás Maduro–Diosdado Cabello leadership succeeded in significantly containing the most critical sectors of the process through a variety of methods, ranging from co-optation to direct intimidation. This process was not straightforward and faced varying levels of resistance depending on the strength and organization of the critical Chavismo sectors within the party structure. Ultimately, by consolidating absolute control over the apparatus, the government gained a powerful tool to suppress the revolutionary left, which questioned its policies and demanded radical socialist transformations.

The bureaucratic consolidation of the PSUV, the persecution and silencing of critical sectors, and the dismantling of grassroots union and popular leadership—replaced by state bureaucracy and army agents—left the right as the only visible opposition when dissatisfaction with the Maduro government and its counter-reforms escalated to mobilization. In the 2015 legislative elections, the right won decisively, securing two-thirds of the deputies, indicating a clear break between the Chavista social base and Maduro. The government's response was to annul the elections in the Amazonas region, challenge the elected deputies, and thereby prevent the right from achieving an absolute majority in the National Assembly. Elections in that region were never held again. The exclusion of critical and revolutionary sectors from the election contributed to this outcome, marking the start of the government's ongoing violation of the principles and laws established in the Bolivarian Constitution—a practice that escalated with the suspension of the Recall Referendum in 2016—serving a polarization disconnected from the demands and interests of the popular majorities.

Mass mobilizations against the high cost of living, democratic deterioration, and other issues of a process once aimed at guaranteeing "happiness to the people" were led by a pro-imperialist and artificial leadership. This leadership broadly shared the bolibourgeoisie-initiated process but sought its share. History once again demonstrated that the alignment of demands does not necessarily imply an alignment of interests, and that consistent revolutionary leadership cannot be replaced by general appeals to the idea of socialism.

Recall Referendum, Mass Mobilizations, and Repression

After its victory in the legislative elections, the right, organized in the Democratic Unity Roundtable (MUD), announced through Democratic Action President Henry Ramos Allup at the inauguration of the

National Assembly that within six months, the MUD would establish a "democratic, constitutional, peaceful, and electoral" mechanism to achieve a change in government.

Despite these declarations, the MUD sought negotiation with the government, aiming for "peaceful coexistence" based on respecting each state institution's powers. This farce reflected the tensions within the right itself and at the same time the shared interests between the government and the opposition. These tensions fluctuated between open confrontation and negotiation. To prepare for this scenario, the government had, in the last session of the outgoing National Assembly, replaced the TSJ to ensure control over it, which immediately began issuing rulings to reduce the National Assembly's powers.

On April 26, 2016, the CNE officially initiated the recall referendum process (as outlined in the 1999 constitution to facilitate the change of government before its terms limits have lapsed if certain terms are met) but delayed the distribution of forms for collecting signatures, extending deadlines and changing requirements to hinder the process. Much of 2016 was marked by political debate around the referendum, with massive mobilizations demanding its realization and the establishment of a date before the government completed two years in office. If the recall succeeded after this period, the vice president would complete the term. However, in October 2016, the CNE halted the referendum, citing irregularities in the signature collection, clearly violating rights enshrined in the 1999 constitution.

It's noteworthy that Chávez himself, during a period of low popularity, called for a recall referendum against his government in 2004, even before the necessary signatures were collected. This contrasts with the current government's approach of prioritizing continuity of government at all costs, marking a shift to bureaucratic consolidation, followed by neoliberal economic measures and greater restrictions on the political regime. Although the pressure of imperialism is undeniable, it is important to emphasize that there is a substantial difference with the period of 2002–4, when progressive measures by the government took precedent.

With the recall referendum suspended, the situation deteriorated again in early 2017, illustrating that the consolidation of authoritarianism aligns with the regressive economic policies of Maduro's government. In March 2017, the PDVSA Board of Directors approved the formation of the mixed company Petrosur, SA. According to the Hydrocarbons Law and the Bolivarian Constitution, the power to approve mixed companies lies with the National Assembly, which had an opposition majority at the time. On March 29, the TSJ issued a resolution assuming legislative functions, bypassing the National Assembly and empowering the executive branch to legislate in key areas without legislative approval, under the current Exception Decree. On March 31, the attorney general of the republic, appointed by the PSUV in December 2015, denounced these rulings as breaches of the constitutional order.

A process of mass mobilization was then unleashed, which the right tried to capitalize on, but it was not similar to the marches between 2001 and 2004 that aimed to overthrow Chávez's government. Martín Poliak, a member of Marea Socialista at the time, describes it:

> In 2002, the right, supported by imperialism, rose up against a series of progressive measures taken by Hugo Chávez's government (Hydrocarbons Law, Fisheries Law, Land Law, fight against the PDVSA technocracy, etc.). The April 11, 2002 coup and the oil sabotage of 2002–2003 were precisely to halt this progressive advance. They disregarded the Constitution endorsed by the Venezuelan people, which they did not recognize.
>
> Now the opposite is happening: the government itself is violating the Bolivarian Constitution, not to advance any progressive measures, but to hand over sovereignty to transnational corporations through the Orinoco Mining Arc (AMO), the Orinoco Oil Belt (OPF), and the 15 "productive engines." The timeline of the current conflict clearly shows that the government's actions are not progressive at all.
>
> That is why, unlike 2002/03 and even the 2014 "guarimbas," often called "revolts of the rich," now a significant sector of the working people, including the Chavista social base, is participating in the protests. A much larger sector, even if not participating in the protests, no longer supports Maduro. It is evident, as even many main official scribes must admit, that the government has lost the support of Venezuelan society and has been governing for almost two years without any elections.[4]

The movement that emerged between April and July 2017 was massive and, at times, multitudinous. It was based on a somewhat confused but progressive sentiment among some sectors of the population participating in it. Many of these citizens believed, albeit mistakenly, that they were fighting to defend democratic rights against unconstitutional abuses toward the National Assembly. They genuinely rejected the elimination of the right to a recall referendum and the suspension of regional elections that were supposed to take place in December 2016.

This progressive yet vague and confused sentiment of democratic struggle was co-opted by the MUD leadership and its elitist and antidemocratic project. The MUD dictated the pace and ultimately dismantled the mobilization by prioritizing isolated, disruptive actions and calls for foreign interference. The MUD also violated the constitution, particularly by abandoning the demand for an electoral solution and attempting to establish parallel government institutions with international support, seeking a coup. The dominance of the MUD leadership over the movement's base, which had diffuse democratic aspirations, led Marea Socialista to discourage participation in the mobilizations. They also warned of the betrayal by the MUD's right-wing opposition leadership. Unable to break the armed forces, the MUD returned to negotiations in the Dominican Republic, agreed to regional elections, and capitulated to the PSUV leadership, abandoning the mobilization process, which was completely dismantled the day after the constituent assembly election was called on May 1, 2017, but not before seventeen lives were lost due to the irresponsible policy of its leadership on that same day.

The shift toward isolated, disruptive actions in the mobilization process against the government that began in April 2017 provided justification for the brutal repression unleashed by the PSUV government, which crushed the movement entirely. With 156 dead, many during marches and rallies, over 3,000 detained (most summarily tried by military courts and imprisoned in military facilities), and more than 1,000 injured, the cost of the conflict was very high for the sectors that came out to mobilize, primarily the popular sectors.

On May 1, amid the mobilizations, the Maduro government resumed its political offensive by calling a Constituent Assembly. Far from signifying a change of course or a radicalization of the Bolivarian Revolution, as some leftist sectors interpreted, the main objective of Maduro's fraudulent Constituent Assembly was to consolidate *authoritarianism by advancing towards a new totalitarian political regime.* Statements made on July 13 by Vice President Tareck El Aissami left no room for doubt: "We need a very strong, very strong institutional framework. And that will be allowed by the Constituent Assembly. [. . .] That Constituent Assembly is not only for the Prosecutor to leave, it is to turn the Public Ministry around."[5] In other words, the Constituent Assembly, which ultimately never drafted a new Constitution, aimed to destroy everything that was not subordinate to it.

A comparison between the Constituent Assembly called by Chávez in 1999 and the one called by Maduro in 2017, laid out in the following table, is clarifying.

The National Constituent Assembly ultimately evolved into a new plenipotentiary state power, serving to establish a new political regime aligned with the ruling elite and its interests. It was dissolved in December 2020, setting the parameters for the new regime without drafting a new constitution. During its tenure, it dismissed the attorney general, revoked the parliamentary immunity of several opposition deputies, passed the Anti-Hate Law, aimed at prosecuting any antigovernment political demonstration, and approved the Anti-Blockade Law, granting Maduro special powers to privatize public companies and enter contracts with private firms. Upon dissolution, its president, Diosdado Cabello, stated that "the main legacy of the constituent assembly was having imposed peace and institutional order in the country," clearly indicating its underlying objectives.

Table 7.1

	Constituent 1999	**Constituent 2017**
Convocation	On April 25, 1999, a national referendum was called where the Venezuelan people were consulted on two questions: (1) Do you convene a National Constituent Assembly with the purpose of transforming the state and creating a new legal system that allows the functioning of a social and participatory democracy? (2) Do you agree with the bases proposed by the National Executive for the convocation of the National Constituent Assembly, examined and modified by the National Electoral Council in session dated March 24, 1999, and published in its full text, in the *Official Gazette of the Republic of Venezuela* No. 36.669 dated March 25 of 1999? The electoral bases contained the duration of the ANC (six months) and the obligation to submit the text of the new constitution to a new referendum. The referendum was approved by 88% (question 1) and 82% (question 2).	No referendum or consultation with the Venezuelan people was held. The electoral bases of the Constituent Assembly proposed by President Maduro and its convocation were approved by the National Electoral Council (controlled by the government) and not by the Venezuelan people. It has no defined period of duration. The gubernatorial elections held in December 2017 were conditional on the recognition of the ANC by the elected candidates.
Election	On July 25, 1999, elections were held to elect 128 constituents by direct election (another 3 were reserved for Indigenous representatives). The Patriotic Pole obtained 65% of the votes. The right-wing opposition grouped in the Democratic Pole obtained 22%. Other parties 12%.	The election, scheduled for July 30, was held without the participation of political parties. 364 territorial constituents were elected and 181 were divided into 8 sectors (students, workers, businessmen, Indigenous people, farmers and fishermen, pensioners, people with disabilities, and communal councils). The location in each of the sectors was decided arbitrarily by the CNE. And, as members of the PSUV itself denounced, the candidacies were accepted or rejected by the CNE without clear rules or criteria.

Approval	Once the new constitution was drafted, it was put to a referendum of the Venezuelan people, who in December 1999, with more than 70% of the votes, approved the Constitution of the Bolivarian Republic of Venezuela.	The ANC resolutions were not put to a referendum. Maduro sent a modification to the electoral rules that urges the ANC to hold a consultation.
Results	The result was an unprecedented process of popular participation in the elaboration of a constitution that, even though it is a capitalist constitution, has many progressive aspects.	Already from the previous process itself, it is explicit that this constituent process does not advance democratic rights, but quite the opposite. Its result was the consolidation of an authoritarian political regime.

Conclusion

Since then, a political regime with increasingly authoritarian characteristics was consolidated: Elections were manipulated, trade unionists and activists were arrested, critical and opposition leaders and media were persecuted, there were cases of dubious disappearances, and procedural rights were eliminated, among other measures. In August 2023, the TSJ questioned the legality of the Communist Party of Venezuela and appointed an "ad hoc board of directors." Similar actions were taken in previous years against other political groups, such as Democratic Action, Primero Justicia, COPEI, Bandera Roja, and Patria Para Todos. Additionally, Marea Socialista was directly banned.

It is increasingly evident that Venezuela is witnessing the emergence of a completely authoritarian and undemocratic political regime, which seeks to avoid being labeled as a dictatorship because of its sensitivity to international pressure and isolation. Nonetheless, it aims to establish a system that represents a lower cost than completely abolishing the electoral process. To achieve this, it holds elections while ensuring opposition to the measure and silencing dissent within its own ranks.

The 2024 presidential elections confirm both assertions. First, the regime's need to carry out some sort of electoral simulation, negotiated and confined within the narrow limits of a tailored opposition, and second, its absolute refusal to tolerate the prospect of an unfavorable outcome, leading to clear delegitimization in the eyes of the world, even after having outlawed all critical expressions with a popular or leftist orientation. This is echoed in the following statement by the International Socialist League:

> The data presented orally and without any evidence was the final chapter of an irregular and undemocratic electoral process. This is a government that for years has intervened in political parties, including those of the radical left, seized their legal records, appointed parallel leaderships, and in the months leading up to the elections, banned candidates from the right, center, and left. Finally, it denied millions of Venezuelans—who were forced by the social and economic crisis to live in other countries—their right to vote. We witnessed a rigged and premeditated electoral process designed to ensure that Maduro would win by any means necessary. And now we are experiencing the consequences of that unjust electoral architecture.[6]

In the aftermath of Chávez's death and Nicolás Maduro's assumption of power along with the PSUV leadership, a process of political and economic counter-reforms commenced, which solidified into a counterrevolution following a significant defeat of the mass movement. This counterrevolution altered the political regime's character and the economic orientation of Venezuelan rentier capitalism and intensified the erosion of workers' and popular rights, whose positive trajectory had begun to stagnate by the end of the first decade of the twenty-first century.

Sanctions and blockades, initiated by sectors of the old Venezuelan bourgeoisie, were utilized by the Maduro regime to obscure its counterrevolutionary and authoritarian tendencies. This authoritarian shift in politics coincided with a pronounced turn toward neoliberal economic policies, exacerbating the country's dependence on primary resources, rent seeking, and extractivism. Through a fraudulent Constituent Assembly, the endorsement of Chinese-style Special Economic Zones, and routine repression, a civic-military regime with clear dictatorial features was established.

These developments were accompanied by ongoing efforts to strike agreements with North American imperialism and growing subservience toward Chinese and Russian imperialism. The Bolivarian process, once the most advanced experience of Latin American progressivism, flirting with the notion of twenty-first-century socialism, was dismantled.

Considering the events outlined here, and the rich history of class struggle throughout these years, it's imperative to recognize a crucial lesson for future revolutionary and socialist endeavors in Venezuela, Latin America, and beyond: Even the most advanced and progressive processes are prone to regression and transformation into their antitheses if they fail to transcend the confines of a historically exhausted system—imperialist capitalism. To achieve this goal, deeply democratic organizations rooted in mass movements are essential, with a steadfast belief that the struggle extends beyond the boundaries of capital. Today, more than ever, in this polarized and declining world, Che Guevara's phrase—"socialist revolution or caricature of revolution"—resonates from the annals of history.

CHAPTER EIGHT

Orinoco Mining Arc as an Expression of the End of a Cycle

Right-Wing Turn and the Economics of Dispossession in the Bolivarian Process

Emiliano Terán

On February 24, 2016, at the beginning of a year marked by severe social hardship in the midst the Great Venezuelan Crisis (2013–21), the Bolivarian government under Nicolás Maduro officially introduced the Orinoco Mining Arc (AMO) through Decree 2248. This initiative outlined an extensive mining project in the northern region of the Venezuelan Amazon, unprecedented in Venezuelan history. Shortly thereafter, a coalition of intellectuals, activists, artists, politicians, and others launched a campaign to expose the environmental, social, and cultural risks and threats to Indigenous communities associated with the implementation of this project.[1]

However, beyond its immediate concerns, the AMO carried historical significance and deeper implications. Since 2016, the campaign against AMO warned that the initiative represented a turning point that signaled a shift in the extractive regime.[2] Not only did it signify the impracticality of the oil-dependent model, which had been in decline and crisis for decades, but it also indicated a reconfiguration of the national territory around a more voracious extractive framework, which was advancing significantly on the Amazon. Consequently, the AMO became a crucial component of the material foundation and economic support for a new power configuration, one that sought to reintegrate transnational corporate influence. From our perspective, we are witnessing a transition from the exhaustion of governmental progressivism to its complete collapse, signaling the conclusion of a cycle in the country.

Since then, a considerable amount of time has passed, and in just a few years, the consequences of the collapse of this oil-dependent nation have brought about significant transformations. The country is no longer recognizable; it has undergone substantial changes. Essentially, the collapse led to a major shift in the extractive system, losing its ability to centralize and establish governance based on oil revenue. This resulted in a fragmented nation, characterized by predatory practices, illegality, dispossession, and a form of neo-feudalization. The AMO stands out as a symbol of this transformation, with the Amazon being the prime territory for (re)conquest. The republican project known as Venezuela has been seriously challenged.

What makes this development unique is that it occurred under a left-wing government that had pledged not only to alleviate poverty and exclusion but also to achieve independence and a socialist revolution. How could such a brutal system of social and political repression, coupled with a predatory extractive regime focused on dispossession, emerge simultaneously from the heart of a political process that generated numerous hopes, promised substantial changes, and declared a challenge to the capitalist system? The development of AMO, from a conceptual idea to a formal project—ultimately becoming a complex apparatus that intertwines legal and illegal mining—offers insights into this process with profound implications for emerging political regimes.

This chapter does not just present an environmentalist critique; it combines economic and political ecology perspectives with critical geography. It aims to emphasize that the crises and historical shifts in power in Venezuela are interconnected with the imperatives of extractivism, the pursuit of the domination of nature, the ongoing dynamics of recolonizing territories (even within left-wing governments), and the emerging geographies of power.

The Emergence of the Bolivarian Process: Historical Ruptures and Continuities and the Antecedents of the Orinoco Mining Arc

Examining the past is crucial for both comprehending the roots of the regressive shift in the Bolivarian process and recognizing the ruptures and continuities between it and the previous political regime. The period leading up to Hugo Chávez's assumption of the presidency in 1999 was marked by intense political and social crises amid the prolonged downturn of the oil-dependent model, which had been in decline since the 1970s.[3] In this context, energy nationalism waned, making room for an increasing influence of neoliberal policies, including the oil industry itself, as part of an Oil Opening initiative. Petróleos de Venezuela (PDVSA) reopened to private investors, advocating for reduced national taxes and royalties, emphasizing the role of the Ministry of Energy and Mines, and establishing contracts favorable to private capital.[4] From the late 1980s, oil production steadily rose, reaching 3,329,000 barrels per day (b/d) in 1998.[5] It is noteworthy that PDVSA's plans during this period (Corporate Guides 1993–98) aimed to boost oil production to 5–6 million b/d to counterbalance the drop in prices resulting from increased supply.

This adjustment sought to "resolve" the crisis by extracting more not only from the labor force and national monetary surpluses but also from nature. However, the extractive expansion during this neoliberal era extended beyond oil. Various investment plans, primarily in the 1990s, encompassed sectors such as mining, forestry, tourism, and regional integration infrastructure, resulting in numerous impacts and socioenvironmental conflicts.[6] This expansion also encompassed the Venezuelan Amazon, a vast biome spanning the southern regions of the Orinoco River (Amazon, Bolívar, and Delta Amacuro states), covering 453,915 km2 (49.5 percent of the continental national territory). The region harbors delicate and invaluable ecosystems (including extensive protected areas) and is home to twenty-nine Indigenous peoples, including three groups in voluntary isolation. Simultaneously, the area boasts significant mineral resources such as gold, diamonds, iron, bauxite, and coltan.

The Venezuelan Amazon has historically been seen, by colonial and, later, republican elites, as a reserve, as a territory yet to be conquered. Venezuelan extractive development has traditionally focused on the north of the Orinoco, encompassing traditional agricultural enclaves, a port economy, and the contemporary oil industry. However, with the crisis of the oil model, the concept of the "conquest of the south" was reevaluated. This shift is evident in policies such as the promotion of mining in the Imataca Forest Reserve (located northeast of Bolívar state, now part of the Orinoco Mining Arc), where mining concessions were granted for over 1 million hectares between 1991 and 1996. In 1997, during the second term of Rafael Caldera's government (1994–99), Decree 1,850 was enacted, authorizing mining and forestry exploitation in 1.2 million hectares of Imataca.[7] Gold extraction levels in the country surged in the 1990s, reaching approximately twelve tons per year in multiple years and surpassing twenty tons in 1997.[8] Despite resistance against the Caldera decree and in defense of Imataca, considered the most emblematic environmental conflict of the time, social and environmental organizations successfully obtained a precautionary measure from the Supreme Court of Justice. This measure aimed to prevent the issuance of new concessions and the development of mining infrastructure within that area through relevant campaigns, mobilizations, and actions.

With Chávez's assumption of the presidency, a series of changes and political ruptures occurred; however, it is essential to analyze them in conjunction with the continuities that persisted from the so-called Fourth Republic. It is worth noting that during Chávez's candidacy, he not only pledged significant political transformations and historical advancements for the population, particularly the disadvantaged sectors, but also proposed a new environmental policy and the resolution of various socioenvironmental issues plaguing the country. For instance, during his presidential campaign, Chávez committed to protecting Imataca, stating in November 1998, "[I]f obtaining gold requires destroying the forest, then I will preserve the forest."[9]

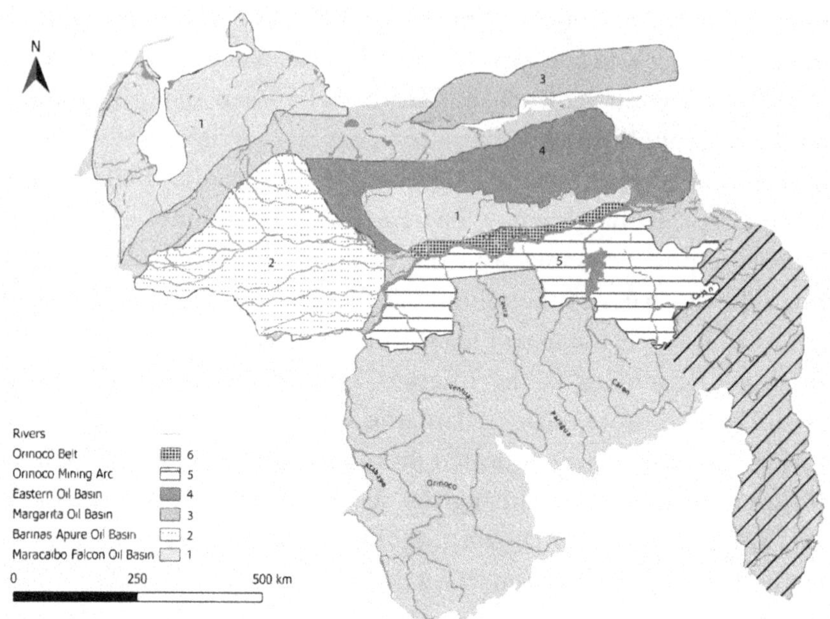

Figure 8.1 Map of Venezuela's oil concentrations north of the Orinoco, and of the AMO polygonal, north of the Amazon. Map by Emiliano Terán.

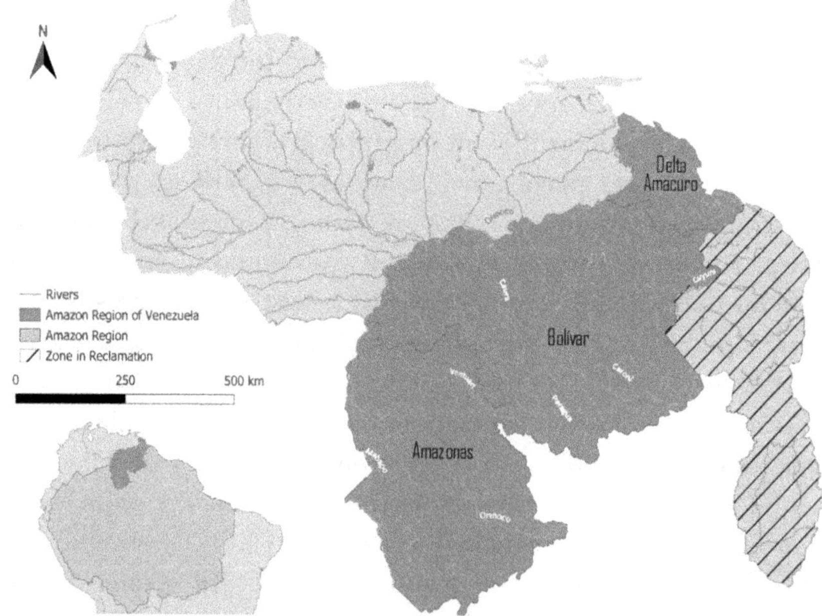

Figure 8.2 Shaded surface of the Venezuelan Amazon. Map by Emiliano Terán.

The inauguration of the Bolivarian process ushered in a new political order based on the 1999 constitution, aiming to revive and reclaim the diminished petrostate. The government's program in the initial period (1999–2004) leaned toward a reformist stance, emphasizing social democracy. There was also a restructuring of the collection and distribution of oil revenue to fund the creation of new institutions and programs for social, economic, and cultural inclusion.[10] In the early years of his administration, Chávez advocated for oil moderation, advocating for no growth in production, defending the price of a barrel of crude oil, and exercising prudence in utilizing oil rents.[11] The new president had delved into Venezuelan literature and discourse on the oil issue, which repeatedly highlighted the dangers of deepening national economic dependence on this sector.

In terms of the environment, rights in this domain were acknowledged in the new constitution, echoing the recognition of the rights of Indigenous peoples. This commitment was further solidified with the subsequent enactment of several laws, including the Biological Diversity Law (2000), the Organic Law of the Environment (2006), and the Water Law (2007). These legislative measures collectively reinforced the regulatory framework for environmental protection in the country. Additionally, laws such as the Organic Law of Indigenous Peoples and Communities (2005) and the Land Law aligned with various policies advocating for a more equitable distribution of land.

However, early on, continuities with the preceding political-economic regime became apparent, underscoring the ongoing expansion of the extractivist model, predatory attitudes toward nature, and a logic of internal recolonization that would shape the trajectory of subsequent years in the Bolivarian process.

Two examples, both from the Amazon, highlight these continuities. First, the aforementioned case of the Imataca Forest Reserve, which, despite originating as a response to Caldera government policies, saw the precautionary measure achieved. Despite Chávez's commitment to preserving these forests, the Bolivarian government revitalized the initiative, leveraging the president's high level of legitimacy and popular-demand discourse and the trust initially placed in government management by broad segments of the population. Through conflicting statements and manipulated consultation strategies, the National Executive ultimately issued Decree 3110 in September 2004. This decree affirmed Caldera's decision to legalize industrial and small-scale mining within the area, rendering the precautionary measure ineffective.[12] This set a negative precedent in the administration of Areas Under Special Administration Regime in the Amazon and overlooked this emblematic socioenvironmental struggle.

As a second example, there is the conflict with the Pemón Indigenous people concerning the installation of a power line in the Canaima National Park. This high-voltage line, intended for exporting electrical energy from Venezuela to Brazil and traversing Pemón territories, was initiated in 1997 during Caldera's administration, and it was under the Chávez government that it was completed in 2001, overcoming opposition from Indigenous communities. The Pemón community resisted by dismantling several towers along the line; however, the Chávez government employed strategies of division and cooptation—aligning with pro-project Pemón factions and reaching agreements with the Indigenous Federation of the Bolívar State. The government also resorted to criminalization, discrediting those who opposed the project and even intervening militarily in the conflict zone.[13] This case holds significance because, over time, it led to the fragmentation of the Pemón people, assimilating many into the development model, and solidified a pattern of intervention in their territories that would intensify in subsequent years.

In both of the aforementioned cases, it was the Bolivarian government that ultimately facilitated, formalized, and executed the policies of extractive and developmental intervention in the Amazon, which the preceding neoliberal Caldera government had failed to fully consolidate or implement.

This initial phase of the Bolivarian process, marked by significant instability and conflicts with opposition factions, tilted in favor of the Chávez government, allowing for its consolidation and the beginning of the shaping of Chavismo's hegemony.

Twenty-First-Century Socialism, Extractivist Expansionism, and the Path to the Recolonization of the Amazon: The Origin of the AMO

During the period spanning from 2005 to 2013, the Bolivarian process experienced phases of ascent, stagnation, and decline, leading to a reorientation of the economic and power structure. This shift took advantage of several years marked by political, electoral, and communicational dominance, as well as alliances with progressive governments in Latin America and favorable regional integration policies. Additionally, a significant surge in raw material revenues flooded the coffers of the Venezuelan petrostate. This reorientation aimed to strengthen the state, establishing a more centralized power structure centered around Chávez, while creating channels for downward influence that shaped a corporate framework affecting the social foundations. The narrative underwent a radical turn toward the left, defining "21st century socialism" as the envisioned horizon and transformative program for the country.

The material foundation for this state and discursive amplification lay in the ambition to transform Venezuela into a "world energy power." This vision involved the revival and expansion of both existing and new large-scale economic projects, many of which were subsequently nationalized. The strategy embraced an expansive extractivism spanning hydrocarbons, mining, industry, agroindustry, infrastructure, forestry, tourism, and more. At its core, the proposal aimed to double oil production, reaching toward six million barrels per day by 2021, with a primary focus on the Orinoco Oil Belt, a region abundant in heavy and extra-heavy crude oil situated on the northern bank of the Orinoco River.[14]

This marked a departure from the moderate extractivism of the initial years, echoing the ambitious oil targets outlined in the PDVSA plans during the era of the Oil Opening. Similarly, there was a revival of the rhetoric of "Great Venezuela," reminiscent of the discourse employed by governments in the previous political regime. This rhetoric inflated development aspirations based on the temporary surge in oil prices, overlooking the subsequent exacerbation of the structural issues in the

Venezuelan economy that had precipitated the preceding crisis. Additionally, the new project signaled a move toward the country's new hydrocarbon frontiers, driven by both the heightened extractive pressure on emerging geographies and the adoption of more polluting, energy-intensive, and economically costly forms of nonconventional oil exploitation. Under Chávez's leadership, production in the Faja Petrolífera del Orinoco increased from 563 thousand b/d in 2006 to 1,228,300 b/d in 2014, altering the percentage of heavy and extra-heavy crude oil from 38 percent of the total extracted in Venezuela to 58.8 percent in 2014.[15]

The "world energy power" vision for Venezuela also aimed to stimulate all forms of extractivism across the national geography, including the Amazon. The advance into the Amazon region was not solely motivated by purported "development" goals for less modernized areas. The historical decline in the profitability of the oil economy, owing to escalating production costs, an increasingly "unconventional" composition, and the waning dynamism of the rentier model, necessitated the opening of new economic niches and commodity frontiers.[16] This underscores the imperative for the ongoing "conquest of the south" that continued with Chávez and the increasing economic importance of the Amazon.

It is crucial to note that the most valuable commodity in the Venezuelan Amazon is gold, which holds special significance in the global market and as a reserve asset. Gold has experienced an extraordinary price increase since the early twenty-first century, coinciding with a substantial surge in illegal mining activities in this bioregion.[17]

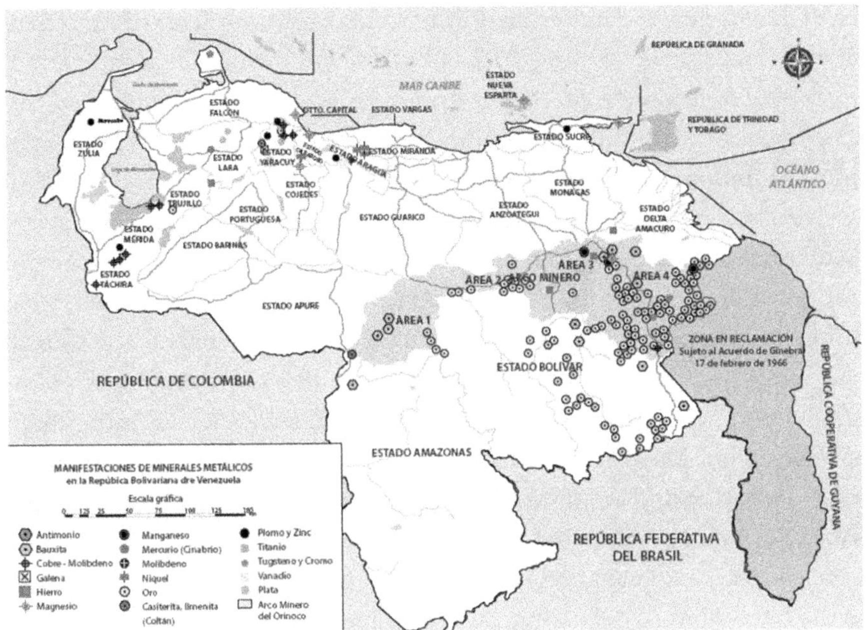

Figure 8.3 Manifestations of metallic minerals in Venezuela (2018).
Source: Ministry of Ecological Mining Development, Venezuela.

Figure 8.4 International price of gold (US$/oz. t), period 2000–2023.
Source: Trading Economics.

The Chávez government aimed to formalize an unprecedented expansion of large-scale mining in Venezuela. Following the legalization of mining in Imataca in 2004, various policies were implemented for the Amazon, including concessions and investments that significantly boosted national gold production—from six tons per year in 1999 to twelve tons in 2009.[18] Measures were also introduced to regularize small miners and transition them to other productive activities through initiatives like the Mining Reconversion Plan and the Piar Mission. The militarization of the Amazon against illegal mining, such as the Caura Plan in 2010, and international agreements, like the one with the Chinese company CITIC Group to create a comprehensive "mining map of Venezuela," played a role. In August 2011, a decree-law nationalized the exploration and exploitation of gold. The apex of this process came with Chávez's announcement in 2011 to initiate a megaproject in the Venezuelan Amazon called the Arco Minero de Guayana—later known as the Arco Minero del Orinoco. This ambitious plan involved creating a polygonal area covering nearly 112,000 km2 across the entire northern region of the Bolívar state, targeting significant deposits of gold, bauxite, coltan, diamonds, and other minerals for exploitation.

The establishment of the Orinoco Mining Arc (AMO) marked a crucial turning point, initiating a complex process of recolonization of the Amazon. This development unfolded alongside the stagnation, decline, and regression of the Bolivarian process. This downturn aligned and intertwined with the onset of the Great Crisis (2013–21), the most severe in the country's history.[19] In this context, the AMO became a pivotal step in the transformations that extractivism would undergo in the subsequent years in Venezuela.

The Great Crisis (2013–2021) and the Formalization of the AMO

From 2013 to 2021, Venezuela underwent its most severe crisis in history, ranking among the worst crises in Latin America.[20] This turmoil witnessed an extraordinary 75 percent collapse of gross domestic product, coupled with the world's highest inflation, which escalated to hyperinflation at 130,000 percent in 2018.[21] Additionally, there was a historic plummet in oil production, reaching 340,000 barrels per day in August 2020.[22]

Under Chávez, dependence on oil reached staggering levels, with oil exports constituting 79.5 percent of total exports in 1999 and soaring to 96 percent in 2012.[23] This expansion intensified the effects of societal and political rentification, leading to a new historical episode of Dutch disease. Corruption, intertwined with bureaucratism, reached unprecedented levels, fostering strong political dependence on Chávez's leadership and weakening grassroots movements and institutional response capacity.[24] These dynamics increased the country's economic, food, and geopolitical vulnerability, compounded by declining crude oil prices since 2014, political instability following Chávez's death, and, later, international sanctions, particularly by the United States since 2019, which severely affected the economy and oil industry.

This crisis profoundly reshaped the social and political fabric, accelerating the petrostate's disintegration. Historical oil governance, marked by hypercentralization and selective income distribution, gave way to fragmented and feudalized power structures, institutional breakdown, escalating violence, and survival-driven dynamics rooted in war and plunder. The collapse of the formal economy enabled underground economies dominated by speculation, corruption, smuggling, and extraction, often tied to international capital and cross-border criminal networks.[25] Gold became a central asset in these networks, driving corruption and extractive policies, with factions of the state, including the military, implicated in their operation. The outcome is a complex and intricate economy, drawing from diverse sources such as the beleaguered oil industry, the illicit gold trade—estimated at a minimum of US$1.7 billion annually—and the shadowy scrap economy, as well as from foreign remittances, which were estimated to range between US$2 and $5 billion in 2020, among other contributors.[26]

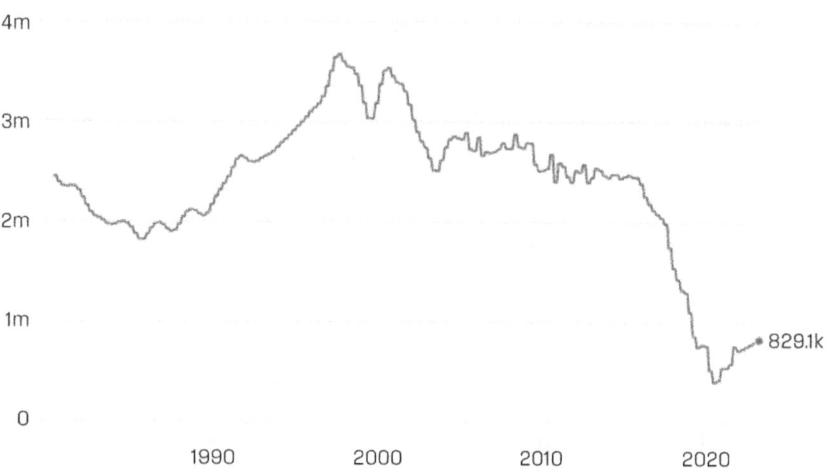

Figure 8.5 Venezuelan oil production, in barrels per day (1980–2023). Chart by Axios Visuals.
Source: FactSet, Oxford Economics

In international terms, this means that Venezuela has become more vulnerable than ever to the unpredictable dynamics of the globalized economy, leading to a strained national landscape shaped by various forces of dispossession and recolonization.

Despite its deconstruction and fragmentation, the state has not disappeared but instead has reconfigured itself under Nicolás Maduro's leadership since 2013. While precarious, unstable, and often contradictory, this state policy has evolved alongside the crisis, developing increasingly dictatorial characteristics. These include intensified persecution, repression, violence, and imprisonment of dissenters, a permanent state of exception since 2016, and the use of para-state groups for control.[27] Additionally, it has manipulated the electoral system, controlled the course of elections, imprisoned and disqualified opponents, and outlawed political parties. Furthermore, it has undermined democratic processes and the framework of rights governing the country, governing without consultation, protocols, respect for the constitution and laws, or consideration for the societal impacts—such as the creation of a National Constituent Assembly in 2017, parallel to the National Assembly, with plenipotentiary and indisputable powers. The regime has manipulated elections, outlawed political parties, and undermined democratic processes, bypassing constitutional norms, exemplified by the creation of the National Constituent Assembly in 2017 with plenipotentiary powers.

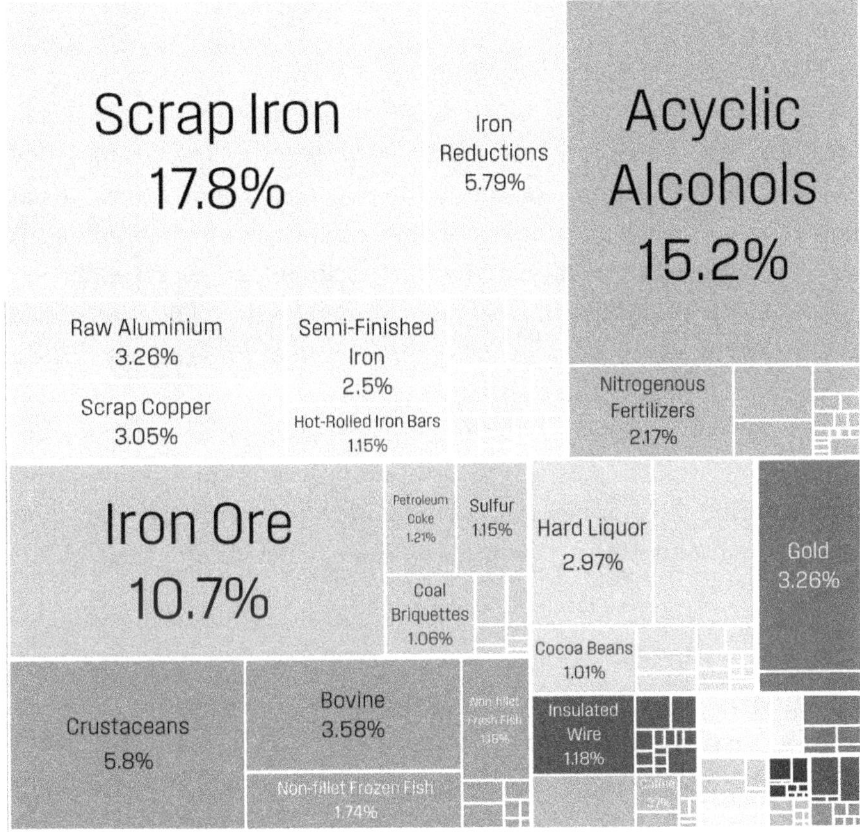

Figure 8.6 Venezuela export income (2021). The graph serves as a reference for the different incomes of the national economy, although in the absence of official data, many of the figures presented may be partial or controversial. Income from underground economies presents difficulties in recording. Note also that oil revenues do not appear, probably because of the veto caused by the sanctions, although they continue to be generated.
Source: Observatory of Economic Complexity

Economically, the state has shifted from a previous progressive format toward a covert neoliberalization, marked by privatizations, foreign investment protections, deregulation, drastic labor cost reductions, persecution of unions, pronounced orientation toward the global market, promotion of the corporate model, allocation of lands and territories to transnational capital, expansion of the extractivist border, and creation of special economic zones, among other measures. This restructuring, promoting transnational capital and extractivist policies, represents one of the most aggressive neoliberal transformations in Latin America's recent history.[28]

These elements collectively indicate a significant restructuring of extractivism within the country, likely signifying the onset of a new historical era. This predatory extractivism involves the coordination of numerous operations for the extraction and dispossession of natural resources, with mining—no longer exclusively or predominantly oil—emerging as a crucial activity for the simultaneous reproduction of power structures at both local and national levels.[29] The central seat of power remains in Caracas, where the national government holds a privileged position in these structures.

The formalization of AMO through a presidential decree is a manifestation of this intricate and multifaceted process. While not exclusive to this period, it is emblematic of the policies characterizing this new phase of extractivism in Venezuela, with a particular emphasis on the Amazon.

Formalization of the AMO and the Strategy of Capturing Gold at All Costs

The backdrop of the Great Crisis exposes an Amazon region that is highly susceptible and laid bare to transnational dynamics involving exploitation, dispossession, and accumulation. While minerals are not the sole economic focus in the Amazon biome, the Maduro government positioned the AMO project as the linchpin of its regional policy. Officially designated as a National Strategic Development Zone through the Comprehensive Regionalization Law enacted in November 2014, it essentially transformed into a Special Economic Zone—a model extensively promoted by China to establish areas characterized by significant deregulation and streamlined operations, facilitating rapid (foreign) capital investment. With the AMO, the government's primary goal has been to escalate resource extraction levels, tighten control over mines, mining territories, and value chains, and capture the maximum possible amount of these resources.

Spanning a surface area of 111,843.70 km2, the AMO is divided into four exploitation areas and a special block situated outside the arc, positioned toward the southern extremity of the Amazon, bordering Brazil.

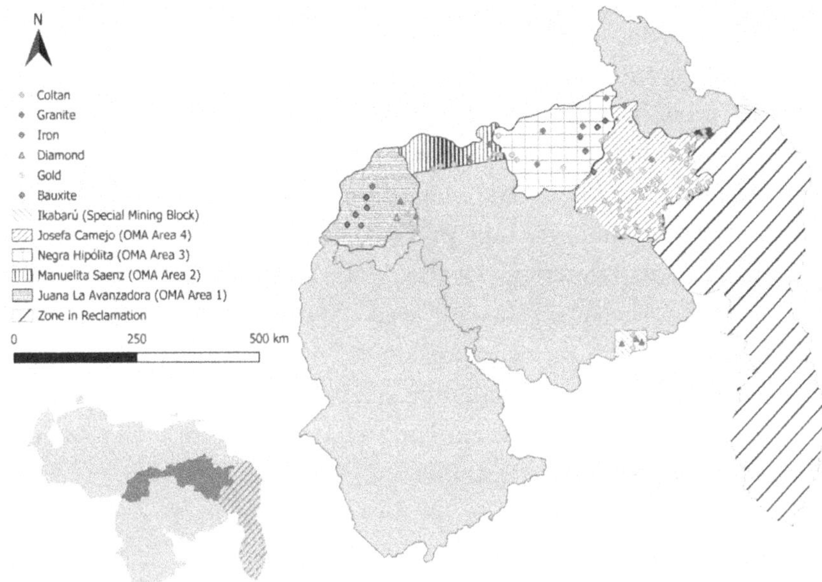

Figure 8.7 AMO areas and main mineral concentrations in them. Map by Emiliano Terán.

The pursuit of extractive goals has been adapted through strategies that respond to the dynamics and evolution of the crisis. In the initial years following the formalization of the AMO, the government announced multiple agreements with over 150 national and international companies, including entities like the Canadian Gold Reserve and Barrick Gold Corporation, the Chinese CAMC Engineering Co. and Yankuang Group, and the Congolese Afridiam, among others. However, details about these agreements remain largely unknown due to a lack of public information and a policy of secrecy regarding new projects by the Maduro regime—a consistent trend throughout the years of the crisis, exacerbated by the enactment of the Anti-Blockade

Law in October 2020, which reaffirmed and legalized the practice of keeping new government initiatives confidential.[30]

Moreover, there is no evidence of prior, free, and informed consultations with Indigenous communities, and the existence of environmental impact studies is unconfirmed.[31] Despite the formal announcements, these undertakings were largely unviable because of economic and institutional collapse, the proliferation of violent irregular armed groups, and the imposition of international sanctions.

On the other hand, since the decree establishing the AMO, there has been a surge in military presence in the area, with special powers granted to the Bolivarian National Armed Forces. The decree stipulated that mining interests take precedence over "private" social interests and introduced sanctions for those interfering in operations. In the same year, 2016, the AMO was declared a "Special Military Zone," and the Military Mining, Oil, and Gas Industries Company (CAMIMPEG) was established—affiliated with the Ministry of Defense. This entity could practically undertake unlimited functions in all processes related to the extraction and commercialization of natural resources, marking a significant and expanding role for the military sector in the economy and in extractivism.

The impracticality of medium- and large-scale formal mining prompted a shift in the government's strategy, with a newfound focus on small-scale mining. The objective was to expand the membership and organization of miners while enhancing mechanisms for collecting gold extracted by them. This involved exerting control over and improving mills, as well as constructing mineral processing plants. The Maduro government, in collaboration with the Ministry of Ecological Mining Development (MDME) established in 2016, actively advocated for the creation of Socialist Mining Brigades and later introduced strategic alliances (AEs) to promote small mining cooperatives. While official information about the number of miners and AEs, as well as their production, remains undisclosed, former MDME Minister Víctor Cano mentioned in 2019 that there were over a thousand AEs, with 946 involving small miners.[32] Regarding the processing of extracted gold, it was reported in 2020 that there were already twenty-one gold-processing plants, the majority located in the El Callao municipality.[33]

The Central Bank of Venezuela (BCV) reported a surge in the internal acquisition of gold from the AMO, increasing from 1.32 tons in 2017 to 9.72 tons in 2018.[34] Nevertheless, it is important to underscore that intricate corruption networks pervade the mining value chains. This was exemplified by the arrest in 2018 of the vice president of the state company Minerven on charges of gold smuggling.[35] There exists substantial opacity regarding the origin and methodologies employed for gold extraction, with numerous companies associated with these alliances having dubious or unknown origins and procedural irregularities or being implicated in corrupt practices.[36]

In a more advanced stage of the Great Crisis, after Juan Guaidó's insurrectional strategy failed and international sanctions were imposed on Venezuelan gold, the Maduro government implemented several measures that unmistakably reflect the shift toward a new morphology of extractivism and its correlation with evolving patterns of statehood and governance. Under the Tricolor Mining Plan (October 2019), productive gold mines were designated to each Bolivarian governorate, formalizing these more decentralized power modalities, characteristic of the Great Crisis.

Another policy introduced in this phase was the establishment of "Military Special Economic Zones," extending this territorial administration format to the military sector. This was evident in the creation of the Military Special Economic Zone for Forestry Development in December 2020, encompassing the municipalities of Sifontes (Bolívar, within the AMO) and Antonio Díaz (Delta Amacuro, outside the AMO but in the Imataca area), which also includes mining.

Throughout the crisis years, military operations persisted for territorial control against illegal mining by the National Bolivarian Armed Forces and other security forces, resulting in numerous fatalities, including members of Indigenous communities, and numerous human rights violations.[37]

Lastly, the national government continued its efforts to encourage joint ventures with national and international capital, propagated a narrative seeking to provide an institutional façade to mining activities in the AMO, and implemented some compensatory social and environmental measures. An example is the creation of the Caura National Park in 2017, situated right where Area 2 of the AMO ends.

Table 8.1 Main State Policies around the AMO and the Amazon in the government of Nicolás Maduro, 2016–2021

Type of Policy	State Policy	Official Publication/ Institution	Description
Mining Expansion	National Strategic Development Zone OMA	Decree No 2,248 February 2016	Sectorial promotion of activities associated with the mineral resources, Bolivar state. Area: 111,843.70 km^2
	Socialist Mining Brigades and strategic alliances with small-scale mining	Organization of Mining in Venezuela/ Small Mining Regulation, Control, and Technical Support Plan Since 2016/2017	Plan to increase the affiliation and organization of small-scale gold mining in partnership with the Venezuelan Mining Corporation (CVM) (belongs to MEMD)
	Strategic alliances with private companies	Guidelines of MEMD	Focused mainly on the increase of the construction of grinding mills and gold recovery plants. Precarious subsistence and very little existence of mixed companies. Opacity and lack of information.
	Mining Sector Plan 2019–2025	Guidelines of MEMD	Strategic document which guides the policy of the Venezuelan state in the mining sector
	Authorization for exploration and exploitation of gold in fluvial spaces	Resolution No. 0010, *Official Gazette* no. 6,526	CVM or the subsidiaries can designate for mining in certain areas of the Amazon rivers and would allow for extraction by means of boats or rafts
Increase of Economic and Territorial Attributions of the BNAF and Local Powers	Security policies	CEOFANB and other security forces Since 2016	Creation of "Special Military Zone" for the OMA (2016); operations against illegal mining, such as Plan Boquete (2017), Tepuy Protector Operation (2019), among others. Military and security forces incursions.
	Military Company of Mining, Oil, and Gas	Decree No. 2,231 February 201	Attached to the Ministry of Defence, focused on multiple functions related to extraction and commercialization of natural resources
	Military Special Economic Zones	Presidency of the Republic May 2019	Establish economic activities and use of natural resources from the military sector within the framework of SEZ
	Allocation of productive gold mine to each governorate	Plan Minero Tricolor October 2019	New strategic alliance model of primary and related activities to strategic minerals with public entities and governorates

Social and environmental protection	Ban of mercury for mining	Decree No. 2,412 August 2016	Prohibition of the use, possession, storage, or transport of mercury as a method of obtaining or treating gold (or other minerals)
	Creation of the Caura National Park	Decree No. 2,767 March 2017	The PN extends over seven NAUSAR. Area: 7,533,952 ha. The territories have been claimed in ownership by Indigenous peoples, in accordance with the national constitution.
National laws	Comprehensive Regionalization Law for the Socio-productive Development	Decree No. 1,425 November 2014	The law establishes the liberalization of geographical units, in the traditional format of the Special Economic Zones
	Anti-Blockade Law	Decreed by the National Constituent Assembly in Gazette no. 6,583 Extraordinary October 2020	It establishes an opening of company and public assets to private capital, extraordinary powers to the government, and severe restrictions to access to information on public projects.

Beyond the AMO: Illicit Extractivism and the Amazon Bioregion as a Basis for New Configurations of Power

Despite the preceding, neither the formal project of the AMO nor the activities within its polygonals can fully explain the complex dynamics of the ongoing extractivist reconfiguration in Venezuela. Beyond the AMO, mining expansion has permeated, to varying degrees, all corners of the Venezuelan Amazon. It is crucial to underscore that all mining activities in the Amazon are essentially illicit for two primary reasons: first, the extensive and pervasive presence, involvement, and control of this activity by irregular armed groups, encompassing national criminal factions, various types of Colombian guerrillas, and garimpo operations organized from Brazil, coupled with criminal elements from that country. The Venezuelan government, various NGOs, and international entities have acknowledged the magnitude of this problem.[38]

Second, these extractive processes and supply chains contravene protocols, laws, standards, and regulations established for the activity and the country's territories. Instances include mining in prohibited and/

or protected areas, as observed in the entire Amazonas state (where it has been prohibited since 1989), and in national parks such as Caura (7.5 million hectares) and Canaima (3 million hectares). The right to information is also blatantly violated, and there is widespread use of mercury—a prohibited substance. There is a lack of respect for environmental and Indigenous laws and, at times, a disregard for the constitution itself, as exemplified by the appeal for annulment filed against the AMO decree and international agreements.[39]

Figure 8.8 georeferences 831 illegal mining points based on spatial analysis using the basic tool on Google Earth. Studies conducted with more sophisticated and exhaustive tools have indicated the existence of a greater number of mining points—RAISG reported 1,423 points in 2020, and Poliszuk et al. identified 3,718 points in 2022.[40] In any case, it is evident that the primary centers of illegal mining in the state of Bolívar, namely Las Claritas, Ikabarú, Caroní, Paragua, and Caura, extend beyond the surface of the AMO, although they may also overlap with it. The location of these unauthorized extractions is fundamentally determined by the geographies of gold and the economic and sociopolitical dynamics of illicit flows and commodity routes on an international scale. AMO zones such as Area 4 and the Ikabarú Special Block exhibit both this overflow and the prevalence of illegal mining, along with the intersections that occur between it and the formal project framework of the AMO.

In the Amazonas state, we observe a substantial growth of this extractive activity in the basins of the Ventuari, Atabapo, and Sipapo Rivers, as well as the headwaters of the Orinoco, leading to significant environmental repercussions and affecting the Indigenous communities that live there.

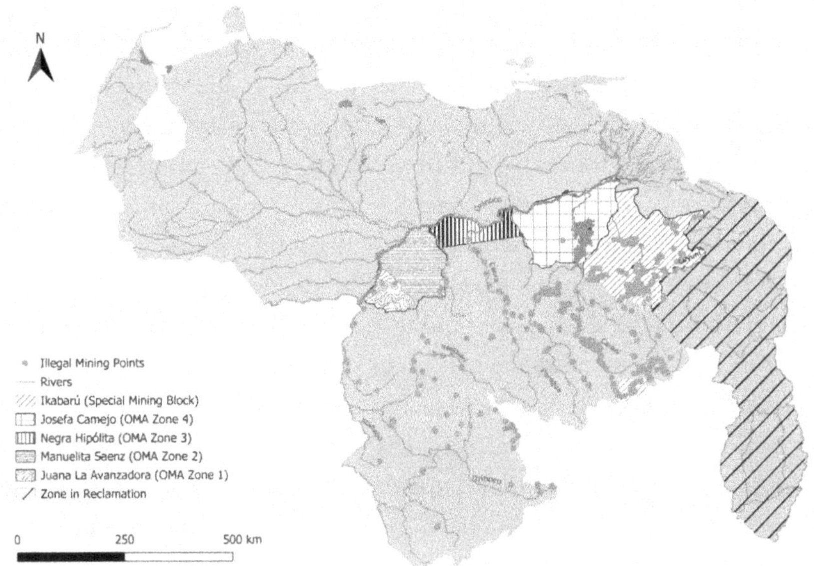

Figure 8.8 Location of illegal mining points in the Amazon and polygonal of the AMO. Map by Emiliano Terán.

Mining stands out as the most destructive activity in the Amazon, with significant environmental impacts, including extensive deforestation in sensitive ecosystems.[41] An estimated loss of 140 thousand hectares of forest between 2017 and 2020 has been linked to mining, along with the destruction of watersheds, protected areas, and the vulnerable soil layer characteristic of the Venezuelan Amazon.[42] Various health impacts are noted, such as contamination of bodies of water, humans, and the food chain with mercury, as well as a substantial increase in malaria resulting from alluvial mining.[43] Additionally, the establishment of violent economies in mining areas has led to incidents of murder and injury due to territorial control, exploitation of the workforce, recruitment of children and youth for labor, promotion of prostitution, and forced displacement.[44]

Criminal groups, including those within the AMO, primarily exercise control over mining territories. In the Bolívar state, examples can be found outside the AMO, such as in La Paragua, Alto Caura, and the Orinoco Delta, which are controlled by entities known as "unions."[45] Violent gangs dominate locations within the project's polygonals, including Las Claritas, El Callao, Ikabarú, El Silencio (Bajo Caura), and Tumeremo.[46]

Colombian guerrilla groups have played a prominent role in illegal mining in Amazonas, particularly in areas like the Yapacana National Park, the Atabapo River, and Manapiare.[47] In Bolívar, their influence is notable in the Cedeño municipality, where concentrations of coltan and diamonds are found.[48] Additionally, organized garimpo activities in border areas with Brazil, especially in Yanomami Indigenous territory, have criminal groups on the Brazilian side promoting the existence and expansion of this extractive activity.[49]

The extensive territorial exploitation in the Venezuelan Amazon at such a magnitude could hardly occur without various levels of complicity, cooperation, coordination, and involvement of state actors. In practically every analyzed mining case and each illicit extraction site, this corrupt collusion with state powers is evident, manifesting itself to different degrees. This occurs both from a macropolitical standpoint to achieve the goal of increasing the capture of natural resources that benefit the central power of the national government—exemplified by the rise in gold purchases by the BCV in recent years—and for provincial state powers. It also occurs at a micropolitical level, primarily benefiting military officials who hold power structures in the territories.

Micropolitical collaboration has taken shape through various mechanisms in the mining chain, such as permissiveness and cooperation with actors engaged in illicit extraction, as reported by Indigenous organizations in Caura, revealing how military checkpoints have protected the continuity of illegal mining.[50] This is exemplified by the arrest in 2020 of several midranking military personnel with ties to criminal groups conducting unlawful mining operations in La Paragua.[51] Another widely adopted method involves payments for "vaccines," often demanded in gold to allow mining activities, as well as the control and distribution of mining supplies, especially fuel, which is diverted to support the mines. Given the widespread issue of gasoline smuggling, its distribution in Venezuela is highly controlled and largely militarized. Individuals in prominent positions, including mayors and senior prosecutors, have faced arrests for crimes associated with illegal mining, such as the case in February 2022.[52] Furthermore, mining establishments, including mills and gold-processing plants, engage in acquiring gold from illegal mining. Miners themselves have highlighted instances, such as in El Callao, where this practice is observed.[53] Finally, another series of policies has acted as encouragement for the strengthening of illegal mining. This includes initiatives like the construction of facilities by the Venezuelan Mining Corporation to provide necessary resources for this activity in the state of Amazonas, where, as mentioned earlier, it is officially prohibited.[54]

Because of this new paradigm of extractivism and recolonization in the Amazon, gold extraction at the national level not only surged during the Great Crisis but also reached unprecedented figures in the country's history. While official data is lacking, various sources suggest that Venezuela's annual gold extraction reached thirty tons in 2021, approaching mining-rich countries like Chile (33.9) and Niger (34.5).[55] However, because of the intricate network of corrupt and multiscalar power, only a fraction of this gold, around 40 percent, finds its way to the BCV's coffers, with approximately 70 percent leaking into local and transnational power networks and international illicit markets.[56]

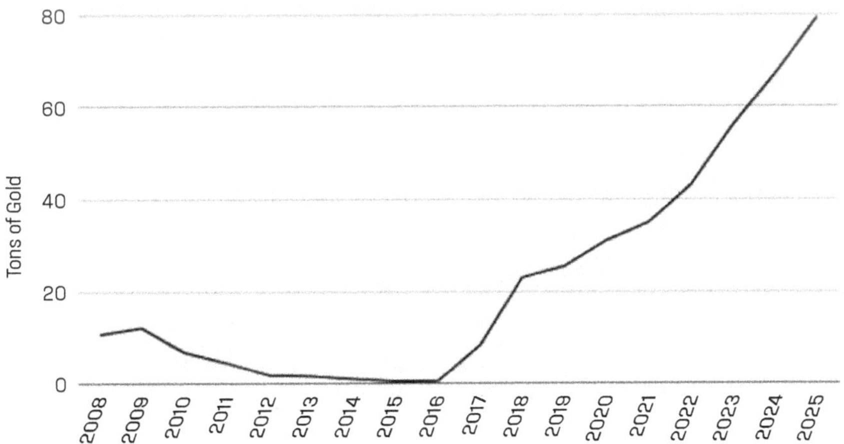

Figure 8.9 Annual gold production in Venezuela (in tons). The figures from 2019 are projections offered by the Ministry of Ecological Mining Development.
Source: MDME

The AMO as a Device and the Centrality of Dispossession in the Chavista Regime

The complex, challenging, and paradoxical integration of criminal forms of extractivism with groups, tools, and/or institutions of the state underscores the expansion and consolidation of hybrid governance rooted in illicit economies. These unique power structures stand out amidst the global rise of organized crime and an extractivism increasingly influenced by criminal networks.[57]

This development carries significant political implications. The progressive framework of the Bolivarian process has all but dissipated, giving way to a profound conservative shift and an internal right-wing trajectory. While the suppression of protests and dissent, the erosion of social and environmental rights, and the implementation of an aggressive neoliberal agenda have been discussed, a crucial aspect is the reconfiguration that has transformed a former left-wing government into a new economic-political regime where dispossession, looting, and plunder take center stage, leaving the country in a precarious state.

The Maduro government, instead of prioritizing the resolution of the crisis experienced by the Venezuelan population, has placed the maintenance of power above all else. Consequently, extractivism has been consciously restructured to embrace this predatory form, one that has essentially served the interests of government factions and foreign capitals. Notably, these foreign capitals are primarily associated with China, Russia, Turkey, Iran, and, since the onset of the war in Ukraine, a rekindling of connections with the West, involving capitals from the European Union and the United States.

The underlying context of this situation stems from a pervasive wave of national-scale accumulation through dispossession, akin to historical processes such as the era initiated by the authoritarian rule of Juan Vicente Gómez (1908–35) and the advent of oil in Venezuela. A century later, this dispossession wave has predominantly unfolded across the Amazon, with mining emerging as a pivotal extractive force. In this new phase of Venezuelan politics, a stark similarity emerges between far-right administrations like Jair Bolsonaro's and the Maduro regime, both of which have spearheaded and executed aggressive forms of assault and recolonization in the Amazon in recent years.

The unprecedented levels of gold extraction, the extensive scope of plundering, and the enduring dynamics of exploitation and resource depletion did not solely result from a 'lack of state intervention' but rather from transformations in the state's inherent structure and character. Consequently, a new political-economic system has emerged from the depths of the Great Crisis, even without a change in government.

The formal establishment of the AMO in 2016 served as an exceptional social and economic incentive for mining activities, occurring amid a backdrop of illicit economies, violence, corruption, and pervasive crisis. Through the AMO, illegal mining became intertwined with the deteriorating state policy, transforming the project into one that blurred the lines between legal and illegal practices. Moreover, this amalgamation extended beyond the designated polygonal areas, effectively governing the entirety of the Amazon.

In this context, it is essential to perceive the AMO not merely as a formal mining megaproject but primarily as a device—an intricate set of strategies designed to promote, legitimize, and coordinate resource extraction and dispossession operations across various scales, modalities, and types. Its fundamental purpose is to facilitate the (illicit) appropriation of natural resources, with the state serving as a privileged arena for such mediations and appropriations.

The AMO has served as the primary mechanism for coordinating and securing the extraction of dozens of tons of gold from the bioregion. Various state-driven actions—such as fuel distribution by the military, the supply of mining materials, the protection of illegal mining operations, the purchase of gold from illicit sources, and the organization of state institutions that operate without regulation or oversight—are interdependent with the illicit economies that drive territorial extraction activities. These systems are interconnected and mutually reinforcing, enabling significant levels of resource extraction, as exemplified in Venezuela.

The perplexing question arises: How did one of the most pronounced neoliberal restructurings in Latin America originate within the framework of a left-wing process, leading to the establishment of a regime focused on violent dispossession and plunder? The Venezuelan experience prompts a profound reflection on internal factors within the left that have not only contributed to the shortcomings of transformative or "revolutionary" political endeavors but also have bolstered right-wing factions, resulting in widespread human suffering and environmental devastation. Engaging in this discourse has proven challenging in certain left-wing circles, some of which rely solely on geopolitical considerations or deem multiple "collateral damages" acceptable to ensure the persistence of "revolutions" in power—essentially implying a desperate clinging to state power at any cost.

Vertical structures, various manifestations of authoritarianism, political dogmatism, the aspiration to monopolize liberation and transformation ideals, challenges in accommodating political diversity, internal colonialism and racism, patriarchal tendencies, and adherence to developmental logic are substantial factors that have constrained numerous left-wing governance experiences. These factors have hindered their transformative potential and, in many instances, have been avoided in discussions to prevent "strengthening the right." Paradoxically, the missteps of the left and progressivism have often bolstered conservative factions, as witnessed in Brazil with the Workers' Party and the ascent of Bolsonaro, in Argentina with Javier Milei's victory and his rejection of progressivism, and in Venezuela with the growing influence of María Corina Machado.

Despite programmatic differences from the right, progressivism and the left have seldom distanced themselves from the prevailing extractivist consensus. This lack of separation has taken a toll in various ways, whether through the deepening of reliance on primary commodities and external dependence, the adverse impacts on local communities leading to a loss of support, or internal fractures within their political coalitions due to divergent perspectives on the matter. In the case of the Bolivarian process, the initial ambition of positioning Venezuela as a World Energy Power eventually devolved into an extreme and decadent form of extractivism, posing a severe threat to life in the affected territories.

Alternatives for the Venezuelan Amazon

The current climate of political stagnation, primarily orchestrated by the Maduro government, has hindered the emergence of dynamic actors and initiatives aiming to transcend the realms of violence, predation, and the state of institutional and economic ruin. As of 2023, María Corina Machado has risen as the dominant political figure, embodying a different facet of violent neoliberal restructuring, heightened extractivism, authoritarianism, elitism, and a preference for transnational capital. Despite this new binary, various actors from diverse backgrounds, including the grassroots, political party bases, and intellectuals, continue to mobilize and advocate for solutions to overcome the crisis, proposing alternative visions that diverge from dispossession-oriented options. However, prevailing fragmentation underscores the need for concerted efforts to consolidate platforms that can facilitate collaborative actions and present society with an alternative national agenda. The progress of these sectors is pivotal for rescuing the Venezuelan Amazon from its current dire situation.

With that in mind, we outline some guiding principles that could shape an alternative vision for the Amazon region:

- Completion of the demarcation and titling processes for Indigenous lands, as mandated by the national constitution. This entails reinforcing the territorial management tools of native communities, recognizing their significant role in the preservation and revitalization of Amazon ecosystems.
- Strengthening and endorsing the emergence of Indigenous guards, serving as unarmed forms of territorial surveillance and monitoring, becomes imperative in light of the escalating presence of irregular armed groups. Collaborative strategies against illegal mining should be devised, avoiding sole reliance on the militarization of territories.
- The extension of co-administration regimes for Indigenous territories and national parks is proposed as a measure significantly enhancing ecosystem management.
- Advocacy for the approval of the Escazú Agreement, introducing regulatory elements for the protection of environmental

defenders in the country.[58] Additional effective protection mechanisms, aligned with international agreements and national legislation, should be guaranteed for these guardians of the Amazon.

- Policies focused on "economic and country recovery" should prioritize the growth and fortification of local Indigenous economies, including agricultural initiatives and community forestry, as well as tapping into the diverse ecotourism potential of the Venezuelan Amazon. Support for forest care strategies, ecological restoration, reforestation, and revegetation is crucial to provide viable economic alternatives for the numerous miners in the bioregion.
- In the context of an Amazon emergency declaration, an immediate suspension of the Orinoco Mining Arc project is needed, coupled with its integration into the proposed country recovery plan, emphasizing a socioecological approach.
- Expanding the discourse on the Amazon and its alternatives within political-party sectors and among candidates for government positions is essential. This broader dialogue aims to strengthen the position of these issues and foster the emergence of new supportive policies and guidelines.
- Lastly, a critical examination and debate on the prevailing development model. Emphasizing that more mining is not an alternative for the Amazon is a key perspective to consider.

CHAPTER NINE

Human Rights Violations of the Maduro Government

Ana Sofía Viloria and Juan García

This chapter examines the human rights violations committed during the era of the Nicolás Maduro administration, from his election in April of 2013 to today. We will pay special attention to the ways in which the Maduro government's human rights violations contrast with the principles outlined in the current Constitution of the Bolivarian Republic of Venezuela (CRBV). This narrative primarily focuses on the period spanning three years (2020–23), while also delving into earlier dates to provide context for relevant events. Such an approach aims to shed light on a situation that has garnered interest from various sectors worldwide for analysis and study. However, the recent focus has shifted, aiming to foster constructive dialogue among different segments of public opinion on the myriad factors contributing to the country's socioeconomic crisis. These factors include job insecurity, mass migration, inefficient management of public resources tainted by corruption scandals, and a growing authoritarianism that infringes upon the human and collective rights of the Venezuelan population, who are the victims of these circumstances.

Asserting and Respecting the Constitution Is Paramount

The section's examination relies heavily on the CRBV of 1999, emphasizing the deep citizen engagement of the popular classes that drove its inception. This process marked a historic moment where citizens actively engaged in debates and discussions, spurred on by President Hugo Chávez's advocacy for the new constitutional project and the referendum as a means of national consultation.[1] A glance at the preamble of the CRBV reveals the values and motivations driving its adoption, which occurred through thᵒe nation's first referendum on December 15, 1999.[2] Venezuelans embraced the new century with the constitution's approval by 3,301,475 "Yes" votes, representing 71.78 percent approval, while "No" votes totaled 1,298,106, accounting for 28.22 percent rejection, according to data from the National Electoral Council.

The preamble sets the stage for the incorporation of human rights, as well as diffuse and collective rights, which extend beyond strict legal interpretations to encompass essential aspects of daily life, such as employment and its impact on family well-being.

During the past three years of Maduro's presidency, Venezuela has faced a severe and widespread crisis, the features of which have been discussed in earlier chapters. For our purposes it is worth reemphasizing that Maduro's policies from 2013 to 2024 have inflicted significant harm on Venezuelan families, who are the primary victims of the challenges created by the crisis. Therefore, it is imperative to comprehend and subsequently discern the individuals affected and the avenues to pursue for restitution. Per the international human rights framework, "victims" encompass those who "individually or collectively, suffer or have suffered harm, including physical or mental injury, emotional suffering, financial loss or substantial impairment of fundamental rights."[3] Moreover, accountability must be identified: "These damages are a consequence of actions or omissions that violate the criminal legislation in force in the Member States, including that which prohibits the abuse of power."[4]

Concerning sanctions against officials implicated in human rights violations, various instruments and principles delineate the obligations of states and the requisite actions to be undertaken, as endorsed by the

United Nations General Assembly. These principles affirm the entitlement of victims to seek remedies and secure reparations. "States must respect and promote these principles, and they apply to law enforcement officials, military and security forces, legislative bodies, the judiciary, victims and their representatives, human rights defenders, the media and the public in general."[5]

Human rights are international in nature; they are not a voluntary or discretionary issue of the government in power, since "states, by being part of international treaties, assume the obligation to respect, protect and guarantee human rights. Serious violations of human rights can constitute crimes against humanity and must be punished."[6]

In theory, it is vitally important that states take effective measures to ensure that officials responsible for human rights violations are brought to justice and that victims receive adequate redress. But in Venezuela today, and in the absence of the state, it is up to the citizens (often victims) and their social organizations to assume this task, given the extensive list of laws in force, which guides the responsible social participation of citizens in matters of the wide range of human rights. A sample can be seen in the CRBV, Chapter X, on Duties in Article 132: "Everyone has the duty to fulfill their social responsibilities and participate together in the political, civic and community life of the country, promoting and protecting human rights as the foundation of democratic coexistence and social peace."[7]

In Title III of Human Rights and Guarantees, specifically Chapter I, Article 31, there is a noteworthy provision aimed at recognizing and emphasizing the courageous actions of victims who raise awareness globally and provide evidence of the situation in Venezuela. This article asserts the following: "Every person has the right, in the terms established by the treaties, pacts and conventions on human rights ratified by the Republic, to submit petitions or complaints to the international bodies created for such purposes, in order to request protection of their human rights."[8] This explains why various international human rights bodies, recipients of multiple complaints, concentrate their efforts to investigate, verify, and demand the protection of these rights and reparations to the Venezuelan victims.

Twenty-Five Years Ago the CRBV Incorporated Collective and Diffuse Rights

With the introduction of the new CRBV in 1999, which for the first time incorporated measures to safeguard the protection of collective and diffuse rights, Article 26 was established, granting "every person the right of access to administrative bodies of justice to assert their rights and interests, even collective or diffuse ones," as well as "to effective protection thereof."[9] This aligns Venezuela with other countries like the United States, which since 1938 has enacted regulations allowing judicial protection for individuals who suffer injuries in their legal sphere, are not holders of a subjective right, and are represented for their collective and diffuse interest.

In addition to Article 26, there are other constitutional provisions, such as Articles 129 and 281, that protect these interests. For example, protections concerning the operation of public services, the rights of Indigenous peoples, the right to a healthy environment as a third generation right, and policy rights that are essentially collective. For instance, voting restrictions not only affect individual subjects but violate the entire society's freedom of choice. Consequently, it enables the ombudsman to exercise protection by filing actions. This means that the ombudsman has the legitimacy and the means to initiate any action capable of protecting rights and defending them against the other branches of the Venezuelan state.

Recognizing the distinction between collective rights and diffuse rights is crucial, although Article 26 of the CRBV ambiguously refers to collective "or" diffuse rights. In practice and jurisprudence in the country, it has been clarified that collective rights pertain to specific groups of people (such as a unions, consumers of a product, a political party, or a neighborhood organization), whereas diffuse rights relate to an indefinite group of people seeking actions for the protection of the environment, biodiversity, the common heritage of humanity, peace, and other similar causes, according to criteria set by the Constitutional Chamber of the Supreme Court of Justice.

With the emergence of new rights come new challenges for the justice system and other entities tasked with safeguarding human rights, including the expanded repertoire of freedoms and rights inherent to every individual, "without distinction of any race, color, sex, language, religion, political or any other opinion, national or social origin, economic position, birth or any other condition."[10] Within this framework, it is reaffirmed that respecting and guaranteeing human rights is the government's obligation, and any failure to do so undoubtedly constitutes a violation of these rights by the government.

The Venezuelan State Violates the Human Rights of Its Population

There is substantial evidence indicating that both the state and the government of Nicolás Maduro are infringing upon the human rights of their population. Therefore, it becomes crucial to juxtapose legal norms such as the CRBV (along with labor laws) and governmental discourse. At both levels, there is an acknowledgment of human rights, aligning with international commitments, including pledges for the implementation of public policies aimed at ensuring compliance. On the surface, it might appear that in theory and rhetoric, the country is upholding human rights standards. However, the stark reality tells a different story: The degradation is so profound that it jeopardizes human lives every passing minute, with the civilian population being the primary victim.

The significant volume of complaints lodged since the beginning of Maduro's administration, documented in the United Nations report since 2014, illustrates a grim picture: extrajudicial executions, forced disappearances, arbitrary detentions, torture, and instances of cruel, inhuman, or degrading treatment, including gender-based violence.[11] These heinous crimes are purportedly committed by Venezuelan state agents. This stark contrast between the government administrations of Chávez (1999–2012) and Maduro (2013–24) underscores a shift indicating not only an economic crisis but also the erosion or abandonment of the original national project based on the CRBV of 1999.

Years of continuous complaints point to a severe and recurrent violation of human rights, particularly intensifying in recent years (2020–23). Solid data substantiates the mention of some cases from the first quarter of 2024, stemming from the government's failure to fulfill its obligations, such as addressing forced migration. This migration crisis has plunged the country into one of the most severe crises in its democratic history, devoid of any warlike conflict.

Reports compiled and disseminated by sources coordinated by the United Nations and various international bodies, facilitated through the host countries of Venezuelan migrants and refugees, reveal staggering figures: "Up to August 2023, an estimated 7,710,887 Venezuelans have become refugees or migrants worldwide, with 6,527,064 of them located in Latin America and the Caribbean."[12]

This paints a bleak picture, signaling the implementation of mechanisms from the core of power to systematically deprive Venezuelans of their rights and instill fear, all while the machinery of state corruption relentlessly advances. Despite the majority of citizens rallying behind the Bolivarian project in pursuit of significant internal reforms, with hopes of catalyzing a positive impact across Latin America, legitimate questions abound, each without a definitive answer. Here, we aim to delve into the allegations concerning human rights violations in a society that legitimately sought to enhance its quality of life and thrive amidst the oil boom of the era.

How can we characterize the institutional decay of the country as the Maduro government depletes natural resources and engages in dealings with external corporations despite facing sanctions? Why is the Maduro administration actively seeking political agreements to ensure impunity? While numerous questions remain unanswered, it remains crucial to continue shedding light on the plight of the victims.

Workers and Families, the First Victims: The Minimum Wage as of January of 2024 Is Bs. 130 (Equivalent to US$3.61)

Pedro Nikken, a Venezuelan jurist and founding judge of the Inter-American Court of Human Rights from 1980 to 1989, and president of the institution from 1983 to 1985, underscored that

> human rights entail duties incumbent upon the government. It is responsible for respecting, guaranteeing, or satisfying them, while on the other hand, strictly speaking, only it can transgress them [. . .]. The defining feature of human rights violations is that they are perpetrated by public authority or facilitated by the resources it provides to those wielding it.[13]

With the previous quote, it can be argued that the Nicolás Maduro government in Venezuela has institutionalized the violation of human, collective, and diffuse rights, with a particular emphasis on the working class and the decline of Venezuelan households, in contrast with what is outlined in the CRBV, as articulated in Article 80:

> The government must ensure that the elderly have full access to their rights and protections. In collaboration with families and society, it is obliged to respect their human dignity, autonomy and guarantee them with comprehensive care and social security benefits to enhance their quality of life. Pensions and retirement benefits provided by the Social Security system must not fall below the urban minimum wage.[14]

And in Article 91:

> Every worker . . . is entitled to a salary that is adequate for maintaining a dignified standard of living and meeting the essential material, social, and intellectual needs of themselves and their family. Equal pay for equal work will be ensured, along with the allocation of profits to workers as appropriate. Salaries cannot be withheld and must be paid regularly and promptly in legal currency, except in cases of legal obligations. The specific procedures and regulations will be determined by law.[15]

In essence, the Maduro-led National Executive is responsible for ensuring that every worker in both the public and private sectors receives a minimum wage and other salary components outlined in Article 104 of the Organic Labor Law.[16] This payment should be made in cash and adjusted annually based on factors such as the cost of the basic basket (as a percentage of the cost of living), the country's economic conditions, and the needs of the working family, known as the "active population."

As of 2022, this active population is estimated at 10,968,535, according to data from the World Bank, out of a total population of approximately 29,257,493, as reported by the United Nations and World Bank portals.[17] Despite the constitutional mandate in Articles 138 and 139 of the CRBV, both the Ministry for Planning and the National Institute of Statistics (INE) have not provided updated information since the last national census, conducted in 2011.[18] The Central Bank of Venezuela (BCV) also fails to comply with this mandate, although there are no administrative consequences for this noncompliance under the Maduro government. This suggests that the government is not concerned about statistical transparency.

It's worth noting that Venezuela has a long-standing tradition of conducting significant censuses, dating back to 1873, when the first census was conducted. Subsequent population censuses were carried out periodically, and from 1941 onward, population and housing censuses were conducted jointly, regulated by the Law of Statistics and National Censuses of 1944. With the enactment of the CRBV in 1999, the Statistical Public Function Law was promulgated in 2001, reaffirming the obligations of organizations such as the BCV and INE to provide necessary data to assist the National Executive in developing and executing public policies.[19] Theoretically, a national census should be conducted every ten years to gather national, regional, and municipal statistics based on objective criteria. These operations should adhere to objective criteria and rigorous processes in design, formulation, and policy monitoring, aligning with scientific standards and international ethical guidelines.

It's essential to emphasize the significant value and importance that accurate statistical data holds for any nation and its inhabitants. Unfortunately, in Venezuela, the standard of good statistical practices has been replaced by obscurity in official institutional figures. Therefore, to gain insight into, comprehend, and forecast Venezuela's situation, one must turn to independent sources: academic institutions, private entities, and nongovernmental organizations.

Is the lack of systematic data production regarding human rights issues in Venezuela merely a temporary setback? Is it a result of government inefficiency, or is there a deliberate strategy to obscure the state of human rights in the country? Does the regime benefit from maintaining opacity regarding human rights matters?

- The absence of accurate and comprehensive data provided by the government under Maduro's administration represents a severe infringement upon the collective and diffuse rights of Venezuelan citizens.
- Among the critical categories of data and information that the government has ceased to produce and publish are the Annual Reports and Accounts of various ministries, the Annual Management reports of Petroleum of Venezuela (PDVSA), the Average Price of the Venezuelan Oil Basket, the Employee Remuneration Index, indicators of scarcity and product diversity, fluctuations in prices of goods and services, epidemiological bulletins, and the Mortality Yearbook. This deficiency extends across vital sectors, such as education, security, and the economy.
- In Venezuela, Maduro has failed to increase the minimum wage for workers for a period of two years (730 days), marking the longest stretch without a wage hike in the past twenty-seven years. Previously, it was customary for the minimum wage to be adjusted annually on May 1. However, Maduro's decision in 2023 fixed the salary at 130 bolivars (Bs), equivalent to approximately US$3.60 per month. This situation underscores the dire state of wages in Venezuela, as illustrated in the accompanying infographic (Figure 9.1) depicting the value of the monthly minimum wage across select Latin American countries in January 2024, compiled by Statista.

Minimum Wage in Latin America in 2024

Minimum monthly salary in US dollars in selected Latin American countries

Costa Rica	$687
Uruguay	$570
Chile	$521
Ecuador	$460
Mexico	$440
Guatemala	$417
Paraguay	$367
El Salvador	$365
Bolivia	$342
Colombia	$335
Honduras	$329
Panama	$326
Brazil	$291
Peru	$277
Dominican Republic	$245
Argentina*	$152
Venezuela	$3.61

Nominal values converted to US dollar on 12/29/2023.
*Includes the increase established only for December 2023.

Figure 9.1
Source: "Ajuste de los salarios mínimos en Latinoamérica," Bloomberg Linea; Statista, https://es.statista.com/grafico/16576/ajuste-de-los-salarios-minimos-en-latinoamerica/.

- The state shirks its obligations concerning labor rights and social security by implementing measures that devalue labor, exacerbate the precariousness of formal employment, erode families' savings capacity, foster heightened levels of uncertainty and insecurity, and fuel an unprecedented wave of Venezuelan migration worldwide, which signals the beginning of the breakdown of family units. Over the past decade (2014–23), the government has failed to assume any internal or external responsibility, despite its robust diplomatic presence and international representation in Latin America and globally, for which official statistics are not provided.
- Venezuelan migration over the past six years (2018–23) has led to a surge in remittance transfers. This substantial segment of the migrant population has become a crucial source of dollar remittances to support their extended families back home, serving as a lifeline for recipients to meet basic needs, such as

food and essential medications. However, remittances have also relieved the Maduro government of its responsibilities, alleviating street protest pressure, while enabling it to tout economic improvements, despite being a mere Band-Aid solution to the population's accumulated needs, with no room for savings. In 2021, remittances accounted for 5 percent of the gross domestic product. Approximately 24.3 percent of Venezuelan households received remittances that year, according to Anova Policy Research, which notes that inflation has diminished the purchasing power of remittance funds, although they remain indispensable for recipient households, often exceeding income from labor (salaries), retirement and pension contributions, and other nonlabor sources (such as state benefits).[20]

- The International Labor Organization (ILO) has identified Venezuela as one of the countries with the highest risk of social unrest globally, owing to its high rate of job insecurity and the limited opportunities available to the majority of its workforce.
- The ILO established a Commission of Inquiry for Venezuela, a decision with few historical precedents within the entity, to investigate recurring complaints from employers and labor organizations regarding the disregard for labor standards and the worsening conditions of informality and precarity in the labor market. A Commission of Inquiry is the highest-level investigative procedure of the ILO and is typically initiated when a member state is accused of persistent and serious violations that it has repeatedly failed to address, among other criteria outlined in the definition.[21]
- The mounting number and variety of cases and complaints have raised alarm within the ILO and various international organizations. These include hindrances to the exercise of collective bargaining rights and the right to strike; the harassment, detention, and prosecution of union members engaged in union activities; suspension of union members; and coercion of workers to resign from non-government-affiliated unions under threat of dismissal, without recourse to defense through Labor Inspectorates, the Ombudsman's Office, or the Public Ministry.

- Additionally, there are reports of multiple collective agreements being disregarded, alongside the endorsement of antiunion and interventionist practices. These practices include promoting parallel unions, establishing bodies aimed at supplanting existing natural union organizations, such as workers' councils and worker militias, and incorporating structures for defense or reserve with specific military training or missions within the public administration and key national enterprises.
- In response to these circumstances, union complaints and conflict levels have escalated. However, the justice system, lacking autonomy and independence, often ignores these grievances. Consequently, union leaders attach significant importance to the sole recourse available to them, namely filing criminal complaints with the ILO. They have been denouncing the imposition of regulations restricting freedom of association, facilitated by government interference that denies them any opportunity for defense, alongside acts of violence hindering access to workplaces during legitimate work stoppages.
- The ILO Commission of Inquiry issued a highly critical report on the country's reality, to which the Maduro administration responded by alleging "partiality" and refuting all allegations. As of the first quarter of 2024, the ILO procedure remains ongoing.
- Regrettably, arbitrary detention and criminal prosecution of union leaders (ignoring their union immunity) and any dissenting workers are recurrent occurrences. Such actions are taken against those who lodge complaints, criticize the government's management, or report corruption to the relevant authorities, demonstrating that harassment and pressure extend to the family members of the targeted worker or leader, as evidenced by several documented instances.

Workers: Victims of Violations of Their Human Rights

Aryenis Torrealba and Alfredo Chirinos, both middle managers in the Commerce and Supply department of Petroleum of Venezuela (PDVSA), were arrested by the General Directorate of Military

Counterintelligence (DGCIM) on February 28, 2020, coinciding with the establishment of the "Alí Rodríguez Araque" Intervention Commission tasked with overseeing the oil industry, under the coordination of Tareck El Aissami. The managers had lodged serious complaints in 2018 regarding a network of corruption within the state oil company, presenting them to the Public Ministry, but no significant investigation was conducted on the matter. On February 28, they were detained at their workplaces and promptly subjected to public exposure by official media outlets, accused of treason and being agents of the United States. Subsequently, they underwent a process of accusation and sentencing overseen by Tarek William Saab, serving as attorney general of the republic. This judicial process was marred by irregularities, including allegations of torture and violations of the rule of law and due process. They were ultimately sentenced to five years in prison and spent three years incarcerated in the cells of the DGCIM in Boleíta, Caracas. The remainder of their sentence, throughout 2023, was served under house arrest. Their arrest sparked widespread condemnation from social organizations, individuals, unions, and industry workers, prompting campaigns for their release across social media platforms, given the constraints faced by conventional media outlets under government interference. Journalist Andrés Izarra captured the situation as follows:

> Alfredo and Aryenis paid for their determination to uphold "living in truth" with torture and imprisonment, but this gesture illuminates the moral fortitude of the Venezuelan collective, further fueling their resilience amid the decade of devastation brought about by the Maduro government.[22]

Luis Alcedo Mora Márquez, a social activist and prominent leftist militant in the Andean and plains regions of the country, was known for his investigations into fuel trafficking to Colombia allegedly involving senior government officials from the state of Mérida, in collaboration with high-ranking military commanders from the Andean states and PDVSA officials. In March 2015 Mora disappeared. He was summoned to SEBIN, the Venezuelan government's intelligence and security agency, after filing a complaint on February 27, 2015, regarding corruption and gasoline trafficking in PDVSA. He informed his family of the risks to his safety via phone calls before disappearing. Despite his family's prompt mobilization and complaints to the authorities, there was no official response or investigation into his disappearance. His case remains unsolved. Two days later, two of his close comrades, brothers Eliécer and Jesús Vergel Prado, also disappeared. They were both aware of the information Mora was investigating. Venezuelan authorities have shown little interest in uncovering the truth behind these disappearances, leading to suspicions that SEBIN itself may be involved, potentially categorizing these cases as "forced disappearances," which are considered crimes against humanity and have been reported to international human rights organizations.[23]

Eudis Girot, a teacher, union leader, and executive director of the Unitary Federation of Oil Workers of Venezuela, was arrested at his home on November 18, 2020, by officials from DGCIM in Puerto La Cruz, in the state of Anzoátegui. His arrest followed his participation in protests demanding fair wages and labor benefits, as well as his role in providing weekly updates on refinery conditions and advocating for better working conditions and the restoration of pension funds for oil workers. Girot also exposed what he termed "PDVSA mafias," led by senior managers, which he claimed were responsible for the fuel shortages experienced by the population at the time. The attorney general's office and the DGCIM charged Girot with multiple offenses, including terrorism, disclosing confidential information, incitement to commit a crime, and unlawful possession of a firearm. During his court hearing, Girot countered, stating, "What is the crime? What is terrorism? Terrorism is what they subject us to with inadequate salaries." Despite numerous irregularities in gasoline and gas production, as well as refinery deterioration, no national PDVSA authority addressed public concerns raised by Girot. His arrest occurred amidst a broader crackdown on employees, middle managers, and union leaders critical of PDVSA's management. Girot was released from prison on April 25, 2022, following the arrival of representatives from the ILO in Venezuela. Various trade union organizations reported that as of April 2022, 121 leaders critical of the Maduro government remained imprisoned.[24]

Rubén González, a prominent union leader and president of the iron workers' union—Sintraferrominera, based in Guayana, Bolívar state—was a staunch supporter of Chávez's presidency following his victory in 1998. He was appointed director of Ferrominera in 2008, where he advocated for the protection of Venezuela's steel industry and better working conditions for employees. However, in 2018, he was detained for two years on charges of conspiring to sabotage Ferrominera. González endured two military trials and was imprisoned for a total of thirty-eight months for defending labor rights, suffering serious health issues from lack of medical attention, which was classified as cruel and inhuman treatment. He was released in 2020 through a presidential pardon issued to 110 individuals as part of government agreements with political factions of the Venezuelan opposition ahead of the December parliamentary elections.[25]

Emirlendris Benítez, a 42-year-old mother and merchant, was arrested in August 2018 and has since been subjected to numerous human rights violations, including arbitrary detention, torture, gender violence, discrimination, unfair trial, and inhumane prison conditions. She was accused of involvement in a drone attack against Maduro without being afforded her right to a fair trial.

Darío Estrada, an engineer at PDVSA, who is neurodivergent and on the autism spectrum, was detained in December 2020 by the Special Action Forces while in isolation because of COVID-19. He was beaten upon arrest and tied to a flagpole at the police command throughout the night. He was accused of belonging to a WhatsApp group planning actions against the government.

María Auxiliadora Delgado and Juan Carlos Marrufo, a married couple aged 50 and 53 respectively, were arrested in March 2019. Delgado worked and was a shareholder in a medical laboratory, and Marrufo worked as an electrical engineer. They are currently held at the DGCIM headquarters in Boleíta-Caracas, a location where the Office of the United Nations High Commissioner for Human Rights and the Ministry of People's Power for Internal Relations, Justice, Peace, and Human Rights (MIIDH) have documented serious and systematic acts of physical and psychological torture, as well as countless instances of cruel, inhuman, and degrading treatment. On December 9, 2022, Delgado and Marrufo were sentenced to thirty years in prison for treason, attempted homicide, criminal association, and conspiracy.

Guillermo Zárraga, a 59-year-old engineer and former union member in the oil sector, was arrested at his home in November 2020. He faced accusations of criminal association, terrorism, and alleged disclosure of national security information, despite a lack of evidence. His health has significantly deteriorated in recent years due to the harsh conditions of his confinement and inadequate nutrition.

Robert Franco, aged 54, a professor and the general secretary of the Carúpano Teachers College in Sucre state, was arrested in December 2020 and is known for his political activism and criticism of the Maduro government. Franco has organized union protests against the Ministry of Education for failing to comply with the country's teachers' collective agreement. His family believes his arrest is politically motivated due to his activism and criticism of the government. He is currently held in a detention center in Caracas.

Javier Tarazona, a 42-year-old human rights defender and director-founder of the NGO FundaRedes, was arrested along with his brother Rafael Tarazona and another collaborator, Omar García, in July 2021. They were conducting training workshops in the state of Falcón and went to the Attorney General's Office to denounce harassment and surveillance by SEBIN officials. Their arrests were carried out on charges of incitement to hatred, treason, and terrorism. Rafael Tarazona and Omar García were conditionally released in October 2021 but are still facing criminal prosecution. Javier Tarazona remains in custody at the SEBIN headquarters in El Helicoide, Caracas, far from his family and city of residence.

Rocío San Miguel, a 57-year-old lawyer and human rights defender, was detained along with her daughter, brothers, father, and ex-partner, at the Maiquetía International Airport on February 9, 2024. They were held without communication, legal counsel, or evidence provided for four days. The attorney general claimed on social media, without evidence, that San Miguel was involved in a plot to attack President Nicolás Maduro. This practice is known in international law as "forced disappearance."

These represent just a fraction of the victims, and without a doubt the situation is much more complex because of the number and conditions that surround them. For a more comprehensive understanding, it is advisable to consult reputable independent organizations, like Provea and others.[26]

Given the limited availability of information on this subject and the difficulty in verifying or accessing official data on cases prosecuted in Venezuela, social media groups play a crucial role in this situation. These groups operate independently of the government and provide platforms for sharing information and raising awareness about human rights violations. Despite government restrictions, several independent digital media outlets have emerged in Venezuela to address the void left by traditional media. These alternative digital platforms have overcome obstacles such as censorship and connectivity issues to provide spaces for information dissemination and advocacy against human rights abuses.

New Context: State Breakdown and Human Rights

In Venezuela, media outlets have faced significant restrictions and censorship under the Maduro administration since 2013. According to a Reporters Without Borders report, the government holds sway over the majority of media channels.[27] Consequently, numerous independent media entities have been shut down, leading to a curtailment of freedom of expression. Over a span of just six years, as reported by the Inter-American Press Association, eighty-four print, radio, and television outlets have been forcibly closed.[28] Moreover, journalists and media personnel have been charged with various offenses, including defamation, slander, espionage, and terrorism, creating a hostile environment for reporting. The media landscape in Venezuela has become heavily influenced by the state, which has become configured as a "state-communicator."[29]

Despite these challenges, some independent digital media platforms have emerged to fill the void left by traditional outlets. "These digital platforms have defied the regime's censorship efforts and continue to provide spaces for freedom of expression."[30]

In Maduro's latest phase of governance, he has prioritized the stability and fortification of his government model. To achieve this, he has established alternative channels outside the framework of the constitution, often justified by a patriotic and anti-imperialist narrative.

In pursuit of objectives such as preserving "peaceful coexistence," combating "hatred" and "terrorism," and upholding "democracy" while confronting "fascism," various measures have been implemented, including the prohibition of disseminating content or expressions that endorse or defend similar ideologies, even extending to the use of social media. These measures serve as familiar pretexts to sustain a regime of fear, resulting in a continuous influx of individuals into detention centers and the active involvement of Attorney General Tarek William Saab in media affairs, a figure whose role merits close examination in the recent history of the country.

Against this backdrop, as of the first quarter of 2024, Venezuelan workers still find themselves grappling with a minimum wage frozen by the national government since 2023 at an unacceptable level of 130 bolivars (Bs), equivalent to just US$3.61 per month. Despite years marked by persistent economic crises, public service failures, and the de facto dollarization of commerce and services, the Maduro government maintains the narrative of Venezuela's purported economic recovery, even as poverty indicators, outward migration, and inequality continue to worsen, according to assessments from academic, labor, and nongovernmental research organizations.

The demand for a living wage from workers is widespread, with particular emphasis from those in the education sector (university, secondary, and elementary teachers) in Venezuela. This is because the average salary in the public sector remains at a meager 130 bolivars (Bs), equivalent to just US$3.38 per month, which is equivalent to "less than one percent of the basic food basket for April 2024, which stood at $535.23, rendering it unattainable for the vast majority of the population," as highlighted by Cendas-FVM.[31]

This means that to afford the basic basket, an individual would require at least 158 monthly minimum salaries. In other words, it would take over thirteen years to earn enough to pay for one month's worth of basic goods. For instance, a worker earning just US$3.39 per month would only be able to afford one package of 250 grams of domestically produced pasta and 250 grams of salt. Such dire circumstances force impoverished individuals to increasingly rely on social assistance programs provided by the Maduro government, such as CLAP (providing low-quality food). Many also seek to register in the Carnet de la Patria system to receive bonuses, which are moderate cash transfers distributed periodically, based on individual circumstances. Additionally, certain bonuses are typically directed toward public sector employees, while women, particularly mothers, often seek registration to access foreign humanitarian aid.

Family Food Basket
January 2024 $535.23

The family food basket (CAF) for January, made up of 60 products, had a price of $535.23, equivalent to 20,541.97 bolivars. Increase 1.6%, 327.93 bolivars compared to the price of the basket last December. In dollars, it rose 0.6%, 3.28. The purchasing power of the minimum wage is 0.6%.

Variation	%
Monthly	1.6
Accumulated	1.6
Annualized	97.2

Required to purchase a food basket	
Monthly minimum wages	158
Daily Bolivars	684.73
Minimum Wages per day	5.3
Dollars per day	17.84

Minimum wage
Bs 130 / $3.38

Price variation of each item	%
Cereals and derived products	2.83
Meats and their preparations	3.28
Fish and seafood	4.09
Milk, cheese, and eggs	3.81
Fats and oils	1.62
Fruits and Vegetables	-1.37
Roots, tubers and others	-9.53
Grains: beans, peas and lentils	9.18
Sugar and salt	4.84
Sauces and mayonnaise	1.87
Coffee	3.96

Exchange rate: Bs. 38.38 per US$1. Minimum Income: SM $3.38 + Food Bonus $40 + Economic War Bonus $30 = $73.38

CENDAS-FVM
Center of Social Analysis and Documentation of the Venezuelan Federation of Teachers

Figure 9.2
Source: Datacendas Oscar Meza. Caracas, February 2024.

Conclusions, Questions, and Dilemmas

There is substantial evidence suggesting that the government's array of laws and decrees fall short of meeting international standards of legality, necessity, and proportionality. Consequently, they serve as tools that promote authoritarianism, further constricting the lives of Venezuelans with narratives and regulations that contradict the tenets of the CRBV. This underscores the strengthening totalitarian inclination within the government, as its new laws are utilized to mold a compliant mass of individuals, who are both persecuted and censored within and beyond the nation's borders.

- The authorities of Maduro's government strive to hinder international bodies from reporting and speaking out about the situation in Venezuela, amidst a progressive tightening of civic space and recurrent violations of the rights to freedom of expression and association, as evidenced by recent decisions of the National Executive and the National Assembly (2024).
- It's noteworthy that over the past year (2023–24), various sectors, including formerly adversarial ones, such as the union movement, social organizations, human rights defenders, and several opposition political parties from both ends of the spectrum, have converged in criticizing and denouncing President Maduro. They accuse him of utilizing the justice and electoral systems to suppress and incapacitate leaders and other critical sectors of his government.
- Since 2020, the United Nations Fact-Finding Mission has identified sufficient evidence to suggest that crimes against humanity have been committed in Venezuela as part of a state policy of repression against various sectors.
- Furthermore, in November 2021, the prosecutor of the International Criminal Court, Karim Khan, initiated an investigation into potential crimes against humanity in Venezuela. Additionally, the Office of the United Nations High Commissioner for Human Rights, which had a presence in Venezuela in 2022, documented the government's obstruction of access to detention centers where individuals were held for political reasons.
- Another alarming manifestation of human rights violations is the exodus of over seven million Venezuelans, constituting one of the largest migration crises globally. Internally, this has dealt a severe blow to family structures, which must navigate this experience amidst widespread deprivation, resulting in significant human losses, vulnerability among certain sectors, and collective challenges without adequate attention or institutional assistance from the state.

- Despite the efforts of international mediation initiatives, such as the Roundtables of Norway, Colombia, Mexico, and Barbados, aimed at fostering conditions for free, transparent, and fair elections in Venezuela, the government's actions remain unchanged. Formal statements and agreements reached at these discussions are swiftly stifled by government actions, undermining any attempts to coordinate electoral efforts by the opposition, regardless of their political orientation.
- The persistence of opacity in national figures represents a violation of the diffuse and collective rights of the Venezuelan population. Consequently, the primary source of data on the reality in Venezuela must be sought within the network of NGOs, universities, and international organizations.
- At the outset of 2024, there are no positive indicators for the Venezuelan population, both within the country and abroad. Corruption, the humanitarian crisis, and human rights violations are the outcomes of a deliberate design by the government system that promotes impunity.
- International actors play a crucial role: their analyses, investigations, pursuit of sanctions, and reparations for human rights violations on behalf of the Maduro government must continue.
- Initiatives should be promoted to stimulate the solidarity and diplomacy of democratic nations and their civil organizations, urging them not to remain impartial in the face of declining quality of life and patterns of violations directly affecting the human rights of Venezuelans, as imposed by the government of Nicolás Maduro.

CHAPTER TEN

Essequibo

Vortex of Confrontations

Simón Rodríguez

Formally appropriated by British imperialism in 1899 and administered by Guyana since its independence in 1966, the Essequibo region has been claimed by Venezuela since 1962. It is the largest territorial dispute recognized by the United Nations. Its 159.5 thousand square kilometers, mostly covered by a dense rainforest, represent more than twice the combined territories of the Donbas and the Crimean Peninsula under Russian occupation.

Despite its enormous size, the Essequibo is sparsely populated, with about 120,000 people living in the area, most of them on the coast. If we consider the legal doctrine of international territorial demarcation, which states that "the land rules over the sea," indicating that land demarcation takes precedence and maritime demarcation extends from the coast, then in the case of the Essequibo, it could be argued that the opposite is true: The sea governs over the land. The focal point of the dispute is in the sea and its oil deposits.[1] Meanwhile, in the vast and lush jungles, with little state presence on either side of the border, where the most common currency is gold, Venezuelan, Colombian,

This chapter is based on Simón Rodríguez, "Essequibo, or the Persistence of El Dorado," *Strange Matters*, September 20, 2024

Brazilian, and Guyanese organized crime mafias wage a subterranean dispute on their own terms and embody the main authority.

On February 9, 2024, a report based on satellite images revealed an increased Venezuelan military presence on the border with Guyana.[2] This deployment took place while the governments of Venezuela and Guyana held meetings under Brazilian mediation, on each occasion concluding with a misleadingly optimistic note. In the preceding months, Brazilian, US, British, Venezuelan, and Guyanese troops, vessels, and military aircraft were mobilized around this territory. As several confrontations converge and overlap, the main driving force in the conflict lies in the shift from Hugo Chávez's detente policy to Nicolás Maduro's irredentism and expansionism, directed against Guyana. This dramatic change has its roots in Venezuela's internal politics, reflecting the regime's degeneration. The dictatorship has found in the Essequibo conflict not only a red herring to distract the Venezuelan people from enduring misery, as an outlet for nationalist agitation, but also an opportunity for military mobilization, criminalization of dissent, and perhaps the opening an external front that can become an asset for future negotiations, not only with Guyana but with US imperialism itself.

There are curious symmetries and oppositions between Guyana and Venezuela. Two nominally leftist regimes are disputing territory, in the name of a Bolivarian Republic and a Cooperative Republic. Returning from a failed rentier utopia after a century as an oil-exporting nation, Venezuela's economy has experienced the most significant contraction of any country in the world over the last decade. In 2024, the Venezuelan economy is approximately one-fifth of what it was in 2013. The economy that has grown the most in the world in the last five years is the Guyanese economy. Between 2020 and 2024 its size has increased fivefold.[3] One-third of the oil discovered since 2015 in the world is located in Guyana, which is on its way to becoming the country with the highest oil production per capita, while Venezuela has the largest proven oil reserves in the world but has a production in sharp decline. Both countries are highly vulnerable to climate change, especially Guyana, with most of its population living in the coastal region, where significant expanses of land are below sea level.

Like Venezuela a century ago, Guyana began oil exploitation by handing over concessions to imperialist companies under unfair conditions. Because of its low level of industrialization upon initiating oil production, this implies the risk of great distortions. In the case of Venezuela, the country went from being an agricultural exporter to a net importer of food. The Guyanese ruling party, the People's Progressive Party/Civic, once persecuted by the United States, has in fact abandoned all Marxist pretensions in favor of the promotion of business interests, while Chavista "socialism" has always had a strong military and bourgeois imprint.[4] Both pose as nationalists and invoke sovereignty while competing to hand over natural resources to transnational corporations. The Guyanese government cultivates political alliances with the United States, the United Kingdom, and India; the Venezuelan government aligns itself with Russia, while both share alliances with China.

Another level of conflict involves the United States and Venezuela, once allies against Guyana. In recent years, US secretaries of state and other senior US officials have visited Guyana, joint military exercises have taken place, and statements of US support for the Guyanese position regarding the Essequibo have been issued.[5] The United Kingdom, the former colonial power that once conditioned Guyana's independence on its acceptance of a territorial dispute with Venezuela, now denies it.[6] Together with the Guyanese government, it asserts that the border was definitively established in 1899. An about-face by both powers, which during the twentieth century took advantage of the Venezuelan claim to put pressure on the Guyanese pro-independence and leftist leadership. Now they see Guyana as an ally against the Venezuelan government. The fact that offshore oil from the Essequibo is being extracted by the US corporation Exxon Mobil also explains this imperialist support for the Guyanese state. However, the Venezuelan government's threat to break ties with corporations involved in offshore exploitation, if carried out, could affect the largest foreign investor in the Venezuelan oil industry, the US corporation Chevron, which is in the process of buying a minority participation in the Stabroek Block, exploited by Exxon Mobil.[7]

Like the arrests of opposition politicians and US citizens that are later used as bargaining chips, mirroring the tactics employed by the US government against Maduro, when detaining key bolibourgeoisie operatives such as Alex Saab, military pressure on Guyana and US oil interests opens possibilities for the Venezuelan government to propose the negotiation of a quid pro quo with the United States.[8]

The Brazilian state has been mostly aligned with Guyana since the era of the military dictatorship. Although Luiz Inacio Lula da Silva, like Maduro, shares an affiliation with the São Paulo Forum and an apologetic vision of inter-imperialist competition, which they both like to brand "multipolarity," Brazilian foreign policy aspires to regional leadership. In that sense, its aim is to dissuade Venezuela from any military action against Guyana.[9] Even while considering Maduro's referendum on the Essequibo as a matter of Venezuelan domestic policy, the Brazilian government also considers Guyana's recourse to the International Court of Justice (ICJ) on the dispute as legitimate. In November 2023, Brazilian presidential adviser and former Foreign Minister Celso Amorim traveled to Venezuela to meet with Maduro, and since then several meetings have been held between the governments of Guyana and Venezuela with Brazilian mediation. Lula has distanced himself from the Chavista position, emphasizing that Brazil, like Venezuela, also suffered territorial losses due to British imperialism in the nineteenth century. Specifically, he refers to the Italian arbitration decision of 1904, which awarded 59 percent of the disputed Pirara territory to British control and 41 percent to Brazil.[10] Despite this historical grievance, Lula abides by the arbitration decision in the case of Guyana.

The Brazilian government aspires to a permanent seat on the UN Security Council. In his efforts to show himself useful to US imperialism, during his first term in office Lula headed the UN military mission that occupied Haiti in 2004. This mission lasted until 2017. For the same reason, he rejects the possibility of a war in South America and tries to counter the Guyanese military dependence on the US, mobilizing his own troops in support of Guyana toward the triple border.[11] Brazil opposes the installation of US military bases in Guyana, a possibility not ruled out in December 2023 by the Guyanese prime minister. While in January it was clarified that there was no concrete request by the US for the installation of a base, in April the Venezuelan government denounced the existence of alleged secret bases.[12] Amorim expressed in December his concern that Guyana would set a precedent that would affect the Amazon region as a whole, although Brazil has also authorized US military exercises in the Amazon.[13] In short, Lula positions himself as a guarantor of Guyanese security, but in a way that does not limit his role as a mediator.

In this context, is a Venezuelan military attack against Guyana likely? Military analysts consider it a highly improbable hypothesis.[14] The Venezuelan government would have around one hundred thousand regular troops of different components, in addition to dozens of war jets and helicopters, and very modest naval forces. The socioeconomic degradation of the country and the starvation salaries suffered by Venezuelan troops are not very auspicious: The invaders could desert. In 2019, in the midst of the political crisis and in the face of the proliferation of street protests, the Venezuelan government even resorted to introducing Russian troops and mercenaries from the Wagner Group.[15] Guyana has a small army of three thousand soldiers and lacks a significant air or naval force. But, as has been seen, Brazil, the United Kingdom, and the United States have shown military muscle in the area to dissuade Maduro from any aggression. On the diplomatic front, Guyana holds the temporary presidency of the Caribbean Community of Nations and has a nonpermanent seat on the UN Security Council. The Venezuelan state currently cannot even vote in the UN General Assembly due to its accumulation of debts.

While the Venezuelan military disseminates images of military exercises, and even some propagandists have spread false news of Venezuelan military attacks through TikTok, the only successes of the armed forces in recent years have been in internal repression.[16] A Venezuelan military maneuver can exert pressure to achieve certain objectives without resorting to an invasion. The Guyanese government criticized the movements of troops and military equipment, alleging that they violated the agreement signed in December in St. Vincent and the Grenadines. The agreements bound both governments to refrain from employing force and coercion in the dispute. The Venezuelan government did not deny the deployment but defended itself by accusing the Guyanese government of violating the agreement in the first place through its economic activities.[17]

Maduro has said that he hopes the Guyanese government will desist from its action before the ICJ and agree to a bilateral negotiation. Maintaining indefinitely the status quo of the Geneva Agreement may be advantageous for the Maduro regime, but not for Guyana nor for the oil transnationals interested in the offshore fields.* In addition to the fact that the bilateral negotiation of a mutually satisfactory delimitation was not achieved in six decades of UN mediation, any concession, no matter how small, may be politically infeasible in Guyana, where the slogan "not even a blade of grass" has been popular for decades. For all these reasons, it would be unreasonable for the Guyanese side to reject the ICJ, an avenue it pursued after considerable delay in utilizing the mechanisms foreseen in the Geneva Agreement itself. Consequently, it may anticipate a favorable resolution from the ICJ. Some analysts consider that Maduro's strategy is to exert pressure to achieve a negotiated agreement that will grant him some participation in the offshore oil business.[18] If foreign policy is considered an extension of domestic policy, this hypothesis is strengthened, since the extortive method has been characteristic of the relationship of the Venezuelan government—representative of an emerging civil-military bourgeoisie, with the country's traditional bourgeoisie.

Chavismo's about-face in relation to Guyana in 2015 was brought together by the discovery of oil deposits in the disputed sea, the departure from power of the People's Progressive Party (PPP), traditionally allied with Chavismo after the electoral victory of David Granger of the People's National Congress Reform (PNC-R), and the economic,

---

* The Geneva Agreement, signed in 1966 by Venezuela, the United Kingdom (on behalf of British Guiana), and British Guiana (now Guyana), was intended to resolve the territorial dispute over the Essequibo region. It established a framework for peaceful negotiation and mandated the formation of a Mixed Commission to seek a practical resolution to the conflict. If no agreement was reached, the matter would be referred to the United Nations secretary-general for mediation or arbitration. However, the agreement did not define a clear resolution timeline, leading to its indefinite continuation.

social, and political debacle of Chavismo itself, which suffered its worst electoral defeat since it came to power in 1999.[19] The regime opted for a reactionary turn, with the suspension of constitutional guarantees and the beginning of a series of measures that would gradually culminate in the establishment of a dictatorship, with elements of right-wing nationalism, such as the persecution of the Colombian immigrant community. In the relationship with the states of the Caribbean, the impossibility of sustaining oil subsidies through Petrocaribe gave way to a rapid abandonment of "integrationist" clientelism and to an openly aggressive policy against Guyana, which would foreseeably alienate a good part of the region. Both inside and outside Venezuela, the progressive façade of Chavismo has fallen and will be difficult to restore.

From Victim to Aggressor

The First World War definitively tipped the balance in favor of the United States in the imperialist arena, and the Second World War further weakened British imperialism and strengthened American imperialism. Subordinate to the US, the Venezuelan regime interpreted these changes to its advantage, and its Congress questioned the arbitration award for the first time in 1944. In 1949, Mallet Prevost, one of the US lawyers who represented Venezuela in the arbitration, stated in a posthumous will that the process was flawed by a pact between British and Russian imperialism.[20]

In the postwar period, Venezuela experienced significant growth, driven by large oil exports. In the Venezuelan Guayana, the metallurgical industry began to develop, again highlighting the mineral wealth of the region. In 1950, the People's Progressive Party (PPP) was founded in Guyana, under the leadership of Cheddi Jagan and Forbes Burnham, as a political expression of a left-wing independence movement.[21] The pro-US military dictatorship of Pérez Jiménez questioned the arbitration award for the first time at a regional meeting of foreign ministers in 1951. The interests of the dictatorship converged with those of British and US imperialism, which sought to politically condition Guyanese independence. This stage of the conflict incorporated these new and contradictory elements.

In 1953 the PPP won the first elections for a government with limited autonomy under British sovereignty. Soon after, the colonialists dissolved the government to prevent it from declaring independence. The maneuvers of US and British imperialism led to the division of the PPP, with the right-wing, led by Burnham, splitting to form the People's National Congress (PNC). This split generated a polarization based on racial alignments. In spite of this, in 1961, the PPP won the elections again with a pro-independence program. The following year the Venezuelan state repudiated the arbitration award before the UN Decolonization Committee, which was discussing the Guyanese question. The postdictatorial government of Rómulo Betancourt took the opportunity to make common cause with imperialism against Guyanese independence and at the same time generate a nationalist distraction from its domestic problems, such as the opposition of the leftist guerrillas inspired by the Cuban Revolution and the right-wing threat represented by the residues of perezjimenismo.* Betancourt was so openly pro-imperialist that he proposed to the British a joint management of the Essequibo. The British rejected the proposal.

In the 1964 Guyanese elections, the Venezuelan government supported Burnham and the PNC, allied to the right-wing United Force (UF) party. The Venezuelan government hatched a coup plot against Jagan, sending arms to Guyana under the coordination of the CIA. Under imperialist instigation, the PNC and UF launched a campaign of political violence. A US embassy memo to the secretary of state in July 1964, declassified in 2005, showed that the US government was aware of a Venezuelan government plan to train mercenaries and kidnap Jagan, imposing Burnham in power. The internal communication recommended pursuing the US policy of imposing Burnham by manipulating proportional representation in the elections, recognizing that preventing a Jagan government was a shared goal of the US and Venezuelan governments.[22] This shameful role of the Venezuelan state as an

* Pérezjiminismo refers to the political ideology and governance style associated with Marcos Pérez Jiménez, who ruled Venezuela as a military dictator from 1952 to 1958. His regime is remembered for its focus on modernization, infrastructure development, and authoritarian control. Pérezjiminismo often symbolizes a combination of state-led economic policies, nationalism, and political repression.

auxiliary of colonialism and imperialism in Guyana is rarely discussed in Venezuela, although President Chávez, between 2004 and 2008, recognized these facts on several occasions, alluding to the declassified memorandum, and condemned the interference of the Betancourt and Caldera governments in Guyana's internal affairs.[23]

In 1965, the official Venezuelan map designated Guyana Essequiba as a Reclamation Zone.[24] In February 1966, the governments of the UK and Venezuela signed the Geneva Agreement, months before the independence of Guyana. Burnham, representing British Guiana, also signed. British imperialism not only officially recognized the existence of a territorial dispute and endowed it to the future independent Guyanese state but also demanded Guyanese recognition of the Venezuelan claim as a condition for recognizing the country's independence.[25]

In any case, independent Guyana came to administer the entire territory colonized by the British. The claim of the Venezuelan state became a mechanism of pressure against an independent country. Corresponding to this change in the character of the conflict, the Venezuelan regime, which had already crushed the leftist guerrillas in a scorched-earth war with thousands of forced disappearances, became even more aggressive, counting as before on US support, but now against an adversary much weaker militarily.

Together with the US government, the Venezuelan government supported the formation of the Guyanese Amerindian party. The Venezuelan military occupied the island of Anacoco in 1968, approximately half of which belonged to Guyana, according to the 1899 borders. President Raúl Leoni issued a unilateral decree of maritime delimitation, initiating the patrolling of waters adjacent to the Essequibo. The culminating point of this policy was reached in 1969, when the Venezuelan regime supported the Rupununi uprising in the Essequibo, a South American caricature of the failed Bay of Pigs imperialist adventure in Cuba. The rebels, a group of cattle ranchers and their employees, who were to declare a secession to allow the Venezuelan government to militarily occupy the territory, were crushed. Burnham's repression left dozens dead, and the Venezuelan government received and protected the fugitives of the rebellion.[26]

As a consequence of this defeat, in 1970 the Venezuelan government signed the Protocol of Port of Spain, which established a twelve-year moratorium on the territorial claim. In this context, in 1974 a rapprochement took place between Carlos Andrés Pérez and Burnham. Pérez took advantage of the increase in oil revenues after the Yom Kippur War and the Arab oil embargo to nationalize the iron and oil companies, paying large indemnities to the imperialist companies and establishing diplomatic relations with countries of the Stalinist bloc. While Burnham, after acting as an agent of US and British imperialism in the 1950's and '60's, turned to China, Cuba, and the USSR, modifying the constitution to rename the country the Cooperative Republic of Guyana in 1970, nationalizing bauxite and the sugar industry.[27] During that decade, Venezuela and Guyana established diplomatic relations with Cuba.

In the 1980s, the Cuban government supported Guyana's position on the Essequibo. The Guyanese government had been providing logistical support to Cuba in its military intervention in Angola and Namibia, where it confronted South African apartheid and the Angolan guerrilla UNITA, supported by China and the United States. In April 1982, in the face of the Argentine military regime's attempt to recover the Malvinas Islands, occupied by British imperialism, the Guyanese government aligned itself with the United Kingdom, while the Venezuelan government aligned with Argentina. When the Port of Spain moratorium ran out, the social-Christian government of Luis Herrera Campins launched a campaign with the slogan "The Essequibo is ours," the exact same slogan that would be used four decades later by Nicolás Maduro. The Venezuelan government, opportunistically, characterized Guyana's support of Cuba as a threat. Under this argument, it obtained the US license for the purchase of F-16 jets.[28] In one of the most striking provocations, in April of 1981, the Venezuelan government sent an expedition of fifty young people, headed by the minister of youth, Charles Brewer-Carías, to camp in the jungle of the Guayana Esequiba. They reached the outskirts of the village of Matthew's Ridge, decorating the route with Venezuelan flags.[29]

Brewer-Carías would later be awarded with a medal for espionage activities in Guyana.

Less than fifty kilometers northeast from there, two and a half years earlier, was the Jonestown Massacre. More than nine hundred members of the sect led by Jim Jones were killed. Burnham's government had leased a twelve-square-kilometer plot of land to the Peoples Temple, presenting its agricultural commune as an example to follow. The presence of US citizens was thought to provide a barrier to Venezuelan military aggression.[30] In fact, its relations with the Peoples Temple and House of Israel sects epitomized the corruption and degeneration of the Burnham regime and its faux socialism.

From Chávez's Lost Opportunity to Maduro's Expansionist Delusions

So-called cooperative socialism had shown its severe limitations as the 1970s reached its end, when international bauxite prices fell, and the government imposed harsh cuts on consumption. With Burnham's death in 1985, the Guyanese regime moved away from statist capitalism, while in Venezuela the oil mirage vanished and inexhaustible cycles of monetary devaluation and inflation began, which continue to this day. While the regime in Guyana adapted to neoliberalism and the PPP returned to power in 1992, Venezuela went through a turbulent period, with a failed attempt to impose the structural reforms recommended by the International Monetary Fund. After a popular rebellion and two failed military uprisings, a bourgeois nationalist government came to power in Venezuela that would eventually claim its version of military petro-socialism, with transnational corporations and patriotic capitalists. During the Chávez government, the possibility of a negotiated solution came closer than ever before, with an apparently minimal political cost.

For most of Venezuelan history, the Essequibo has been outside the national imaginary. For decades, it represented nothing more than stripes on a map. Even today, many in Venezuela do not believe Maduro's threats, which they interpret as just another one of his bluffs. The Guyanese experience has been very different, with Venezuelan threats weighing heavily in national politics and to some extent influencing a defensive national identity. The convergence of Venezuela's territorial claim with the imperialist maneuvers aimed at undermining Guyanese independence during the 1950's and 1960's, along with events such as the traumatic Rupununi rebellion and the naval and air incursions, highlight the aggressive character of the Venezuelan state. This real threat was also exploited and weaponized by successive Guyanese governments. During the 1980s, the Burnham government thus justified the militarization of Guyanese society and the postponement of social demands. On May 1, 1981, in response to the demand for a minimum wage of fourteen Guyanese dollars a day, Burnham responded, "We can discuss the fourteen dollars; we can discuss twenty-one dollars; but right now we have to defend the Essequibo." He directly called on the workers to choose between the fourteen dollars and the Essequibo.[31]

At the turn of the century, Venezuelan politics revolved around incipient Chavista reforms and right-wing coup attempts. In 2004, just six months before the recall referendum that Chávez would win by a landslide, the Venezuelan president visited Georgetown and announced that he would not oppose any economic project in the Essequibo region for the benefit of the population, placing the bilateral relationship outside the framework of the territorial dispute.[32] The construction of a binational road to link Caracas with Georgetown was even discussed. This gesture did not have a significant impact on the national political debate, despite the fierce opposition campaign for the recall of the presidential mandate, which showed that the political cost of a cessation of the claim in exchange for minor concessions by Guyana would be low for the Venezuelan government.

Relations improved as they never had before. The Venezuelan government provided humanitarian aid to Guyana when it was affected by floods. Chávez also incorporated Guyana to the Petrocaribe scheme of oil credits and subsidized prices in 2005, which allowed it to acquire 5,200 barrels of oil daily and supply half of the country's demand.[33] The fortieth anniversary of the Geneva Agreement was reached in 2006, with indifference. In 2008, the Venezuelan government canceled the Guyanese debt contracted in 1974, in the Pérez and Burnham era.

In an interview in mid-2005, the Guyanese ambassador in Caracas, Odeen Ishmael, described the relationship between Presidents Chávez and Bharrat Jagdeo, an economist trained in the USSR in the 1980s, as friendly. Jagdeo, who is currently vice president, presided over Guyana between 1999 and 2011. Ishmael pointed out that the undefined maritime border had generated difficulties, such as the detention of Venezuelan and Guyanese fishermen. He was of the opinion that both governments should concentrate on reaching an agreement on the maritime issue. "Both sides will have to make concessions, both sides will have to take giant steps," he added, showing a flexible attitude. He went further and offered the Venezuelan state participation in the exploration and exploitation of oil: "Venezuela is a country with many resources. It could assist us with the exploration of oil, we just started looking for it in the east of our country. We can cooperate in this field within Petrocaribe."[34]

In February 2007, Ishmael again offered statements along the same lines:

> Hugo Chávez proclaims himself as anti-imperialist and only anti-imperialism can solve the problem by abandoning the Essequibo claim. . . . Chávez has given great assistance to Guyana. . . . All these aids show us that brotherhood exists, and fraternity between two socialist countries implies abandoning the border dispute. Brothers are called to live in peace. That is why we believe that Chávez may take a step forward to obtain a quick solution and abandon the claim over the Essequibo. . . . We believe that the two countries may continue talking to reach some type of concession or agreement for the control of the maritime area off the Essequibo coast, given that those limits have not been defined.[35]

The Chávez government fell short. It did not take advantage of the favorable situation that its own policy of rapprochement had created, including the disposition of the Guyanese government to make concessions in matters of maritime delimitation, possibly even some land concessions. Without the need for military threats, in a friendly manner, the Venezuelan state could have secured an outlet to the Atlantic between the territorial seas of Guyana and Trinidad and Tobago. This would have given the Venezuelan state a share in any oil exploitation on a binational oil field. A binational, mutually beneficial road could have been built. None of this was achieved.

The failure is characteristic of the Petrocaribe policy: lacking a strategic vision and limited to short-term objectives guided by clientelism and corruption.[36] In addition to the irrationality of subsidizing right-wing and corrupt governments in Haiti and the Dominican Republic and accepting overpriced payments for agricultural products like Guyanese rice while the Venezuelan agricultural sector was in shambles, there was also a complete lack of strategic vision to consolidate truly lasting ties with the Caribbean region. These ties would not be contingent on the fluctuations of the capitalist energy market. The result of this blind policy is that with the fall of oil prices and the ruin of the Venezuelan oil industry, the vaunted but artificial and precarious regional integration vanished. The relationship with Guyana, which went from friendly to openly hostile, is just the most extreme example. The only legacy of Petrocaribe are the accounts in tax havens of corrupt politicians from Venezuela and the Caribbean and a set of debts that the Venezuelan government will only be able to collect with huge discounts. A years-long effort was undertaken, at great economic cost, to achieve nothing solid or lasting, in any meaningful way. It is hard to imagine a more categorical failure. In a very short time, the Chavista regime went from representing a wealthy and wasteful energy patron of the Caribbean, with a discourse on fraternity and integration, to a bankrupt and threatening regime.

In July 2015, the last shipment of oil to Guyana through Petrocaribe was made, and Maduro requested the UN appoint a mediator.[37] The government of Guyana in turn issued a straight baseline decree for the coast of the Essequibo. The United Kingdom and the Commonwealth positioned themselves in support of Guyana, sending a warship as a sign of support. David Granger announced that he would take the Essequibo case to the International Court of Justice. The Venezuelan government continued with the interception of oil tankers. In December, Chavismo lost its parliamentary majority, initiating an authoritarian turn that would culminate in the adoption of dictatorial features. The right-wing majority in the National Assembly, de facto deprived of its powers through the courts under government control, appointed a Parliamentary Commission for the Defense of the Essequibo to compete with Maduro in the issue.

The international tide was turning. In December 2016, UN Secretary-General Ban Ki-moon announced that the next secretary-general, in the absence of progress, would refer the case to the ICJ, unless both states requested he not do so. Massive popular protests against Maduro erupted in 2017. In September of that year, Granger affirmed that he would resort to the ICJ. Shortly thereafter, Guyanese media revealed that Exxon Mobil paid $18 million for legal fees to defend the case at the ICJ.[38] In January 2018, the new UN secretary-general, António Guterres, referred the case to the ICJ, and in March the Guyanese government formally submitted the request for it to resolve the dispute. In December 2020, the ICJ declared itself competent to hear Guyana's claim in spite of Maduro's opposition.

In a July 2015 interview with Telesur, Maduro regretted that there is a perception that "now Venezuela is the imperialist power," saying, "We are the country that was dispossessed. . . . That land of the Guayana Esequiba was not given to us by the British or Spanish empires, it was earned by our grandparents fighting on the battlefield, it is sacred land."[39] Ex-colonial countries can indeed claim to have won in the course of the struggle against colonialism the administration of the totality of the formerly colonized territory. But, if this is the source of postcolonial state legitimacy, the Guyanese people also fought for their independence from British imperialism. If British territorial conquest was theft, so was the Spanish conquest.

At various times in our common history there have been sectors willing to reach a just solution, outside the zero-sum calculations of nationalism. In April 1981, the Working People's Alliance of Guyana (WPA) issued a statement questioning Burnham's foreign policy:

> The WPA makes it very clear that our Party neither accepts the Venezuelan claim to Guyana nor any attitude that is so blind as to ignore the aspirations of the masses on one side or the other—whether in Guyana, Suriname or Venezuela, all of which lay claim to being part of the oppressed world. Patriotic and non-chauvinistic organizations in Guyana and Venezuela should at once set about organizing a people's

> congress to explore deeply and expose approaches to the dispute and to set up a standing body of lawyers, scholars and trade unionists to propose solutions by a date to be agreed on. . . . WPA sees the border dispute as having its origin in Spanish and British colonialisation under monarchies of the old order. It asserts without fear of contradiction that the *blade of grass* diplomacy on both sides has failed and threatens to engulf the peoples in profitless conflict. . . . The patriotic masses of the countries involved must impose on the governments who have bungled and mishandled the border issue a commitment to a settlement in which the Caribbean sense of values prevails.[40]

In November 2023, calling for abstention in the referendum on the Essequibo, the Socialism and Freedom Party of Venezuela (PSL) described the conflict as alien to

> the needs of the peoples and the working classes of Venezuela and Guyana. . . . Without any doubt, British imperialism took over a territory that belonged to the Captaincy General of Venezuela as it became independent. Already since colonial times, the British had been progressively occupying territory not controlled by the Spanish crown. And then they took advantage of the disaster in which the country was plunged after the bloody war of independence. However, although in its origin this claim had legitimacy because it confronted British imperialism, when Guyana became independent it was lost to the extent that it became an instrument of aggression against a brotherly Caribbean people, which could lose 74% of its territory.[41]

The mirage of the Essequibo represented in official maps with the stripes of the reclamation zone, or even assimilated by the new maps issued by Maduro's government, a seemingly uninhabited territory without history, took for too long the appearance of a harmless-looking lie. Almost nobody took it seriously. Today it is very costly. It represents the risk of uncontrolled escalation and armed confrontation. But even without that danger materializing, as the perspective of military conquest is evidently not viable, that mirage of territorial possession appears as a tool for the indefinite prolongation of a capitalist dictatorship disguised as socialist, by serving as an alibi for pseudonationalist demagoguery, militarization, and repression.

Conclusion

Gonzalo Gómez

This book has attempted to provide a comprehensive and nuanced understanding of Venezuela's current crisis and the trajectory of the Bolivarian process. The analysis highlights several key factors, including labor policy, the state of democracy, the government's repressive actions, and the role of corruption in both the onset and escalation of the crisis. It also examines how these factors are intertwined with the increasing bureaucratization and bourgeoisification of the political leadership. This degeneration has been further exacerbated by the adoption of reactionary policies, where extractive practices reinforce the persistence of a rentier capitalist economic model heavily dominated by the state—a defining feature of Venezuela's economy. These challenges are further complicated by a contradictory framework that combines regional imperialist aggression and the impact of sanctions with the realities of global economic dynamics that remain deeply dependent on hydrocarbons. As a nation heavily dependent on oil and raw materials, Venezuela has been particularly vulnerable to these forces. These dynamics have profoundly influenced the political distortions experienced by the Bolivarian process, especially under Nicolás Maduro's presidency.

From this analysis emerges the conclusion that the process has been fundamentally disfigured, marking the end of the revolutionary cycle initiated during Hugo Chávez's era. However, despite the reactionary shifts in the country's economic, social, and political spheres, the ongoing conflict with imperialism continues to necessitate solidarity with Venezuela. This solidarity is vital in resisting interventionism and efforts to fully integrate the nation into the global imperialist order.

The current situation calls for a dual approach: combining the struggle for liberation and the recovery of rights and achievements taken from the people with the defense of sovereignty and Venezuela's resistance to imperialist subjugation. This requires empowering Venezuelan people with their own independent social and political tools, free from bureaucracies and bourgeoisies. It also involves reviving the idea of socialism in their collective consciousness, enabling them to take power and advance toward breaking with capitalism to build a truly new society. These are essential tasks for the international left, forming a key part of its broader struggles for justice and equality.

Throughout the preceding chapters, a comparison between the governments of Hugo Chávez and Nicolás Maduro demonstrates that the Bolivarian Revolution effectively ended in the years following Chávez's death, having failed to achieve the envisioned "Socialism of the 21st Century." Tragically, it has devolved into a regressive phase of decomposition and general reversal, cloaked in pseudorevolutionary rhetoric.

However, the Bolivarian Revolution was never grounded in a strictly socialist agenda. Rather, it prioritized national sovereignty, Latin American unity, a mixed economy with state ownership and private partnerships, expanded popular participation among Bolivarian supporters, and strong social policies for wealth redistribution—all within the framework of capitalism.

Under Maduro's leadership, the path charted by Chávez was quickly reversed, although the seeds of its downfall were already present or emerging during Chávez's tenure. These included bureaucratic degeneration and the persistent legacies of Venezuelan capitalism, particularly in the continuation, and in some cases the intensification, of dependent rentier capitalism. As Carlos Carcione argued in chapter 7, this shift resulted in "the transformation of an advanced progressive regime, within the framework of capitalism, to a deeply authoritarian regime."

Under Maduro, the deterioration and regression of the process accelerated, reaching counterrevolutionary proportions. This period has been characterized by the erosion or dismantling of key economic, social, democratic, and national sovereignty spheres that had been promoted or realized in Venezuela before 2013. It was also evident in the decline of efforts toward Latin American integration, a cornerstone of Chávez's vision. While this regression and dismantling began before the US sanctions were imposed in 2017, the effects of those sanctions significantly worsened the situation.

As explained in chapter 7, "the change in economic conditions at the international level, the modifications in the class composition of the Bolivarian government, the growing pressures from inter-imperialist disputes, the absence or extreme weakness of an alternative working-class and revolutionary leadership, and the subsequent defeat of profound street mobilizations built the stage for this regressive transformation." These "multiple factors combined, impacting the political regime and transforming it into what it is today."

A key element in this transformation was an offensive against the left, mirroring other historical instances where revolutionary or progressive movements were undermined from within by their own leadership. Maduro and the bureaucratic caste systematically attacked sectors of "critical Chavismo" at political, union, and institutional levels to consolidate their political and economic power.

This analysis leads to the conclusion that the blockade and sanctions were not the primary cause of the revolution's deterioration. Many of the measures adopted by the Maduro government were driven by its own political choices (or those of the establishment it represents). Rather than pursuing alternative paths, the government opted to place the burden of the crisis on the working class, adopt neoliberal-style economic policies, and restrict democratic rights and public participation.

A significant factor in Venezuela's decline was the drop in oil revenues within an economy that failed to diversify or move beyond rentierism and the monoproduction of fossil fuels. This decline, compounded by economic sabotage and widespread bureaucratic corruption, forced the reallocation of resources to satisfy the demands of a lumpenbourgeoisie nurtured within institutions of power. In this already precarious context, international sanctions exacerbated the situation. By the time sanctions were imposed, corrupt bureaucratic elites and sectors of capital had already squandered hundreds of billions of dollars from the public coffers and state-owned enterprises, severely undermining the state's productive capacity.

By the time the sanctions were imposed, the rampant looting of public resources had already tripled the country's external debt, which was itself riddled with corruption. New instances of corruption emerged as high-ranking political-administrative leaders competed over substantial portions of the nations' remaining resources.

The policies adopted by the Maduro government further dismantled the earlier achievements of the Bolivarian Revolution. Social services were effectively dismantled, wages were rendered meaningless, though certain inadequate and questionable clientelist "benefits" were maintained, primarily as tools for sociopolitical control. This destruction was largely driven by the adoption of measures that, in many respects, resemble neoliberal policies (despite the government's claims to the contrary), marked by antiworker and deeply authoritarian measures. These neoliberal elements operated alongside a framework of state capitalism, creating a dynamic that ultimately served the interests of the United Socialist Party of Venezuela (PSUV) bureaucracy, the military, and the new bourgeoisie. This is the group—which has self-identified as the "revolutionary bourgeoisie"—that is referred to in chapter 6 as a "lumpenbourgeoisie."

In essence, rather than "deepening the revolution" as promised during Chávez's era, the government stifled it, implementing regressive and even reactionary policies that plunged the population into severe hardship. All the while it maintained a pseudoleftist rhetoric that was starkly at odds with its actions. As noted in chapter 3, this is a "complex and contradictory reality that shows that the interests of multinational capital can be executed by governments that formally declare themselves enemies of that same neoliberalism."

The sanctions imposed by imperialist powers, coupled with sabotage and right-wing offensives, exacerbated an already dire situation. At the same time, Maduro's government has leveraged these sanctions as a pretext to justify its politics and failures.

Major conflicts with American imperialism have persisted and continue, driven by the United States' desire to control Venezuelan resources and its preference for different actors and a government more aligned with its sphere of influence, rather than a government with geopolitical relationships that favor the US's Chinese and Russian capitalist competitors or regimes with whom the US has significant conflicts. Meanwhile, the sanctions have pushed Maduro's government to seek economic and military support from these nations, despite attempts to "normalize" aspects of its relationship with successive US administrations.

In the face of the blockade, economic-financial sanctions, interference, and interventionist threats, it is essential for the international left to show solidarity with the Venezuelan people and call for an end to such sanctions and interventionist practices. However, this solidarity should not translate into support for Maduro's government, which has maintained an oppressive and exploitative relationship with its own people.

It is vital for progressives and the international left, including those identifying as Marxists, to recognize that Maduro's government does not represent a continuation of Chávez's government or of the Bolivarian process. While it originates from that process and though Chávez himself endorsed Maduro for the presidency, the current government has abandoned the proclaimed socialist vision. Instead, it has driven the population and the working class into conditions significantly worse than those that existed before Chávez came to power.

Recognizing the harm inflicted by Maduro's government on the working class and the general population, it is unacceptable to remain silent or to justify support for this bureaucratic and increasingly right-leaning government under the guise of opposing imperialism. It is essential to distinguish between solidarity with the people and support for the government and avoid conflating the two. The Venezuelan people must defend themselves against the oppression imposed by their government while simultaneously defending national sovereignty—a challenge made more difficult by the government's contradictory policies, which often undermine this very objective.

Some sectors of the international left acknowledge the regression of the Bolivarian Revolution but primarily attribute it to sanctions and the ongoing imperialist conspiracy in collaboration with the traditional bourgeoisie. However, as detailed in this book, sanctions have served more as an aggravating factor than as the root cause of a crisis fundamentally rooted in bureaucratization and the preservation of the capitalist system.

Adopting a position that misdirects solidarity with an oppressed nation toward a government, which oppresses its people and worsens their suffering, is a dead end. A more constructive political approach from the left would involve grappling with the dialectical contradiction of a government that, while in conflict with imperialism, is simultaneously at odds with the needs and interests of the vast majority of Venezuelans.

This perspective would allow the left to more effectively campaign against sanctions and foreign intervention while also supporting the social and democratic demands of Venezuelan workers and the broader population. It would counter the traditional right's attempt to dominate political space and challenge the excuses used by the bureaucracy to curtail freedoms, suppress wages, and exploit public resources. Such an approach would pave the way for a leftist opposition that is firmly anti-imperialist, anticapitalist, antibureaucratic, democratic, and antiauthoritarian—distinct from the oppressive and antiworker capitalist policies of Maduro's government.

We believe that a different approach, informed by the data, analyses, reflections, and perspectives presented in this book, provides valuable guidance for the left's stance on the Venezuelan situation. This approach emphasizes accurately characterizing the government while aligning with the people and the working class. It involves defending the sovereignty of a nation under threat or violation by imperialism without supporting those in power, their exploitative systems, or their subordination to foreign interests, whether American, European, Chinese, or Russian.

The rapid and pronounced increase in poverty in Venezuela since Chávez's departure cannot be ignored. This deterioration began before the imposition of economic sanctions but was undoubtedly exacerbated by them. It is critical for the left to acknowledge how Maduro's government has systematically dismantled all independent union structures outside the control of the PSUV and the state apparatus. The left must avoid being misled by caricatures of communal organizations that lack true autonomy or by so-called productive workers' councils that are effectively subordinated to state control.

The left must remain vigilant about the severe repressive responses to dissent, criticism, denunciations, and workers' struggles in Venezuela. These actions strip the working class of its most fundamental rights, often in ways more brutal than those seen in many capitalist countries governed by neoliberal right-wing administrations.

The evidence and arguments presented in these chapters are clear and irrefutable. It is therefore unacceptable to echo official propaganda that dismisses all criticisms as manipulation or lies by the right-wing opposition or imperialism, even while acknowledging that such manipulations do exist. Rejecting this propaganda does not mean, under any circumstances, aligning with the pro-imperialist traditional right. If sectors of the left choose to support Maduro's government or choose to align themselves with the right-wing opposition, which claims to represent the people's desire for liberation, they will hinder the emergence of a revolutionary alternative that opposes both Madurismo and the traditional bourgeois right, represented by figures like María Corina Machado, who is increasingly capitalizing on public discontent and protests against Maduro. This surge in support for the traditional right stems from the absence of strong revolutionary alternatives capable of effectively standing against both imperialism and the traditional bourgeoisie on one side and bureaucratic corruption and the new bourgeoisie on the other. This new bourgeoisie has ultimately choked the life out of the Bolivarian process that defined the first decade of the twenty-first century.

Learning from the Venezuela experience is essential to offering meaningful solidarity to nations facing imperialist pressure or aggression without endorsing their governments or misrepresenting the reality. This is critical for advancing future struggles for socialism that avoid the seizure of power by oppressive and counterrevolutionary bureaucracies cloaked in anti-imperialist rhetoric or deceptive appearances. Such outcomes only alienate and repel the working masses and popular sectors, driving them into the hands of the right-wing opposition.

This understanding is vital for the left to navigate its approach to future revolutionary movements, which must be supported to succeed rather than allowed to degenerate. The degeneration of the Bolivarian process, falsely labeled as "socialist," has had a profoundly damaging effect on the left and political consciousness across the globe. It has distorted the concept of socialism, associating it with severe failures and disgraceful political practices more aligned with the right, or even the far right.

In the case of Venezuela, it is crucial to recognize these realities to avoid abandoning the people and the working class, who are enduring a massive counterrevolutionary assault and a devastating decline in living conditions. They urgently need to defend their democratic and social rights, rebuild their trade unions and social and political organizations, and overcome the colossal defeat they have suffered—a task in which they must be supported.

Under these circumstances, attempts to raise the banners of socialism often face rejection or mistrust from large sectors of the working class and population, who have been misled into equating "socialism" with the practices of the current government. As a result, reclaiming the concept of socialism has become an extremely difficult political and cultural challenge.

It is necessary to reclaim the true essence of socialism and its core values, ensuring it does not become a false promise, a "poisoned candy," or merely a façade used to mask brutal regimes that betray revolutionary processes. Without this clarity, it will be impossible to chart a credible path toward socialism, especially in light of the civilization-level challenges humanity faces today. These challenges—such as the climate crisis, war, migratory catastrophes, and capitalist efforts to intensify exploitation and all manifestations of the global crisis of capitalism—underscore the stark choice between "socialism or barbarism."

As previously noted, "[e]ven the most advanced and progressive processes tend to regress and become their opposites if they are not able to overcome the limits of a historically exhausted system, imperialist capitalism." A critical discussion lies in how to truly achieve this goal. It is evident that this cannot be done through bureaucratized political organizations, tainted by corruption and capitalist ambition and marked by undemocratic practices and violations of people's rights.

Such organizations inevitably undermine and destroy the very processes they once led, often leaving conditions far worse than those they initially sought to overcome and promised to transform.

Ultimately, what is at stake in this discussion is reclaiming hope and ensuring the continuity of the struggle for socialism, free from false flags and deceptions. With this compilation, we aim to contribute to this critical effort while reaffirming the genuine solidarity that the Venezuelan people—and other oppressed peoples worldwide—deserve in their struggles for freedom and against exploitation.

AFTERWORD

The 2024 Venezuelan Elections and Their Aftermath

Anderson M. Bean

The 2024 Venezuelan elections and their aftermath have provided stark confirmation of the arguments laid out in this book. The events surrounding the election and the subsequent inauguration of Nicolás Maduro illustrate the deepening authoritarianism of his regime, the suppression of political opposition—including of the left—and the increasing detachment of the government from the needs and aspirations of the working class. Rather than representing the continuation of the Bolivarian process initiated under Hugo Chávez, Maduro's rule has marked a profound reversal of its progressive elements, turning the state into an apparatus of repression against popular mobilizations and independent workers' movements.

The Road to the 2024 Elections: The Illusion of Democratic Openings

The preelection period was marked by a series of negotiations between the United States, the Maduro government, and the US-backed opposition under the Barbados Agreement and the Qatar Agreement. The former agreement included both Maduro and the domestic opposition and focused on domestic electoral conditions and political rights aiming to ensure fair elections. The latter were just between the US and the Maduro government, excluding the Venezuelan opposition and centered on international relations, particularly US sanctions and diplomatic normalization. These agreements, which involved prisoner swaps—Maduro accepting Venezuelan deportees, and Washington providing temporary sanctions relief on oil, gas, and gold sectors in exchange for electoral guarantees—initially appeared to open a pathway for a more competitive electoral process. However, as the election approached, it became evident that these guarantees were hollow. Maduro's government systematically blocked individual candidates and entire political parties, ensuring that only acceptable opposition forces could compete.

María Corina Machado, who won the primaries of the right-wing electoral alliance Democratic Unitary Platform (PUD), was barred from running, along with her designated replacement, Corina Yoris. Edmundo González was ultimately chosen as the PUD candidate, but his candidacy was overshadowed by Machado's continued dominance in the opposition campaign. The reality of González's role was clear—he was a figurehead, while Machado dictated the campaign's direction. This situation not only revealed the authoritarian manipulation of the electoral process but also underscored the limitations of the mainstream opposition's strategy, which relied on individual figures rather than building a genuine political alternative.

Maduro's repression extended beyond the right-wing opposition. Three hundred political organizations had requested legalization from the National Electoral Council in the year leading up to the elections but never received a response.[1] The Maduro government banned the Communist Party of Venezuela (PCV), the country's oldest political party and a long-standing ally of Chávez, from running in the election after it distanced itself from Maduro's government. Their headquarters was also raided, and several of their supporters were arrested. The Supreme Court (TSJ) effectively dissolved the PCV, handing its legal representation and electoral registration to a group of Maduro loyalists who had no ties to the party. As a result, two factions now claim the PCV identity. The first is the state-recognized PCV, led by a TSJ-appointed board composed of Maduro loyalists aligned with the PSUV. The second, now known as PCV (Dignidad), consists of the party's original leadership and members who oppose the TSJ's intervention. While this faction lacks legal recognition and is consequently stripped of its electoral card, it continues to operate independently and maintain its political activities.

Other left parties, such as Marea Socialista and the Socialism and Freedom Party of Venezuela (PSL), were denied their electoral cards in 2015 and 2017, respectively. Marea was denied its electoral card from the beginning, while the PSL had one, but it was revoked. Despite repeated efforts by the parties to obtain or regain an electoral card, their requests have been consistently rejected since then. The PCV was the last remaining left party that still had the right to stand for political office. With its exclusion, all left parties were effectively banned from the elections. This maneuver symbolized the broader crackdown on independent leftist organizations, ensuring that no legitimate left-wing alternative to the PSUV exists, thus allowing the government to present itself as the sole leftist force in the country. It is not convenient for the Maduro government to have a revolutionary left force exposing the contradiction between the PSUV's rhetoric and Maduro's actual policies. Even Enrique Márquez, a center-left presidential candidate who ran with the support of the PCV and dissident Chavistas, was detained incommunicado for months without being formally charged with any crime. Márquez was eventually released but then detained again. He remains in prison to this day. Another presidential candidate, María Alejandra Díaz, a critical left-leaning Chavista, was banned from running for office. After taking part in a lawsuit challenging the July 28 elections, she was also stripped of her right to practice law and was forced into hiding to evade persecution. These are just a few instances of the regime's efforts to squash anything that could be seen to challenge its leftist credentials.

Election Day: Fraud and Manipulation

The election itself was plagued by irregularities. Voter registration abroad faced significant delays, with many Venezuelans reporting that they were unable to register or update their information. Despite twenty-one million

Venezuelans being eligible to vote abroad, only sixty-nine thousand—just 1 percent—were able to do so, largely because of the extralegal requirements demanded of voters, such as presenting residence papers issued by foreign governments. Meanwhile, opposition candidates and their supporters faced repression throughout the campaign. They were harassed when attempting to rent sound equipment for rallies and similarly persecuted when securing venues for campaign events, severely limiting their ability to mobilize voters. On Election Day, initial tallies from electoral monitors suggested that González was leading Maduro by a wide margin. However, the National Electoral Council (CNE) abruptly suspended the transmission of results following an alleged cyberattack—the origins of which the CNE changed repeatedly, blaming North Macedonia, then Elon Musk, and later even blaming George Soros. When the system was restored, Maduro was suddenly declared the winner.

The CNE's Unprecedented Refusal to Release Election Results

For the first time since Venezuela introduced its electronic voting system in 2004, the CNE has refused to publish election results. This marks a stark departure from the standard practice of the last two decades, during which disaggregated results have always been made publicly available within hours—or at most, a few days—after an election. This practice is not only a long-standing tradition but also a legal requirement in Venezuela.

By law, the official election results must be publicly released, allowing voters to access detailed data by state, city, voting center, and even by individual voting machines. However, in this latest election, the CNE has failed to provide this information at any level. The Venezuelan government has never before withheld such fundamental presidential electoral data, making this a historic first.

Ironically, Venezuela's electronic voting system was once celebrated as one of the most transparent in the world. In 2006, the Carter Center praised the country's double-check electronic voting system, stating that Venezuelan elections were among the most free and fair in the world. This system's strength was its ability to quickly and reliably verify election results, allowing for a high degree of confidence in the democratic process.

Although pro-Maduro forces continue to reference the 2006 endorsement, the very electoral system that once distinguished Venezuela as a model has now been abandoned. The CNE's refusal to release the results directly undermines the election's credibility and reveals the process as fundamentally unfair.

The refusal to publish the election results has led to widespread concern across the political spectrum, both domestically and internationally, about the election's credibility. In Venezuela, both right- and left-wing opposition groups have demanded the release of the results. Even internationally, left-of-center governments in Latin America—such as those of Brazilian President Luiz Inácio Lula da Silva, Colombian President Gustavo Petro, and former Mexican President Andrés Manuel López Obrador (AMLO)—have issued statements urging the CNE to publish the election data.

Additionally, international election observers, including the Carter Center, have weighed in. The Carter Center has now stated that the 2024 electoral process "did not meet international standards" and that the elections "cannot be considered democratic."[2] While Western NGOs should always be approached with skepticism due to their political biases, it is important to note that it was this same Carter Center that once validated Venezuela's elections during the Chávez era. It is also important to note that the Carter Center was one of the few foreign organizations invited by Maduro's government to observe the elections. Their shift in position underscores just how much Maduro's government has deviated from past transparency norms.

In previous elections, the right-wing opposition frequently issued baseless claims of electoral fraud, most of which have been debunked. However, this history does not automatically mean fraud is impossible this time. The key difference this time is that, in past elections, the government was able to swiftly counter these allegations by releasing a significant number of electoral returns. In 2013, when the opposition claimed fraud, the government published the full set of disaggregated results, which conclusively disproved their accusations.

This time, however, independent analysts who have examined the available electoral returns published by the opposition have found no evidence of tampering. These returns suggest that opposition candidate González won with two-thirds of the vote—more than double Maduro's tally—based on 80 percent of the tallies they have reviewed. If Maduro had actually won, the simplest way to prove it would be to release the full, disaggregated results. And if the PSUV claims the tallies published by the opposition were forged, they could publish the "authentic ones." The government's reluctance to do so raises serious suspicions about the legitimacy of the election outcome.

In response to calls for transparency, Maduro's government has claimed that the results have not been published because of a supposed hacking attempt. This explanation fails to hold up under scrutiny. If a hacking attempt had truly disrupted the election system, how is it that the CNE was still able to announce approximate figures on television and claim a victory for Maduro? Furthermore, while the results have not been released to the public, they were reportedly provided to Venezuela's Supreme Court (TSJ), which is widely known to be under Maduro's control. This contradiction raises an important question: If the government is capable of releasing the results to the TSJ, why can't it release them to the public as required by Venezuelan law? By withholding the election results, the Maduro government has created a crisis of legitimacy that extends beyond Venezuela's borders. The refusal to release data not only contradicts Venezuela's own electoral laws but also betrays the transparency that was once a hallmark of the country's voting system.

If Maduro's government truly won fairly, then transparency should be in their best interest. The refusal to release the results only fuels suspicion and further isolates the administration both domestically and internationally. Until the full, disaggregated results are made public, the credibility of Venezuela's electoral process will remain in question.

Popular Resistance and State Repression

In the wake of the election, a wave of protests erupted across Venezuela. Unlike previous opposition-led demonstrations, these mobilizations were not limited to the middle and upper classes but saw mass participation from the working class and residents of popular barrios—many of whom had historically supported Chávez. The mass mobilizations on July 28–29 were not called for by Machado and González. After this initial wave, there were more traditional protests in Eastern Caracas organized by the opposition, but the main popular protests were spontaneous and came from barrios that used to be electoral and political bastions of Chavismo. These protests reflected the growing discontent with Maduro's government, not just from the right but also from broad sectors of the population that have suffered under the country's economic collapse and political repression.

The government responded with brutal force. Within the first week, over two thousand people were arrested, and at least twenty-five were killed. The vast majority of those arrested came from working-class backgrounds, disproving the government's claims that these protests were solely driven by the traditional right-wing opposition or foreign interference. Security forces conducted raids, detained activists without warrants, and imposed severe restrictions on prisoners, many of whom faced sentences of up to thirty years for so-called terrorism or "hateful instigation."

As the January 10, 2025, inauguration of Maduro approached, repression intensified. Members of the opposition, including leaders from the Centrados party and the Frente Democrático Popular, were arrested. The use of paramilitary groups, house raids, and judicial maneuvers to silence dissent underscored the deepening crisis of democracy in Venezuela.

A Divided Opposition and the Absence of a Working-Class Alternative

While opposition to Maduro spans the political spectrum, it remains deeply fragmented. The mainstream right-wing opposition, led by González and Machado, is primarily focused on ousting Maduro rather than on presenting a coherent alternative program. The right wing is divided between those advocating for a centrist approach and the more extreme free-market policies of Machado, which include privatizing Petroleum of Venezuela (PDVSA) and social services.

On the left, the situation is equally complex. While some former supporters of Maduro have defected to the right-wing opposition in desperation, others remain committed to an independent socialist alternative. The Popular Revolutionary Alternative (APR), composed of leftist groups such as the PCV, PPT-APR, and MRT, represents a significant effort to build a working-class movement outside of both Maduro's PSUV and the traditional opposition. Other leftist formations, including Marea Socialista, PSL, and the League of Workers for Socialism (LTS), have taken a more radical stance, advocating for voting null as a form of protest against both the fraudulent election and the broader political exclusion of independent socialist forces.

As a united front for action (but not electoral participation), the PCV (Dignidad), PPT-APR, PSL, Marea Socialista, and Revolución Comunista (formerly Lucha de Clases) have been jointly organizing protests for the past two years under the banner of the Encuentro Nacional en Defensa de los Derechos del Pueblo (National Meeting in Defense of the People's Rights). LTS also collaborates with the National Meeting in Defense of the People's Rights, though it is not formally a member.

Despite the differences in orientation, all these left groups do have some points of unity, such as campaigning for the freedom of political prisoners and for fair wages as stipulated in the constitution and against corruption and antiworker policies, and in solidarity with the Palestinian people.

This rupture with the left demonstrates that Maduro's claim to be the only legitimate socialist force in Venezuela is false. His government has embraced neoliberal policies, prioritized debt repayment to foreign creditors over social spending, and violently suppressed workers' struggles. The very movements that once formed the backbone of Chavismo—organized labor, peasant groups, and community organizations—are now among the most repressed under Maduro's rule unless they strictly adhere to the government's directives

Conclusion: The Path Forward for the Venezuelan Left

The 2024 election and its aftermath have confirmed the central arguments of this book: Maduro has overseen a reactionary transformation of the Venezuelan state, reversing many of the progressive achievements of the Chávez era. His government is not a vehicle for socialist change but a deeply authoritarian regime that represses all opposition—not only the right but also independent trade unionists and leftist critics from the working class.

For the Venezuelan working class and the left, the path forward does not lie with Maduro or with the traditional opposition, both of whom ultimately serve elite interests. The challenge is to construct an independent political force that represents the real interests of workers, peasants, women, and marginalized communities. The growing mobilization of the left against state repression and the emergence of alternative socialist formations suggest that such a force is beginning to take shape. Rebuilding organization, strengthening mobilization capacity, and fostering independent political action will be essential to forming a force that rejects both the corrupt bureaucracy and the US-backed capitalist opposition. This effort is also crucial for resisting the authoritarian regime and reclaiming the rights that have been taken away. Whether it can coalesce into a viable movement capable of challenging the existing political order remains an open question, but what is clear is that Venezuela's crisis will not be resolved through fraudulent elections or authoritarian rule.

The struggle continues.

Acknowledgments

First, I would like to thank all the incredible contributors to the book: Carlos Carcione, Juan García, Gonzalo Gómez, Roberto López Sánchez, Gustavo Márquez Marín, Oly Millán Campos, Simón Rodríguez, Emiliano Terán, Omar Vázquez Heredia, and Ana Sofía Viloria. I want to thank these authors not just for their contributions in this volume but also for all their past writings, contributions, and organizing that have inspired the creation of this edition in the first place. It was bringing these voices to an Anglophone audience that inspired this book. I would also like to thank a list of other people who contributed in one way or another in the completion of this project: brian bean, Bryson Brewer, Martín Carcione, Phoenix Carter, Gabriel García, Erik Kerl, John McDonald, Héctor Navarro, Martín Poliak, Jason Smith, and Stephanie Teixeira-Poit. I would also like to thank Haymarket Books for its dedication and commitment to publishing radical, activist-oriented literature and all the staff at Haymarket who worked tirelessly to bring this volume to print. Finally, I want to express my deepest gratitude to Ana Sofía Viloria and Mara García, without whom this book could not have been possible.

Notes

Introduction

1. Gregory Wilpert, *Changing Venezuela by Taking Power* (London: Verso, 2007).
2. Jeffery Webber, "What Is Hugo Chávez's Legacy?," *Socialist Worker*, March 8, 2013.
3. Reuters, "Venezuela's Chávez Raises Venezuela's Minimum Wage by a Third," May 1, 2008.
4. Kevin Voigt, "Chávez Leaves Venezuela Economy More Equal, Less Stable," CNN, March 6, 2013.
5. Datos Observatorio Venezolano de Finanzas, OVF.
6. Wladimir Abreu, "Economía informal y cuarentena, una pareja dispareja," *Aporrea*, May 12, 2020.
7. Abreu, "Economía informal."
8. Cira Pascual Marquina, "Working-Class Struggle in Venezuela: A Conversation with Leander Perez," *Venezuelanalysis*, February 21, 2020.
9. Deutch Welle, "ACNUR: 'Nos preocupa que se invisibilice la crisis de refugiados y migrantes de Venezuela,'" *Aporrea*, November 29, 2019.
10. United Nations High Commissioner for Refugees (UNHCR), "Emergency Appeal: Venezuela Situation," UNHCR, www.unhcr.org/us/emergencies/venezuela-situation#:~:text=Nearly%207.9%20million%20people%20have,Latin%20American%20and%20Caribbean%20countries.
11. Aporrea-Agencias, "Venezuela es el segundo país del mundo con mayor número de desplazados, según Acnur," *Aporrea*, June 20, 2020.
12. UNHCR, "Venezuela Situation."
13. William I. Robinson, "Latin America's Pink Tide: The Straightjacket of Global Capitalism," in *Latin America's Pink Tide: Breakthroughs and Shortcomings*, ed. Steve Ellner (New York: Rowman & Littlefield, 2020); Jeffery R. Webber, *The Last Day of Oppression and the First Day of the Same: The Politics and Economics of the New Latin American Left* (Chicago: Haymarket Books, 2017).
14. Robinson, "Latin America's Pink Tide."
15. Rene Rojas, "The Latin American Left's Shifting Tides," *Catalyst* 2, no. 2 (2018): 7–71; Robinson, "Latin America's Pink Tide."
16. Giovanni Andrea Cornia, "Inequality Trends and Their Determinants: Latin America Over the Period 1990–2010," in *Falling Inequality in Latin America: Policy Changes and Lessons*, ed. Giovanni Andrea Cornia (Oxford Scholarship Online, 2014), 25; Webber, *Last Day of Oppression*; Jeffery R. Webber, "The Retreat of the

Pink Tide in Latin America," interview by Phil Gasper, *International Socialist Review*, no. 110 (April 2018).

17. Robinson, "Latin America's Pink Tide."
18. Eduardo Gudyas, "Estado comprensador y nuevos extractivismos: Las ambivalencias del progresismo sudamericano," *Nueva Sociedad*, no. 237 (January–February 2012): 128–46.
19. John Ficenec, "Commodity Prices Collapse to Lowest in 12 Years," *Telegraph*, January 29, 2015.
20. Gabriel Hetland, "Why Is Venezuela in Crisis?," *Nation*, August 17, 2016.
21. Frederick Mills, "Chavista Transition to the Communal State," *openDemocracy*, July 22, 2015.
22. Branko Marcetic, "Sanctions Are Murder," *Jacobin*, May 6, 2019.
23. Joe Emersberger, "Trump's Economic Sanctions Have Cost Venezuela About $6bn Since August 2017," *Venezuelanalysis*, September 27, 2018
24. Marcetic, "Sanctions Are Murder."
25. Edward Wong and Nicholas Casey, "U.S. Targets Venezuela with Tough Oil Sanctions During Crisis of Power," *New York Times*, January 28, 2019.
26. Marc Weisbrot and Jeffrey Sachs, "Economic Sanctions as Collective Punishment: The Case of Venezuela," Center for Economic and Policy Research, April 2019.
27. Weisbrot and Sachs, "Economic Sanctions."
28. United Nations Human Rights Office of the High Commissioner, "Venezuela Sanctions Harm Human Rights of Innocent People, UN Expert Warns," press release, January 31, 2019.
29. Marcetic, "Sanctions Are Murder."
30. Luis Salas, "Venezuela ha realizado un ajuste ortodoxo a rajatabla," *La Vanguardia*, January 12, 2020.
31. Mike Gonzalez, *The Ebb of the Pink Tide: The Decline of the Left in Latin America* (London: Pluto, 2019).
32. Gonzalez, *Ebb of the Pink Tide.*
33. Gonzalez, *Ebb of the Pink Tide.*
34. Gonzalez, *Ebb of the Pink Tide*, 130.
35. Gonzalez, *Ebb of the Pink Tide.*
36. Orlando Chirino, "El memorándum 2792 es una reforma laboral antiobrera y reaccionaria," *Deslinde 2011* (blog), June 21, 2019, deslinde2011.blogspot.com/2019/05/orlando-chirino-el-memorandum-2792-es.html.
37. Surgentes Colectivo, "Giro a la derecha y represión a la izquierda: Violaciones a los derechos humanos en el campo venezolano (2015–2020)," Rosa Luxemburg Institute, no. 24 (May 2021): 20.
38. Paul Garver, Austin Gonzalez, and Carrington Morris, "The International Question in DSA," *Socialist Forum* (Summer 2021).
39. Max Blumenthal and Ben Norton, "The Real Humanitarian Aid: Inside Venezuela's State Subsidized Communal Markets," *Grayzone*, February 24, 2019.

Chapter 1: Continuities and Ruptures in the Bolivarian Process

1. Polo Patriotico was the name for the bloc of Venezuelan left-wing parties that supported the project of the Bolivarian Revolution led by Hugo Chávez in the 1998 presidential elections. The parties included the party founded by Chávez, the Fifth Republic Movement, as well as Movement to Socialism, Patria Para Todos, and the People's Electoral Movement.
2. Plan Bolívar 2000 was the social emergency plan advanced by President Hugo Chávez, immediately after he assumed the presidency in 1999 and before the constituent process began, to address the urgent needs of the population with the support of the National Armed Forces.
3. The second OPEC summit was held in Caracas in 2000, forty years after the first summit was held, in which its role was reaffirmed not only as a defense mechanism for the interests of oil-exporting countries but also as an instrument to regulate the hydrocarbon market.
4. The Constitution of the Bolivarian Republic of Venezuela contains the programmatic bases of the transition from a liberal democracy to a deep democracy, based on the participation and protagonism of the people in the management and control of the established public powers.
5. The Fourth Republic is the Venezuelan republican period that spans from 1830 to 1999.
6. Free Trade Area of the Americas (FTAA) was a trade agreement proposed by the United States with the aim of establishing a free trade area in the Americas under the neoliberal principles of the Washington Consensus.
7. The military rebellion of February 4, 1992, was an uprising by middle and lower officers of the Venezuelan Armed Forces, who tried unsuccessfully to depose social democratic president Carlos Andrés Pérez (1990–93).
8. The Bolivarian Revolutionary Movement 200 (MBR-200) was the movement formed within the national armed force, made up of middle and lower commanders of the military structure, with the aim of promoting a revolutionary transformation based on the ideology of Simón Bolívar.
9. Hugo Chávez Frías, Agenda Alternativa Bolivariana (Caracas: Edciones Correo del Orinoco, 2014).
10. The Fifth Republic began with the constituent process that gave rise to the Constitution of the Bolivarian Republic of Venezuela (1999).
11. Democratic Action party (AD), a social democratic party founded by Rómulo Betancourt in 1941.
12. Francisco Solórzano y Tom Grillo, eds., *El Caracazo* (Caracas: El Perro y la Rana, 2022).
13. Social Christian Party (COPEI), founded in 1946.
14. Movement for Socialism is the democratic left-wing socialist party founded in 1972 by Pompeyo Márquez, Teodoro Petkoff, and Rafael Guerra Ramos, from a split from the Communist Party of Venezuela. People's Electoral Movement, a party founded by a split from Democratic Action, was born from a current that defined itself as socialist, democratic, revolutionary, and nationalist, founded by Luis Beltrán Prieto Figueroa and Jesús Ángel Paz Galarraga. Communist Party of Venezuela was founded in 1931 by Juan Bautista Fuenmayor and Kotepa

Delgado. The National Convergence party formed from a split with COPEI, led in 1993 by its own founder, Dr. Rafael Caldera.

15. Agustín Lewit and Luis Wainer, "La Venezuela pactada: Entre el El Punto Fijo y el paquete neoliberal," Centro Cultural de la Cooperación "Floreal Gorini" (Edición 20). The Puntofijista democratic system was established from the so-called Punto Fijo Pact, which was a governance agreement between the AD, COPEI, and Democratic Republican Union parties after the fall of the Marcos dictatorship. The pact was signed at the residence of Dr. Rafael Caldera, called Punto Fijo.
16. Fifth Republic Movement, a party founded by Hugo Chávez, originating from a civic-military union that had as its predecessor the MBR-200.
17. Mark Weisbrot, Rebecca Ray, and Luis Sandoval, *El gobierno de Chávez después de diez años: Evolución de la economía e indicadores sociales* (Center for Economic and Policy Research, 2009).
18. Coup d'état of April 11, 2002, against President Hugo Chávez, promoted by the US government and the right-wing opposition, triggered by the first measures taken by the revolutionary government to take control of the oil industry and reestablish sovereignty over oil and advance agrarian reform. Federation of Chambers of Commerce (Fedecámaras) is the leadership of the organization that brings together most of the national business community. The Confederation of Workers of Venezuela is the federation of unions controlled fundamentally by AD and COPEI.
19. The oil strike in 2002–3 was a lockout aimed at causing the collapse of PDVSA and the consequent economic crisis of the country.
20. The 2004 presidential recall referendum was called by the opposition, making use for the first time of the mechanism provided for in the Bolivarian Constitution, which was won by Hugo Chávez, ratifying his legitimacy and the leadership that the opponents sought to ignore.
21. Alberto Müller Rojas, "Nuevo pensamiento militar venezolano," *Revista Venezolana de Economía y Ciencias Sociales* 12, no. 6 (2006). The Bolivarian military doctrine derived from the military thought that Simón Bolívar developed in the war for the independence of Venezuela and South America, in which concepts such as security and comprehensive defense, asymmetric war, and war played an important role, among others, which changes the conception of the role and mission of a national armed force.
22. The São Paulo Forum is a space for dialogue among the different leftist currents of Latin America and the Caribbean. It was founded in 1990 in the Brazilian city of São Paulo, and everyone from center-left reformists to the revolutionary left participates.
23. Plan for the Homeland was the government plan presented by Hugo Chávez during his candidacy for reelection in the 2006 presidential elections, for the constitutional period 2007–13.
24. Asdrúbal Baptista, "El capitalismo rentístico: Elementos cuantitativos de la economía venezolana," *Cuadernos del Cendes* 22, no. 60 (2005).
25. Poverty graph with respect to GDP 1990–2021.

26. Ministry of Popular Power for the Communes (MPPC) is the state ministry of the new territorial organization (geometry of power) and the constitution of Popular Power.
27. As part of the shift toward socialism, the PSUV was founded with the intention of becoming the sole party of the revolution, which did not happen.
28. The idea of "sowing oil," first used by Alberto Adriani and then by Arturo Uslar Prietri, suggests that since oil is a nonrenewable natural resource with a finite duration, it is essential to allocate oil income to the development of a sustainable non-oil economy.
29. Hugo Chávez Frías, *Aló Presidente*, Venezolana de Televisión, July 29, 2007.
30. Mercedes De Freitas and Christi Rangel, *Fonden, una estrategia política para gastar sin control* (Caracas: Transparencia Venezuela, 2021).
31. Mercedes De Freitas, Christi Rangel, Negocios Chinos, *Acuerdos qu socavaron la democracia en Venezuela* (Caracas: Transparencia Venezuela, 2020).
32. The new productive model proposed by the Bolivarian Revolution sought to replace the extant petro-dependent extractivist rent model with an endogenous, diversified, sustainable model capable of promoting the development of an economy with its own dynamics, autonomous from oil rent. The social and solidarity economy (SSE) is a set of socioeconomic and cultural initiatives that are based on a paradigm shift based on the cooperative work of people and the collective ownership of goods. The SSE seeks to generate relationships of solidarity and trust and community spirit and participation in society and to strengthen processes of productive integration, consumption, distribution, and savings and loans to satisfy the needs of its members and communities where they develop.
33. There were separate statements from the Food and Agriculture Organization of the United Nations and the Economic Commission for Latin America and the Caribbean (ECLAC) recognizing the social advances of the Bolivarian Revolution.
34. Neritza Alvarado Chacín, "La estrategia de inclusión en Venezuela: Una acercamiento a la experiencia de las misiones," *Convergencia* 16, no. 51 (2009): 85–128.
35. Hugo Chávez Frías, Propuesta del Candidato de la Patria Comandante Hugo Chávez para la Gestión Bolivariana Socialista 2013–2019 (Caracas: Comando de Campaña Carabobo, 2012).
36. The implementation of the exchange rate anchoring policy in Venezuela, aimed at combating inflation for over a decade, resulted in a consistent and increasing influx of oil revenues. However, this strategy prioritized the generation of significant capital exports, detrimentally affecting domestic productive development.
37. Comparison of economic performance between the Chávez and Maduro governments. Chart from Statista.
38. Álvaro Merino, "La producción y exportación de petróleo de Venezuela," El Orden Mundial, January 23, 2023.
39. United Nations Refugee Agency, "Llamamiento de emergencia: Situación de Venezuela," UNHCR ACNUR, retrieved January 3, 2024.
40. Ángel Bermúdez, "Cuanto se ha reducido la población en Venezuela y como impacta en su desarrollo," *BBC*, August 9, 2021.

41. Sanciones y Bloqueo: Crimen de lesa humanidad contra Venezuela, Gobierno Bolivariano.
42. José Francisco López, "El impacto de las sanciones de EEUU a Venezuela," *Economipedia*, May 16, 2019.
43. This graph shows the evolution of the value of oil exports before and during the governments of Chávez and Maduro.
44. Executive Order 13692; Manuel Sutherland, "Informe especial | Sanciones económicas contra Venezuela: Consecuencias, crisis humanitaria, alternativas y acuerdo humanitario," *PROVEA*, November 25, 2020.
45. Plataforma Ciudadana en Defensa de la Constitución, "Maduro consolida Régimen Autoritario Neoliberal Extractivista al margen de la Constitución," *Aporrea*, June 21, 2021.
46. The so-called Anti-Blockade Law was dictated by the government of Nicolás Maduro outside the constitution, with which it grants extraordinary powers and legitimizes a neoliberal authoritarian regime.
47. Ana Barrios Benatuil, Martha Lía Grajales Pineda, and Antonio González Plessmann, "Giro a la derecha y represión a la izquierda: Violación de los derechos humanos en Venezuela," Surgentes: Colectivo de Derechos Humanos, Fundación Rosa Luxemburg, May 2021.
48. Gustavo Márquez Marín, "El gobierno de Maduro construye un régimen autoritario neoliberal periférico y extractivista ampliado," *Aporrea*, July 30, 2021.
49. Puerto Rican word adopted in Venezuela in the 1940s. *Pitiyanqui* is used to describe people who, without having American nationality, adopt their customs and imitate their lifestyle, considering it better, even when it is discordant with their environment or local traditions.
50. This move had the consent of the Supreme Court of Justice (TSJ) and the National Electoral Council (CNE), which was by this time attended only by the government party bloc and its allies.
51. The Lima Group was established by fifteen right-wing governments in Latin America to support the US government's "regime change" policy of ignoring the government of Nicolás Maduro, reelected in 2018, and recognizing the parallel government of Juan Guaidó.
52. The so-called group of four (G4) is made up of the parties Democratic Action (Henry Ramos Allup), Un Nuevo Tiempo, Voluntad Popular, and Primero Justicia.
53. The Democratic Unitary Platform (PUD) is made up of the G4 parties.
54. Andrés Cañizales, "La rendición de cuentas que nos debe Guaidó," *Confidencial*, October 28, 2021.
55. CERLAS, "Informe sobre la situacion de derechos humanos en el arco minero y el territorio venezolano ubicado al sur del rio Orinoco," *Transcontinental Human Trajectories*, August 2019; Gustavo Márquez Marín, "El gobierno construye un Régimen Autoritario Neoliberal Periférico y Extractivista Ampliado," *Aporrea*, July 30, 2021.
56. The policy of the new Oil Opening reverses the process of nationalization and rescue of oil sovereignty implemented by the government of Hugo Chávez, in even more surrendering terms than those that occurred in the Fourth Republic.

57. Surgentes Colectivo, "Giro a la derecha y represión a la izquierda: Violaciones a los derechos humanos en el campo venezolano (2015–2020)," Rosa Luxemburg Institute, no. 24 (May 2021): 20.
58. Mora Contreras, "Venezuela: el petróleo y el socialismo del siglo XXI," *Enciclopédie d' La énergie*, May 4, 2020.
59. Carlos Peña, ed., *Venezuela y su tradición rentista: Visiones, enfoques y evidencias* (Caracas: CENDES, 2017).
60. Juan José Pérez, "El papel del petróleo en la conformación del socialismo del siglo XXI," *Temas de Coyuntura*, no. 66 (2012).
61. Plataforma Ciudadana en Defensa de la Constitución, "No a la nueva apertura petrolera inconstitucional y entreguista: Construyamos una alternativa posrentista y soberana," *Aporrea,* October 5, 2022.

Chapter 2: The Venezuelan Economy During the Bolivarian Process, 1999–2024

1. Statista. "Oil Production in Venezuela from 1998 to 2021 (in 1,000 Barrels per Day)," last modified 2021, www.statista.com/statistics/265185/oil-production-in-venezuela-in-barrels-per-day.
2. Observatorio Venezolano de Finanzas, OVF, observatoriodefinanzas.com.
3. Universidad Católica Andrés Bello, *Encuesta Condiciones de Vida de los Venezolanos 2022* (Caracas: Universidad Católica Andrés Bello, 2022). This same survey mentions the increase in income inequality (Gini) for 2022, the indicator stood at 0.603, while in 2014 it was 0.407.
4. Population and Housing Census, National Institute of Statistics.
5. Refers to the "main and second enemy."
6. It is important to avoid falling into the campist vision of "the enemy of my enemy is my friend."
7. Parties: Democratic Action (AD) and the Social Christian Party (COPEI).
8. Boaventura De Sousa Santos, *Construyendo las Epistemologías del Sur, Volumen 1* (Buenos Aires: CLACSO, 2018).
9. Asdrúbal Baptista, *El relevo del capitalismo rentístico. Hacia un nuevo balance de poder* (Caracas: Fundación Polar, 2004).
10. Baptista, *El relevo del capitalismo*, 18.
11. Armando Córdova, "Lineamientos de política económica de largo plazo," in *Una estrategia para Venezuela*, ed. Elías Eljuri (Caracas: IIES–FACES-UCV y Academia Nacional de Ciencias Económicas, 1990), 45–63.
12. Celso Furtado, *Notas de la economía venezolana y perspectivas actuales* (Caracas: Ediciones Cordiplan, 1981), 4–5.
13. Moisés Ikonicoff, *De la cultura de la renta a la economía de producción* (Buenos Aires: Editorial Legasa, 1989).
14. The proposal was formulated by the Economic Commission for Latin America and the Caribbean (CEPAL/ECLAC).
15. Domingo Maza Zavala, "Hacia un programa de transición," in *Una estrategia para Venezuela*, ed. Elias Eljuri (IIES–FACES-UCV y Academia Nacional de Ciencias Económicas, 1990), 33–44.

16. Edgardo Lander, "El impacto del ajuste neoliberal 1989–1993," in *Neoliberalismo, sociedad civil y democracia: Ensayos sobre América Latina y Venezuela* (Caracas: Consejo de Desarrollo Científico y Humanístico, 1994).
17. In various interviews conducted by journalist Ángela Zago (1998) with leaders of the "military rebellion" of February 4, 1998, the leaders all refer to corruption as an important factor that led them to rebel.
18. Herrera Campins was the president of Venezuela from 1979 to 1984.
19. Armando Córdova, "Crisis económica Venezolana: Causas y perspectivas," in *Homenaje Carrillo Batalla, Tomo I* (Caracas: Universidad Central de Venezuela, 2009), 406.
20. Ángela Zago, *La Rebelión de los ángeles*, cuarta ed. (Caracas: Warp, Ediciones, 1998). The Caracazo is the name given to a wave of protests, riots, and looting. The state responded to these protests with extreme violence and human rights violations. Thousands of Venezuelans were murdered by state security forces.
21. Mireya Lozada, "Conflicto y polarización en tiempos de revolución: Representaciones e imaginarios del otro en Venezuela," *Revista SOMEPSO* 1, no. 1 (2016).
22. Domingo Maza Zavala, "Hacia un programa de transición" in *Una estrategia para Venezuela*, ed. Elías Eljuri (Caracas: IIES-FACES-UCV y Academia Nacional de Ciencias Económicas, 1990), 33–44; Córdova, "Lineamientos de política económica de largo plazo," 45–63; Baptista, *El relevo del capitalismo rentístico.*
23. Baptista, *El relevo del capitalismo rentístico*, 295.
24. Maza Zavala, "Hacia un programa de transición," 35.
25. Carlos Mendoza Pottellá, "Venezuela, petróleo y transición energética," *Petróleo Venezolano* (January 7, 2022). In 1970, the country achieved its peak production of 3,758,333 barrels per day (b/d), followed by a decline that reached its lowest point in 1985 at 1,564,000 b/d. Later in 2005, there was a rebound leading to a second peak, although it was lower than the levels experienced in the 1970s, reaching 3,067,000 b/d. From that point onward, there was a progressive and systematic decrease in national oil production, culminating in the oil collapse of 2019. This collapse was the result of internal factors combined with the sanctions imposed by the US Department of State, which carried significant weight.
26. Córdova, "Crisis económica Venezolana."
27. Córdova, "Crisis económica Venezolana," 440.
28. Edgardo Lander, *Crisis civilizatoria: Experiencias de los gobiernos progresistas y debates en la izquierda latinoamericana* (Guadalajara: CALAS, 2019).
29. Hugo Chávez's proposal to transform Venezuela in 1996, the Economic Transition Program 1999–2000, Economic Program 2001, Development Plan 2001–7, Homeland Plan 2007–13.
30. Plan de la Patria, 18.
31. Remember that Venezuela was a founding member of OPEC.
32. Carlos Mendoza Pottellá, "Del debate petrolero," *Petróleo Venezolano* (blog), December 18, 2020.
33. Disregarding the crucial discussion and the historical impact associated with "Socialism of the 20th century."
34. General Lines of the National Economic and Social Development Plan 2007–2013, 40.

35. General Lines of the National Economic and Social Development Plan 2007–2013, 41.
36. These figures are according to OPEC.
37. Wilmer Torrealba and Oly Millán, "La crisis económica venezolana en el contexto del Covid-19," *Cuadernos del Cendes*, no. 106 (2021): 80.
38. Oly Millán, "Desfalco a la nación y quebrantamiento a la dignidad," *Provea*, March 11, 2019.
39. Sergio Sáez, "Los Informes financieros de la PDVSA de Ramírez," in *¿Quién Destruyó PDVSA?*, ed. Sergio Sáez and Gustavo Coronel Sánchez (Caracas: Dahbar, 2021), 47–85.
40. This reorganization was marked by internal conflicts within the PSUV and the departure of some of Chávez's longtime ministers.
41. For the year 2013, international reserves stood at $21.4 billion (see table 2.1 in annex).
42. It is prohibited to use US dollars to issue new debt. The sanctions have been escalated to the extent of prohibiting any commercial negotiations with Venezuelan state institutions, which has had an impact on the commercial activities of PDVSA (the national oil company) and the financial operations of the Central Bank of Venezuela.
43. The G4 is made up of four right-wing opposition groups: Primero Justicia, Voluntad Popular, Acción Democrática, and Un Nuevo Tiempo.
44. By the end of 2015, the outgoing National Assembly (AN) altered the composition of the Supreme Court of Justice (TSJ) to establish control over it. Subsequently, in 2016, this newly constituted TSJ issued a ruling declaring the new AN in a state of "contempt." This decision effectively granted the Maduro government the authority to govern without requiring congressional approval.
45. We should remember the statements made by the Lima Group and the alleged entry of "humanitarian aid" across the border with Colombia in April 2019, whose strategy was to produce a fracture within the Bolivarian National Armed Forces.
46. Between January 14, 2016, and May 14, 2020, the Executive issued a total of twenty-seven decrees under this State of Exception and Economic Emergency.
47. In 2016 the Arco Minero del Orinoco National Strategic Developmental Zone was established through Decree 2248.
48. Gobierno Bolivariano de Venezuela, "Presidente Nicolás Maduro aprobó entrega de una mina de oro 'Productiva a cada Gobernación Bolivariana,'" *Ministerio del Poder Popular de Desarrollo Minero Ecológico*, October 16, 2019.
49. A group of Venezuelans publicly raised concerns and denounced the "new Oil Opening" on October 4, 2022. They presented an alternative proposal as an approach to address these issues. The PDVSA Executive Directorate of Planning presented a proposal for the restructuring of PDVSA in April 2020. PDVSA document: Venezuela a safe investment.
50. To not exceed 1.5 degrees Celsius; a goal that does not seem to be achievable.
51. Published in the *Extraordinary Official Gazette* 6,710 on the 20th of July, 2022.
52. Oly Millán, "¿Qué tiene de 'Especial' la Ley Orgánica de las Zonas Económicas Especiales?," *Aporrea*, September 6, 2022.

53. As defined in the preamble of the Constitution of the Bolivarian Republic of Venezuela. Karl Polanyi said that it is not true that the market system and intervention are not mutually exclusive terms.
54. This is alluding to one of the protagonists of the novel *Conversations in the Cathedral* by Peruvian writer Mario Vargas Llosa.

Chapter 3: A Comparative Analysis of the Governments of Hugo Chávez and Nicolás Maduro

1. Margarita López Maya, "Venezuela: El impacto de sus reformas políticas durante el lapso crítico de 1989–1993," *Cuadernos del Cendes*, no. 26, (May–August 1994): 32; Gastón Carvallo and Margarita López Maya, "Crisis en el sistema político venezolano," *Cuadernos del Cendes*, no. 10, Universidad Central de Venezuela, Caracas (1989): 49.
2. Gonzalo Barrios-Ferrer, "Los sucesos del 27 y 28 de febrero de 1989: Una aproximación histórico-política," *Argos no. 11, Revista de la División de Ciencias Sociales de la Universidad Simón Bolívar*, Caracas (1990): 55; Luis Pedro España, "Un estallido social no esperado," *Revista SIC*, no. 513, Centro Gumilla (April 1989): 118–19; Elio Colmenarez, *La insurrección de febrero* (Caracas: Ediciones La Chispa, 1989).
3. A power bloc made up of the AD and COPEI parties, the military high command, the business elite grouped in Fedecámaras, the church hierarchy, the mass media, and the trade union bureaucracy of the CTV (Confederación de Trabajadores de Venezuela). The formation of this power bloc is considered by historians to be based on the Punto Fijo Pact, signed in October 1958 by the AD, COPEI, and Democratic Republican Union (URD) parties. The governments between 1959 and 1999 are called "Punto Fijo" governments.
4. Edgardo Lander, "Comentarios sobre el acuerdo con la Gold Reserve," *Aporrea*, August 16, 2016. In 1979 the social-Christian government of Luis Herrera Campins (1979–84) timidly applied some neoliberal measures, such as price liberalization. But the strong social protest presented made him give up after a few weeks.
5. The neoliberal economic plan applied by Rafael Caldera as of 1996 was called "Venezuela Agenda."
6. Steve Ellner, "Las reformas neoliberales y la crisis política venezolana, 1989–1999: Antecedentes de la llegada de Hugo Chávez al poder," *Diez años de revolución en Venezuela: Historia, balance y perspectivas (1999–2009)* (Buenos Aires: Editorial Maipue, 2009), 42.
7. Ibsen Martínez, "Chávez, Maduro y la Tercera Vía," *El País*, August 20, 2018.
8. Javier Biardeau, "Hugo Chávez y la Declaración del 'Socialismo' en el Foro Social de Porto Alegre (2005)," *Aporrea*, June 22, 2015.
9. Rubén Alayón, *La rebelión latinoamericana a la globalización neoliberal* (Caracas: Instituto de Altos Estudios "Pedro Gual," 2007), 181.
10. Alayón, *La rebelión latinoamericana*, 184.
11. Eric Toussaint, "Latinoamérica: En pro de una integración regional y una desvinculación parcial del mercado capitalista mundial," *Respuestas del Sur a la crisis económica mundial* (Caracas: Centro Internacional Miranda, 2009), 255; Juan Pablo Mateo Tomé, "La evolución de los salarios en Venezuela," *Boletín Económico de Información Comercial Española*, no. 2994 (2010): 44. The Caldera government

privatized the Siderurgica del Orinoco, CANTV (the national telephone company), and the airline Aeropostal. It sold to the private sector the banks that had gone bankrupt and had been under state control since the banking crisis of 1994.

12. Pedro Rodríguez Rojas, "Venezuela: Del neoliberalismo al socialismo del siglo XXI," *Revista Política y Cultura*, no. 34 (2010): 195.
13. Roberto López Sánchez, "El movimiento de trabajadores durante el gobierno de Hugo Chávez (1999–2012)," *Revista Notas Históricas y Geográficas*, no. 19 (September–December 2017): 34.
14. In the main Western capitalist countries, labor rights do not have constitutional status but appear in specific laws and regulations. Venezuela was one of the first countries, after Mexico (Constitution of Querétaro 1917), to constitutionally endorse the fundamental rights of the working class, with the constitution that emerged from the Constituent Assembly of 1947.
15. Orlando Chirino, *Orlando Chirino responde* (Caracas: Equipo Editorial Aporrea, 2005).
16. López Sánchez, "El movimiento de trabajadores," 34–50.
17. Roberto López Sánchez and Carmen Alicia Hernández, "Control obrero y consejos de trabajadores, nuevas formas de gestión productiva," *Revista Opción* 32, no. 80 (2016): 184–214.
18. López Sánchez and Hernández, "Control obrero y consejos de trabajadores," 184.
19. Alexis Adarfio, "El control obrero en el nuevo modelo productivo," *Revista Comuna*, no. 3 (2011): 43.
20. Carlos Carcione, "Experiencias de Democracia Obrera en la Venezuela Bolivariana," *Revista Comuna*, no. 2 (2010): 56.
21. National Institute for Prevention, Health and Safety at Work.
22. Roberto López Sánchez, *El movimiento de trabajadores en Venezuela durante la revolución bolivariana: 1999–2012* (Caracas: Fundación Editorial El perro y la rana, 2017), 201.
23. The main point, which had been a central element of Chávez's programmatic discourse during the 1998 election campaign, was the reinstatement of the retroactive calculation for the payment of seniority (payment of social benefits on the basis of the last salary). In addition, double compensation in the case of unjustified dismissal was reinstated.
24. Organic Law of Labor and Workers; López Sánchez, *El movimiento de trabajadores*, 234.
25. Roberto López Sánchez, "El movimiento de trabajadores durante el gobierno de Hugo Chávez (1999–2012)," *Revista Notas Históricas y Geográficas*, no. 19 (September–December 2017): 35.
26. Carlos Carcione, "Lo que fue privatizado, nacionalícese," *Revista Comuna*, no. 1 (2009): 14.
27. Compañía Anónima Nacional Teléfonos de Venezuela (National Telephone Company of Venezuela).
28. It had been privatized during the second government of Rafael Caldera in the 1990s.
29. Rita Giacalone, "Privatización del acero e internacionalizacion de empresas en Argentina, México y Venezuela," *Iberoamericana. Nordic Journal of Latin American*

and Caribbean Studies XXXIII, no. 2 (2003): 53–87. The Amazonia Consortium, in which the Techint Group of Argentina held a majority stake. Other companies participating in the consortium were Siderar (Argentina), Tamsa (Mexico), Hylsa (Mexico), Sivensa (Venezuela), and Usiminas (Brazil).

30. Stalin Pérez Borges et al., "La nacionalización de Sidor," *Revista Comuna*, no. 1 (2009): 24.
31. Comisión de Sistematización, "Sistematización del Balance del Plan Guayana Socialista," *Aporrea*, October 23, 2013, https://www.aporrea.org/trabajadores/a175676.html.
32. Pérez Borges et al., "La nacionalización de Sidor," 64. The trade union most closely aligned with the anti-Chávez government bureaucracy throughout the Chávez-Maduro period was the FSBT, or FBT (Fuerza Socialista Bolivariana de Trabajadores), which followed in the steps of the old CTV and the Trade Union Bureau of Acción Democrática.
33. Carlos Carcione and Martin Poliak, "El Plan Guayana Socialista en la encrucijada," *Revista Comuna*, no. 3 (2010): 58.
34. Data provided by Andrés Izarra, Minister of Communication under President Chávez.
35. "Gobierno ofrece 350 empresas públicas al capital privado nacional para que invierta y asuma su gestion," *Banca y Negocios*, November 7, 2024.
36. Juan Pablo Mateo Tomé, "La evolución de los salarios en Venezuela," *Boletín Económico de Información Comercial Española*, no. 2994 (August 1–15, 2010): 43–57.
37. Manuel Sutherland, "Venezuela es el cuarto salario más bajo del mundo, luego de 60 aumentos: ilusión monetaria," *Politikaucab*, April 4, 2023.
38. Néstor Kirchner (Argentina), Luiz Inácio Lula da Silva (Brazil), and Tabaré Vásquez (Uruguay); J. M. Karg and A. Lewitt, "Del No al ALCA a Unasur: Diez años después de Mar del Plata," *Revista Idelcoop*, no. 217 (November 2015): 193–98.
39. Impeached by the legislative branch in her second presidential term.
40. Impeached by the legislative branch in 2012.
41. Overthrown by a military coup in 2009.
42. The seminar "Intellectuals, Democracy, and Socialism" was held in June 2009 at the Miranda International Center in Caracas.
43. "Intelectuales, democracia y socialismo," *Comuna*, no. 0 (June 2009). A compilation of thirty-one interventions and twenty-three articles from the debate seminar held at the Centro Internacional Miranda.
44. Antonio García Romero, "La contrarrevolución obrera: FBT," *Aporrea*, June 20, 2011; Alcides Rivero, "La coherencia de la FBT en Guayana," *Aporrea*, November 19, 2010.
45. Johnny Alarcón Puentes, "Maduro y su 'socialismo' neoliberal," *Aporrea*, October 30, 2017; Marcos Luna, "El paquetazo de Moreno nos distrae del paquetazo de Maduro," *Aporrea*, October 11, 2019; Javier Vivas Santana, "Maduro aplica disimulado y tardío plan de ajuste neoliberal y apuran venta de Pdvsa a chinos y rusos," *Aporrea*, June 5, 2019; Manuel Sutherland, "Venezuela: Salario Cero," *Aporrea*, May 2, 2020. Maduro was a union activist in the Caracas Metro, where he worked as a bus driver in the 1980s. In the dispute staged within the Chavista trade union forces from 2003 onward, the FBT tendency prevailed, thanks to the

backing given by Chávez to its main leader, Nicolás Maduro. The formation of the Central Bolivariana Socialista de Trabajadores (CBST) in November 2011 took place under almost total control of the FSBT, with the more radical tendencies being completely displaced. Maduro's first militancy was in the Socialist League party, a Marxist-Leninist organization that existed from the 1970s until its integration into the PSUV when the latter was formed by Chávez in 2007. The Socialist League sent Maduro to Cuba sometime in the 1980s for political training.

46. Ángel Bermúdez, "Cómo Venezuela pasó de la bonanza petrolera a la emergencia económica," *BBC Mundo*, February 25, 2016; Leonardo Vera, "¿Cómo explicar la catástrofe económica venezolana?," *Revista Nueva Sociedad*, no. 274 (2018).
47. Tomás Straka, "20 años de P: El quiebre del 'estado mágico,'" *Revista Nueva Sociedad*, no. 280 (March–April 2019).
48. Manuel Sutherland, "¿Nicolás Maduro tiene un plan? 'Socialismo,' hiperinflación y regresión social," *Nueva Sociedad*, August 2018.
49. Leonardo Vera, "¿Cómo explicar la catástrofe económica venezolana?," *Revista Nueva Sociedad*, no. 274 (2018).
50. Mario Ayala, "Estructura y coyuntura en la crisis venezolana," *Cuadernos de Coyuntura*, no 4 (2019): 23.
51. Edgardo Lander, "Comentarios sobre el acuerdo con la Gold Reserve," *Aporrea*, August 16, 2016.
52. El Estímulo, "Venezuela indemnizará a Gold Reserve con $769 millones por expropiación," *Redacción El Estímulo*, August 9, 2016; "Venezuela indemnizará a Gold Reserve por $759 millones y conformará empresa mixta tras acuerdo del Arco Minero," *Aporrea*, August 8, 2016. During the 1998 election campaign, Chávez emphasized that such clauses in the Oil Opening contracts (allowing disputes to be arbitrated in foreign courts) were tantamount to an act of treason. Later, he ignored the concession made by the Caldera government to the Canadian mining company, Gold Reserve, and refused to pay ICSID compensation when the company appealed to the tribunal. Maduro, acting in reverse, contracted again with Gold Reserve and paid the compensation that Chávez had refused.
53. Edgardo Lander, "Comentarios sobre el acuerdo con la Gold Reserve," *Aporrea*, August 16, 2016.
54. Manuel Sutherland, "Venezuela: Salario Cero," *Aporrea*, May 2, 2020.
55. Fapuv, "Significado y alcance de la recuperación del salario y la seguridad social de los profesores universitarios de Venezuela," *Federación de Asociaciones de Profesores Universitarios de Venezuela*, June 10, 2020.
56. Javier Biardeau, "Estructura de repetición del rentismo y conciencia sumisa-enajenada," *Aporrea*, June 14, 2020. The minimum wage in Venezuela was, as of July 4, 2020, 400,000 Bs. per month. At the official exchange rate of 202,000 bolivars to the dollar, this is equivalent to US$1.98 per month. By March of 2022, the minimum wage was 7 bolivars per month, the equivalent of US$1.59 per month. In August of 2023, the minimum wage is 130 bolivars per month, the equivalent of US$4.12 per month.
57. "Trabajadores marcharon en Caracas contra el plan de ajuste de Maduro y los empresarios," *La Izquierda Diario*, November 28, 2018.

58. Orlando Chirino, "El memorándum 2792 es una reforma laboral antiobrera y reaccionaria," *Deslinde*, June 21, 2019.
59. "Trabajadores marcharon en Caracas."
60. "Conozca el precio en dólares que impuso el gobierno a 27 productos regulados," *Aporrea*, April 27, 2020.
61. Omar Vásquez Heredia, "Maduro anunció privatización y liberalización de facto del mercado interno de gasolina," *Aporrea*, June 1, 2020.
62. Ministerio del Trabajo, "Memorando-circular no. 2792. Lineamientos para ser implementados en las negociaciones colectivas de trabajo en el marco del programa de recuperación, crecimiento y prosperidad económica," *La Izquierda Diario*, 2018.
63. Transparencia Venezuela, "Clap llega a su cuarto aniversario marcado por la corrupción y la improvisación," Transparencia Venezuela, April 4, 2020.
64. Aula Abierta, "Carnet de la Patria: Discriminación para el control político," Aula Abierta, August 31, 2018. Food box provided by the government to workers and families through the Local Supply and Production Committees (Comités Locales de Abastecimiento y Producción). In major cities in the province, CLAPs arrive about twice a year. The vouchers distributed through the carnet de la patria are not regular in their delivery, nor do they have fixed amounts. They do not provide any kind of stability to working families. Generally, the amount is between $1 and $2. A carnet holder can go several months without receiving a bonus.
65. Gustavo Márquez Marín, "El gobierno de Maduro construye un Régimen Autoritario Neoliberal Periférico y Extractivista Ampliado," *Aporrea*, July 20, 2021. The justification for passing this law has been the economic sanctions imposed by the US government against Venezuela.
66. Márquez, "El Ggobierno de Maduro."
67. Márquez, "El gobierno de Maduro."
68. "Detienen al dirigente sindical Rubén González regresando de la marcha convocada por la Intersectorial de Trabajadores," *La Izquierda Diario*, November 29, 2018; "Luego de 8 días presos, fueron liberados los tres sindicalistas de Sucre," *Crónica Uno*, February 7, 2020; Provea, "Provea reclamó libertad para trabajadores petroleros presos," *El Nacional*, August 8, 2021.
69. Pascualina Curcio, "La economía: Números imposibles de manipular y no para insultar," *Diario Ultimas Noticias*, July 27, 2020. It only goes to 2017 because that is the last year in which the Central Bank of Venezuela (BCV) published statistics.
70. Curcio, "La economia."
71. Curcio, "La economia."
72. Caritas Venezuela, "Nutrición infantil y seguridad alimentaria," *Caritas Venezuela*, April 2020; Plataforma Ciudadana en Defensa de la Constitución, "Acuerdo pre-electoral para atender la emergencia social," *Aporrea*, July 2, 2020.
73. Anti-imperialist in relation to the West but aligned with China and Russia, which, in economic terms, is not distanced from the neoliberal philosophy. In fact, some analysts such as Hernández Parra (2020) point to China as the new model that inspires the International Monetary Fund.

Chapter 4: The Venezuelan Workers' Movement During the Bolivarian Process

1. Roberto López Sánchez and Carmen Alicia Hernández Rodríguez, "Trayectoria del movimiento de trabajadores en un siglo de historia de Venezuela," *RIHALC. Red Intercátedras de Historia de América Latina Contemporánea* 2, no. 4 (2016): 41.
2. Constitution of the Bolivarian Republic of Venezuela; Organic Law of Work and Workers.
3. The rights outlined in this article enhance an expansive interpretation of the "working class." Notably, it emphasizes gender equality in the access to employment opportunities, while also recognizing homemakers as "workers."
4. The labor reforms initiated by the International Monetary Fund across Latin America since the late 1970s have consistently aimed at curtailing workers' rights, leading to the relinquishment of long-standing accomplishments. This curtailment of labor rights is presently being implemented in European Union nations, England, and the United States as well. The current Maduro administration has disregarded these legal advancements, implementing labor flexibility reminiscent of the methods advocated by the IMF.
5. In the past ten years, the labor reform in Europe has pursued the objective of extending the duration of the workday in various countries, such as Portugal, where it has been proposed to add thirty minutes to the workday.
6. Neoliberal reforms often disregard collective agreements, undermine union structures, and advocate for individual contracts between employees and employers, thereby disrupting the bargaining power that the labor movement had built through its historical struggles in the nineteenth and twentieth centuries.
7. Federation of Chambers of Commerce, the main employer union in Venezuela.
8. YVKE Mundial, "Denuncian Corrupción en la CTV," *Aporrea*, March 13, 2012.
9. Ultimas Noticias, "En la UNETE la lucha por la presidencia es peleando," *Aporrea*, March 12, 2006. United Revolutionary and Autonomous Class-Struggle (C-CURA), led at that time (2006) principally by Orlando Chirino and Stalin Pérez Borges. Pérez Borges later contributed to the formation of Marea Socialista. CTR (Collective of Workers in Revolution).
10. Siderúrgica del Orinoco (SIDOR) is the largest Venezuelan steel corporation.
11. When SIDOR was privatized in 1997 under President Rafael Caldera, 60 percent of its stake went to the Argentine company Ternium.
12. Roberto López Sánchez, "La renacionalización de Sidor es un triunfo de la clase trabajadora contra la burguesía internacional y la derecha endógena," *Aporrea*, April 10, 2008.
13. Roberto López Sánchez and Carmen Alicia Hernández Rodríguez, "Control obrero y consejos de trabajadores, nuevas formas de gestión productiva," *Revista Opción* 32, no. 80 (Agosto 2016): 197.
14. Alexis Adarfio, "El control obrero en el nuevo modelo productivo," *Revista Comuna*, no. 3 (2011): 52.
15. Carlos Carcione, "Experiencias de Democracia Obrera en la Venezuela Bolivariana," *Revista Comuna*, no. 2 (2010): 70.

16. Norton Rose Fulbright, *La Ley Constitucional de los Consejos Productivos de Trabajadores*, www.nortonrosefulbright.com/-/media/files/nrf/nrfweb/imported/la---ley-constitucional-de-los-consejos-productivos-de-trabajadores.pdf?la=es-es.
17. Milton D'Leon, "Ajuste en toda la línea: El neoliberalismo extremo de Maduro y los mitos sobre la 'recuperación económica,'" *La Izquierda Diario*, September 21, 2022.
18. "Memorando oficial 2792 del Ministerio del Trabajo," Las Comadres Púrpuras, September 2019.
19. "Instructivo de la Onapre violenta media docena de disposiciones constitucionales," editorial, *Acceso a la Justicia*, August 23, 2022.
20. "Los venezolanos necesitan 118 salarios mínimos para cubrir gastos de alimentos, dice ONG," editorial, *La Economista*, August 21, 2023.
21. "Venezuela registra una inflación anual de casi 430 %," editorial, *DW*, June 7, 2023.
22. Emiliano Terán Mantonvani, "Zonas Económicas Especiales y neoliberalización: Una alerta ante la encrucijada histórica venezolana," *Observatorio de Ecología Política de Venezuela*, August 8, 2022.
23. Roberto López Sánchez, "Maduro y su plan neoliberal: Traidores siempre," *Aporrea*, August 7, 2022.
24. "Venezuela: Condenan a seis sindicalistas a 16 años de cárcel," editorial, *DW*, August 8, 2023. Those sentenced to sixteen years in prison include Reynaldo Cortés, Alonso Meléndez, Alcides Bracho, Néstor Astudillo, Gabriel Blanco, and Emilio Negrín. All of them are labor activists and affiliated with opposition parties. These detained workers were released in December 2023, as a result of the Barbados Agreements between the Maduro government and opposition sectors.
25. Reynaldo Mozo Zambrano, "Trabajadores de Sidor detenidos en Bolívar fueron imputados y enviados a Caracas," *Efecto Cocuyo*, June 13, 2023.
26. Brayan Silva, "Sector construcción denuncia que exdirector de la DGCIM en Bolívar estaría detrás de la detención de sindicalista," *NTA*, August 3, 2023.
27. Bianile Rivas, "Víctor Venegas, líder sindical detenido: 29 anos al servicio del magisterio," *El Pitazo*, January 17, 2024.
28. "Excarcelan al sindicalista Víctor Venegas tras casi dos meses detenido," editorial, *Tal Cual*, March 11, 2024.
29. Bolivarian Republic of Venezuela, "Constitución de la República Bolivariana de Venezuela, December 1999–March 2000," amendment no. 1, *Gaceta Oficial*, no. 5,908.
30. The National Coordination of the National Committee for Conflict-Workers in Struggle was initially made up of: CNProfesores, APUCV, CUTV, SINATRA/UCV, FUTPV, SITRALUMINA Bolívar, Col. Enfermería DC, FVM, UNETE, FADESS, ASOCEJUPRC, FENATEV, FORDISI, Comité Pensionados del IVSS, FAPUV, Col. Enfermería Barinas, AEUC Carabobo, Corpoelec Lara, APUNELLARG Guárico, Sindicato CANTV Mérida, SITRAENSEÑANZA DC Caracas, Central ASI, UDSE Caracas, USB La Guaira, SITRAIUT Sucre, DDHH CTV, CCURA, FETRASINED Monagas, CTL Miranda, Coalición Magisterio Yaracuy, SOLUZ Zulia, Colectivo 2 de Junio Caracas, CTL Aragua, CTL Aragua, Trab. del Campo Guárico, SUNEP Amazonas, Sirtrasalud Caracas,

Fetracarabobo, FETRASINED, Zulia, Sindicato Minero, Comité Conflicto Padres y representantes Trujillo, UDO Sucre, SUTICEZ Zulia, Palabra Obrera, ATAUNEG Guárico, CAIT, UPTOS Sucre, FENAJUPV, Sindicato Obreros Alcaldía Caracas, and others who have subsequently been designated.

31. "Constituido el Comité Nacional de Conflicto y convocada Protesta Nacional para el 27 de Marzo. Comunicado 01 de la Asamblea Nacional de Trabajadores en Lucha," editorial, *Aporrea*, March 21, 2023.

Chapter 5: US Sanctions as a Factor Exacerbating the Crisis and Stagnation of the Venezuelan Economy

1. Economic Commission for Latin America and the Caribbean (ECLAC), *Balance Preliminar de las Economías de América Latina y el Caribe* (Santiago, Chile: ECLAC, 2021).
2. ECLAC, *Balance Preliminar de las Economías de América Latina y el Caribe* (Santiago, Chile: ECLAC, 2023).
3. Dany Bahar et al., *Impact of the 2017 Sanctions on Venezuela: Revisiting the Evidence* (Global Economy and Development, 2019), 9.
4. Francisco Rodríguez, *Sanciones, Política Económica y la Crisis Venezolana* (Fourth Freedom Forum, 2022), 33.
5. ANOVA, "Impacto de las Sanciones Financieras Internacionales contra Venezuela: Nueva Evidencia," ANOVA *Policy Research* 3, no. 1 (2021).
6. Manuel Sutherland, "Impacto y naturaleza real de las sanciones económicas impuestas a Venezuela," *Provea* (2019): 26.
7. Sutherland, "Impacto y naturaleza real," 22.
8. Central Bank of Venezuela: Exports and Imports of Goods and Services According to Sectors.
9. Central Bank of Venezuela: International Investment Position.
10. Central Bank of Venezuela: International Reserves.
11. PDVSA, Consolidated Financial Statements, December 31, 2007, and 2006; with the Report of the Independent Public Accountants, PDVSA, 2013. Consolidated Financial Statements December 31, 2013, 2012, and 2011; with the Report of the Independent Public Accountants.
12. Central Bank of Venezuela: External Debt.
13. PDVSA, Consolidated Financial Statements, December 31, 2016; with the Report of the Independent Public Accountants.
14. ECLAC, *Balance Preliminar de las Economías de América Latina y el Caribe* (Santiago: ECLAC, 2023); Central Bank of Venezuela: National Consumer Price Index.
15. Central Bank of Venezuela: Exports and Imports of Goods and Services According to Sectors.
16. ECLAC, *Balance Preliminar de las Economías de América Latina y el Caribe* (Santiago: ECLAC, 2023).
17. Central Bank of Venezuela: Exports and Imports of Goods and Services According to Sectors; OPEC, *Annual Statistical Bulletin* (Vienna: OPEC, 2018).
18. PDVSA, Consolidated Financial Statements, December 31, 2013, 2012, and 2011; with the Report of the Independent Public Accountants; PDVSA, Consolidated

Financial Statements, December 31, 2016; with the Report of the Independent Public Accountants.

19. Central Bank of Venezuela: External Debt.
20. Omar Vázquez Heredia, "La situación económica de Venezuela en el período 2014–2018 y disputa intellectual: Socialismo, guerra económica o ajuste económico," *OLAL*, no. 3 (January–June 2019).
21. Central Bank of Venezuela: Consolidated Accounts of the Nation.
22. ENCOVI, "Encuesta Nacional de Condiciones de Vida 2016," *UCAB-UCV-USB* (2016).
23. Food and Agriculture Organization (FAO), "Panorama de la seguridad alimentaria y nutricional en América Latina y el Caribe 2017," *FAO-OPS* (2017).
24. Anna Ayuso and Sussane Gratuis, "Sanciones como instrumentos de coerción: ¿Cuán similares son las políticas de Estados Unidos y la Unión Europea hacia Venezuela?," in *Venezuela en la encrucijada: Radiografía de un colapso*, ed. Susanne Gratius and José Manuel Puente (UCAB, 2020).
25. Ayuso and Gratius, "Sanciones como instrumentos de coerción"; Alena Dohaun, "Report of the Special Rapporteur on the Negative Impact of Unilateral Coercive Measures on the Enjoyment of Human Rights" (UN Human Rights Council, 2021).
26. Omar Vázquez Heredia, "La cuestión chavista: Estado extractivista y nación petrolera," *Grupo de investigación en ciencias sociales e historia* (2018).
27. Ayuso and Gratius, "Sanciones como instrumentos de coerción"; Sutherland, "Impacto y naturaleza real."
28. Dohaun, "Report of the Special Rapporteur."
29. Sutherland, "Impacto y naturaleza real."
30. US Department of the Treasury, *Guidance to Address Illicit Shipping Practices and Sanctions Evasion* (US Department of the Treasury, May 2020).
31. Ayuso and Gratius, "Sanciones como instrumentos de coerción."
32. Rodríguez, *Sanciones*.
33. Rodríguez, *Sanciones*.
34. Luis Oliveros, *Impacto de las sanciones financieras y petroleras sobre la economía venezolana* (Washington, DC: Washington Office on Latin America, 2020).
35. OPEC, *Annual Statistical Bulletin* (Vienna: OPEC, 2012); OPEC, *Annual Statistical Bulletin* (Vienna: OPEC, 2021.)
36. OPEC, *Annual Statistical Bulletin* (Vienna: OPEC, 2021.)
37. OPEC, *Annual Statistical Bulletin* (Vienna: OPEC, 2021.)
38. Oliveros, "Impacto de las sanciones financieras."
39. Rodríguez, *Sanciones*.
40. Rodríguez, *Sanciones*.
41. ECLAC, Balance Preliminar de las Economías de América Latina y el Caribe (Santiago, Chile: ECLAC, 2023).
42. ENCOVI, "Encuesta Nacional de Condiciones de Vida 2021," *UCAB-UCV-USB* (2016).
43. FAO, "Panorama."

44. Benedicte Bull, Rosales Antulio, and Manuel Sutherland, "Venezuela: Lujo, desigualdades y 'capitalismo bodegonero,'" *Nueva Sociedad*, no. 298 (2022). A bodegón is a high-end store that sells overpriced imported goods. More on bodegónes in chapter 6.
45. VenAmCham, "Perspectivas económicas marcó el camino para enfrentar este año," VenAmCham, March 2023.
46. "Chevron activa nueva fase de operaciones en su plan de recuperación de deuda en Venezuela," editorial, *Tal Cual*, May 10, 2023.

Chapter 6: Bureaucracy and Lumpen Capitalist Management in the Maduro Government

1. Andre Gunder Frank, *Lumpen-burguesía: Lumpen-desarrollo: Dependencia, clase y política en Latinoamérica* (Buenos Aires: Ediciones Periferia, 1973)
2. Jorge Giordani, "Testimonio y responsabilidad ante la historia," *Aporrea*, June 18, 2014; "Presidenta del BCV: Parte de los $59.000 millones entregados en 2012 fueron a 'empresas de maletín," editorial, *Aporrea*/AVN, May 24, 2013; "A sólo tres meses de ser nombrada, Edmée Betancourt es reemplazada por Eudomar Tovar en la presidencia del BCV," editorial, *Aporrea*, August 13, 2013.
3. Luis Enrique Gavazut Bianco, "Dólares de maletín, empresas extranjeras y modelo económico socialista," *Aporrea*, March 24, 2014.
4. Ministro Miguel Rodríguez, "Fuga de divisas vía empresas de maletín en 40%," *Aporrea*, December 13, 2013.
5. Equipo de Investigación de Marea Socialista, "Sinfonía de un Desfalco a la Nación: Tocata y fuga . . . de Capitales," *Aporrea*, August, 9, 2014.
6. Carlos Carcione, "Corrupción en PDVSA: Apenas la punta de un iceberg. Recordando qué pasó con los dólares petroleros de Venezuela," *Aporrea*, September 5, 2017.
7. "Marea Socialista solicita derecho de palabra ante la AN para denunciar desfalco a la nación," editorial, *Aporrea*, February 25, 2016.
8. Gonzalo Gómez Freire, "Venezuela 2008: Balance del proceso revolucionario," *Aporrea*, December 8, 2008.
9. Wilmar Castro Soteldo, "Cultivando Patria," YouTube, 15:52, October 25, 2018.
10. Joseph Poliszuk and Antonio María Delgado, "La revolución también termina en Miami," *Armandoinfo*, October 30, 2022.
11. "Sunbiz – Division of Corporations – Florida Department of State," Florida Department of State.
12. Transparencia Venezuela, "IPC 2019: Venezuela es el país más corrupto en América y el Caribe," Transparencia Venezuela, January 23, 2020.
13. "Estos son los 10 escándalos de corrupción que sacudieron a Venezuela en 2017," editorial, *El Estimulo*, June 4, 2018; Ángel Bermúdez, "Qué pasa con los millones de dólares de la corrupción en Venezuela decomisados en EE.UU," *BBC News Mundo*, May 20, 2021; Ramón Cardozo Álvarez, "Gran Corrupción' e impunidad continuada en Venezuela," *DW*, February 6, 2023.
14. Radio Fe Y Alegria, "Transparencia Venezuela: 42 mil millones desfalcados en PDVSA: '¿Para qué quieren tanto dinero?" *Aporrea*, March 24, 2023.

15. "Transparencia Venezuela: Economías ilícitas al amparo de la corrupción," editorial, Transparencia Venezuela, June 2022.
16. Marea Socialista, "Comunicado de Marea Socialista: Nuestras denuncias, exigencias y propuestas de lucha. Lancemos una marea obrera y popular contra la corrupción," *Aporrea*, March 26, 2023; Florantonia Singer, "Las economías ilícitas producen un quinto del PIB de Venezuela," *El País*, September 10, 2022; "Actividades ilícitas' generaron 21,74% del PIB de Venezuela en 2021, según informe," editorial, *Banca y Negocios*, July 27, 2022; Transparencia Venezuela, "Economias ilicitas en venezuela: una renta creciente repartida entre aliados," Transparencia Venezuela, September 2023.
17. Clark Gasciogne, "Reporte de Global Financial Integrity 2008–2017: Nueva entrada del blog de GFI revela que Venezuela perdió más de US$33 mil millones en salidas ilícitas en 2008," *Global Financial Integrity*, October 11, 2010.
18. Unidad de Inteligencia de The Economist, "El Índice del Entorno Global del Comercio Ilícito," *Economist*, 2018.
19. Transparencia Venezuela, "Más de USD 9.400 millones al año dejan las economías ilícitas en Venezuela," Transparencia Venezuela, June 26, 2022.
20. Transparencia Venezuela, "Economías ilícitas al amparo de la corrupción: Entre el contrabando de oro, drogas, gasolina y la extorsión en los puertos," Transparencia Venezuela, June 2022.
21. Transparencia Venezuela, "Economías ilícitas."
22. Transparencia Venezuela, "Economías ilícitas."
23. Transparencia Venezuela, "Economías ilícitas bajo el manto de la impunidad: Entorno, caracterización, tecnología, impacto regional y otros ilícitos," Transparencia Venezuela, July 2023.
24. "Corrupción en Venezuela durante la Revolución bolivariana," Wikimedia Foundation, https://es.wikipedia.org/wiki/Corrupci%C3%B3n_en_Venezuela_durante_la_Revoluci%C3%B3n_bolivariana#cite_note-8.
25. ICIJ, "Los paraísos fiscales de políticos y multimillonarios quedan al descubierto en los Pandora Papers," *Armandoinfo*, October 3, 2021.
26. Mission Mercal, launched in 2003 under Chávez, was a state-run program that provided subsidized food and basic goods through a nationwide chain of stores. Abasto Bicentenario was another state-run food program which operated from 2010 to 2019.
27. Cecilia Barría, "Venezuela no es un país socialista. Es un país con una economía capitalista de bodegones," *BBC News Mundo*, February 7, 2022; Benedicte Bull, Antulio Rosales, and Manuel Sutherland, "Venezuela: de la crisis económica al capitalismo elitista bodegonero," *Revista Nueva Sociedad*, no. 298 (March–April 2022).
28. "Maduro se rinde y abre la puerta a privatizar el sector petrolero tras 45 años de monopolio de PDVSA," *El Economista / Bloomberg*, March 20, 2021.
29. Rafael Ramírez Carreño, "La privatización de PDVSA: El gran negocio de Maduro y el peor error para Venezuela," *Aporrea*, February 2, 2020.
30. Carreño, "La privatización de PDVSA."
31. Carreño, "La privatización de PDVSA."

32. La Izquierda Diario, "Trabajadores de Petropiar: 'Chevron nos está desmejorando, estamos trabajando con las uñas,'" *Aporrea*, August 29, 2023.
33. "El reino de las mil y una noches de un clan sirio crece en Barinas," *Armandoinfo*, August 29, 2021.
34. Joy Uricare, "¿Qué hay detrás de las privatizaciones de empresas del Estado?," *El Diario*, December 3, 2020.
35. "Entrevista a Diosdado Cabello sobre Tramo Tinaco Anaco de Ferrocarriles de Venezuela," Venezolana de Televisión (VTV), July 30, 2009.
36. "¿Qué pasa con la deuda externa venezolana?," *HispanoPost*, September 18, 2020.
37. "Caso PDVSA-Cripto," Wikimedia Foundation, 2023; "Fiscal de Venezuela confirma: Desde la Sunacrip se evadían pagos por venta de petróleo," *CriptoNoticias*, March 25, 2023; "Inusual ola de arrestos internos en Venezuela incluye al superintendente de criptoactivos," *Bloomberg Línea*, March 18, 2023; Eligio Rojas, "(VIDEO) Revelaciones: Oficina clandestina funcionaba en PDVSA para cocinar los guisos," *Aporrea*, June 26, 2023; Agencias, "Diputado de la Asamblea Nacional, Hermann Escarrá: No estamos hablando de poca cosa, 3 mil millones de dólares por un lado, 8 mil millones por el otro, 12 mil millones," *Aporrea*, March 23, 2023.
38. Marea Socialista, "Sinfonía de un Desfalco a la Nación: Tocata y fuga de Capitales," *Aporrea*, September 8, 2014.
39. "CENDAS-FVM: Canasta Alimentaria Familiar de julio 2023 se ubicó en US$ 502,27," editorial, *Aporrea*, August 22, 2023.
40. Fabrizo Sánchez Di Camillo, "Transparencia Venezuela: Al menos 246 obras públicas quedaron inconclusas en el país desde 1999," *El Diario*, September 30, 2022.
41. Sara Crespo Cárdenas, "Tocoma: Mega construcción millonaria e inconclusa," *Los Sin Luz*, December 8, 2023.
42. Banco Mundial, "Venezuela–Gross Domestic Product (GDP) 2024 (1986–2024)," Statista, November 24, 2023; Banco Mundial, "Datos Venezuela," 2022.
43. Gaceta Oficial, "Ley Constitucional Antibloqueo para el Desarrollo Nacional y la Garantía de los Derechos Humanos," *Gaceta Oficial*, no. 6,583 Extraordinario, October 12, 2020; Luis Britto García, "Proyecto de Ley Antibloqueo," *Aporrea*, October 3, 2020; Asamblea Nacional, "Ley Orgánica de las Zonas Económicas Especiales," Asamblea Nacional, July 20, 2022; "Marea Socialista: No es una 'Ley Anti-bloqueo'; es un instrumento para el despojo y la entrega del país," editorial, *Aporrea*, October 7, 2020.

Chapter 7: Revolution and Counterrevolution in the Bolivarian Process

1. The Water and Gas Wars in Bolivia, the uprisings in Ecuador, and the process that began with the Caracazo in Venezuela and continued until 2001 in Argentina all serve as examples of this wave of struggles.
2. Gonzalo Gómez, "Venezuela: De la Revolución Bolivariana de Chávez al régimen lumpenburgués, antiobrero y autoritario madurista," *Liga Internacional Socialista*, October 20, 2023.
3. Gonzalo Gómez, "¿Un congreso del PSUV para enterrar a la revolución o para resucitarla?," *Rebelión*, May 14, 2014.

4. Poliak Martin, "La Constituyente de Maduro vs la Constituyente del '99," MST, July 26, 2017.
5. Diario Panorama, "Tareck El Aissami: Una vez instalada la Asamblea Nacional Constituyente, la Fiscal debe irse," YouTube, July 13, 2017, www.youtube.com/watch?v=93iwrkPUPDI.
6. Liga Internacional Socialista, "Venezuela: Los trabajadores no tuvieron candidato. Que se respete la voluntad popular, no a la represión," *Liga Internacional Socialista*, August 1, 2024.

Chapter 8: Orinoco Mining Arc as an Expression of the End of a Cycle

1. "Detener el ecocidio minero en la cuenca del Orinoco es urgente: Un exhorto al Gobierno Nacional," editorial, *Aporrea*, April 15, 2016.
2. Emiliano Terán-Mantovani, "Arco Minero del Orinoco y fin de ciclo en Venezuela," *Aporrea*, August 17, 2016.
3. Asdrúbal Baptista, *Teoría económica del capitalismo rentístico* (Caracas: Banco Central de Venezuela, 2010).
4. Bernard Mommer, *La cuestión petrolera* (Caracas: Fondo Editorial Darío Ramírez, PDVSA, 2010).
5. Ministerio del Poder Popular para la Energía y Petróleo, "Petróleo y otros datos estadísticos," Gobierno Bolivariano de Venezuela, 2006.
6. Marianella Carrillo, "La inversión extranjera directa y los conflictos ambientales locales en Venezuela," *Cuadernos Del Cendes* 53 (2000): 155–96.
7. Environmental Justice Atlas, "Imataca Forest Reserve, Guayana Region, Venezuela," *Environmental Justice Atlas*, https://ejatlas.org/conflict/reserva-forestal-imataca-region-guayana-de-venezuela.
8. CEIC, "Venezuela Gold Production," 2022.
9. SOS Orinoco, "Cuyuni Corazón de Imataca. Epicentro del Arco Minero de Maduro," SOS Orinoco, July 13, 2020.
10. Emiliano Terán-Mantovani, *El fantasma de la Gran Venezuela* (Caracas: Fundación Celarg, 2014).
11. Ministro del Poder Popular de Petróleo y Minería, Pensamiento Petrolero del Comandante Chávez.
12. María Pilar García-Guadilla, "Ecosocialismo del Siglo XXI y modelo de desarrollo bolivariano: Los mitos de la sustentabilidad ambiental y de la democracia participativa en Venezuela," *Revista Venezolana de Economía y Ciencias Sociales* 15, no. 1 (2009): 187–223.
13. Miguel Ángel Mellado and Iokiñe Rodríguez, "Proyecto de Tendido Eléctrico en el Parque Nacional Canaima," *EJAtlas*, 2018.
14. Terán-Mantovani, *El fantasma*.
15. PDVSA, "INFORME de Gestión Anual 2015," PDVSA, 2015.
16. Asdrúbal Baptista, *Teoría económica del capitalismo rentístico* (Caracas: Banco Central de Venezuela, 2010).
17. Peruvian Society of Environmental Law (SPDA), "La realidad de la minería ilegal en países amazónico," SPDA, December 16, 2014.
18. CEIC, "Venezuela Gold Production."

19. José Manuel Puente and Jesús Rodríguez, "Venezuela en etapa de colapso macroeconómico: un análisis histórico y comparativo," *América Latina Hoy*, no. 85 (2020).
20. CEPAL, "Balance Preliminar de las Economías de América Latina y el Caribe, 2021: República Bolivariana de Venezuela," CEPAL, 2022. The year 2021 does not necessarily mark the end of this crisis; we have placed it as a referential limit for our analysis of the dynamics in the Amazon.
21. BCV, "Statistics from the Central Bank of Venezuela."
22. OPEC, "Monthly Oil Market Report," OPEC, 2020.
23. BCV, "Informe económico 2012," BCV, 2013.
24. Terán-Mantovani, *El fantasma*.
25. Crisis Group, "A Glut of Arms: Curbing the Threat to Venezuela from Violent Groups," Crisis Group, February 20, 2020; Organization for Economic Co-operation and Development (OCDE), "Flujos de oro desde Venezuela: Apoyo a la diligencia debida sobre la producción y el comercio de oro en Venezuela," OCDE, September 8, 2021.
26. OCDE, "Flujos de oro desde Venezuela"; Observatory of Economic Complexity (OEC), "Venezuela"; International Trade Center, "Trade Map"; Alex Vásquez and Nicolle Yapur, "Venezuela Moves Closer to Dollarization with New Bank Rules," *Bloomberg*, January 12, 2021; *El Economista*, "A pesar de la crisis, Venezuela ganó más por remesas que exportando petróleo," *La República*, October 12, 2021.
27. Keymer Avila, "El Covid-19 como dispositivo. Inquietudes securitarias en tiempos de pandemia," *Territorios Comunes*, no. 4 (2021): 80–93; InSight Crime, "La delegación del poder estatal: Los 'colectivos,'" InSight Crime, May 18, 2018; United Nations, "Situación de los derechos humanos y la asistencia técnica en la República Bolivariana de Venezuela," Informe de la Alta Comisionada de las Naciones Unidas para los Derechos Humanos, 2021.
28. Emiliano Terán-Mantovani, "Las metamorfosis del progresismo: Neoliberalización y derechización del proceso bolivariano en La Gran Crisis venezolana (2013–2020)," in *Derivas y dilemas de los progresismos sudamericanos* , ed. Salvador Schavelzon, Pabel López Flores, and Mila Ivanovic (Red Editorial, 2022).
29. Emiliano Terán-Mantovani, "Venezuela: extractivismo predatorio y política del saqueo," *Observatorio de Ecología Política de Venezuela*, August 12, 2019.
30. Emiliano Terán-Mantovani, "La ley antibloqueo es parte de un proceso neoliberalización de la economía, que viene desde el 2014," *La Clase.info*, October 14, 2020.
31. GTAI, Provea y Laboratorio de Paz, "Derechos humanos en el contexto del proyecto 'Arco Minero del Orinoco' en Venezuela," Audiencia ante la Comisión Interamericana de Derechos Humanos (CIDH), November 2016; UN, "Situación de los derechos humanos."
32. MippCI, "Arco Minero del Orinoco cuenta con más de 1.000 alianzas estratégicas," MippCI, May 17, 2019.
33. MDME, "Ministra Magaly Henríquez participó en encuentro con representantes de plantas de lixiviación del estado Bolívar," MDME, September 24, 2020.
34. BCV, "Compras de oro en el mercado interno," BCV, 2018.
35. Mónica Martiz, "Sector Minero: La Sangrienta Fiebre Del Oro" Transparencia Venezuela, 2018.

36. OCDE, "Flujos de oro"; Lisseth Boon, María Ramírez, and Lorena Meléndez, "El Arco Minero: La corporación de la molienda," *RRES, Correo del Caroní*, 2022.
37. Amnistía Internacional, "Acción urgente: Comunidades indígenas atacadas y en riesgo," Amnistía Internacional, December 19, 2018; CDH-ONU, "Informe de la misión internacional independiente de determinación de los hechos sobre la República Bolivariana de Venezuela," CDH-ONU, 2022; OVV, "2018–La violencia presenta nuevos rostros en el país: El empobrecimiento y la letalidad policial," OVV, 2018.
38. MDME, "Arco Minero del Orinoco (AMO): un modelo de minería responsable"; FundaRedes, "El Arco Minero del Orinoco y la destrucción de la reserva natural más importante de Venezuela," July 14, 2022; SOS Orinoco, "Presencia, actividad e influencia de los Grupos Armados Organizados en la actividad minera al sur del río Orinoco," SOS Orinoco, March 29, 2022; Consejo de Derechos Humanos ONU, "Informe de la Alta Comisionada de las Naciones Unidas para los Derechos Humanos," Consejo de Derechos Humanos ONU, 2020; HRW, "Venezuela: Violentos abusos en minas de oro ilegales," HRW, February 4, 2020.
39. Appeal for annulment due to illegality and unconstitutionality with request for a precautionary measure of the general administrative act contained in Decree No. 2,248, dated February 24, 2016, published in No. 40,855 of the Official Gazette of the Bolivarian Republic of Venezuela on February 24, 2016, through which the National Strategic Development Zone "Arco Minero del Orinoco" is created, May 31.
40. RAISG, "Amazonía bajo presión," RAISG, 2020; Joseph Poliszuk, María Ramírez, and María Antonieta Segovia, "Las pistas ilegales que bullen en la selva venezolana," *El País*, January 30, 2022.
41. ORPIA, Wataniba, Plataforma contra el Arco Minero del Orinoco, et al., "Situación de la Amazonía venezolana en tiempos de pandemia," *Observatorio de Ecología Política de Venezuela*, 2020.
42. MAAP, "MAAP #155: Hotspots de deforestación en la Amazonía venezolana," June 14, 2022.
43. Leopoldo Villegas and Mary Ann Torres, "Una epidemia resurgente como parte de una emergencia humanitaria compleja," *Icaso*, September 3, 2019.
44. HRW, "Venezuela: Violentos abusos"; UN, "Situación de los derechos humanos."
45. Jhoalys Siverio, "Procesan a jefes militares y subalternos por nexos con el pranato minero de La Paragua," *Correo del Caroní*, May 21, 2020; Joseph Poliszuk, María Ramírez, and María Antonieta Segovia, "El quién es quién de los cárteles criminales al sur del Orinoco," *Armando Info*, February 3, 2022; InSight Crime, "¿Por qué el ELN está detrás de la ruta del río Orinoco en Venezuela?," InSight Crime, February 8, 2022.
46. Transparencia Venezuela, "Economías ilícitas en Venezuela"; InSight Crime, "La última movida de una banda de minería ilegal en Venezuela," InSight Crime, May 17, 2021; SOS Orinoco, "Minería en Icabarú, Cuenca Alta del Caroní: De la Incoherencia a la Anarquía Criminal de Estado," SOS Orinoco, April, 2020; Laura Clisánchez, "Asesinan a capitán general del pueblo jivi y a otras tres personas en mina en el Bajo Caura," *Correo del Caroní*, April 29, 2021; Transparencia Venezuela, "Economías ilícitas en Venezuela: Organización R," Transparencia Venezuela, June 2022.

47. La Amazonía Saqueada, https://saqueada.amazoniasocioambiental.org/story/protectedareas; Katie Jones, Javier Lizcano, and Maria Fernanda Ramirez, "Bajo la superficie de la minería ilegal de oro en el Amazonas," InSight Crime, November 8, 2022; FIP, "¿Cómo se mueven el ELN y las disidencias de las FARC en la Orinoquía colombiana y la Guayana venezolana?," FIP, March 7, 2018.
48. SOS Orinoco, "Coltán: El Contrabando del "Oro Azul" por el Régimen en Venezuela," SOS Orinoco, March 2020.
49. SOS Orinoco, "Reserva de Biósfera Alto Orinoco Casiquiare: Invasión garimpeira en auge con apoyo del gobierno venezolano," SOS Orinoco, May 2022.
50. Cerlas, Plataforma contra el Arco Minero, "Informe sobre la situación de derechos humanos en el Arco Minero y el territorio venezolano ubicado al sur del río Orinoco," *Observatorio de Ecología Política de Venezuela*, September, 2020.
51. Jhoalys Siverio, "Detienen en Bolívar a militares que permitían el tráfico de combustible y minería ilegal," *Crónica Uno*, May 20, 2020.
52. Transparencia Venezuela, "Economías ilícitas en Venezuela"; Correo del Orinoco, "Desarticulado un grupo de delincuencia organizada por desviar gasolina a minería ilegal," Correo del Orinoco, February 3, 2022.
53. Explorando el Arco Minero, "Malestar en la cuna de las minas de oro de Venezuela."
54. Minerva Vitti, María De Los Ángeles Ramírez, and Joseph Poliszuk, "La veda a la minería se levanta en 'La Nueva Amazonas," *Armando Info*, February 16, 2022.
55. OCDE, "Flujos de oro"; World Gold Council, "Global Mine Production," 2022; MDME, "Plan Sectorial 2019–2025," 2018; MDME, "Arco Minero del Orinoco"; World Gold Council, "Global mine production."
56. OCDE, "Flujos de oro."
57. Christian Nellemann, Jürgen Stock, and Mark Shaw, "World Atlas of Illicit Flows," *Global Initiative*, 2018.
58. The Escazú Agreement is a regional treaty focused on environmental rights, officially titled the "Regional Agreement on Access to Information, Public Participation and Justice in Environmental Matters in Latin America and the Caribbean." It was adopted in 2018 and entered into force in 2021, aiming to strengthen the implementation of environmental democracy in participating countries, including Venezuela. Venezuela is a signatory but has not ratified the agreement as of December 2024.

Chapter 9: Human Rights Violations of the Maduro Government

1. "Constitution of the Bolivarian Republic of Venezuela," *Official Gazette* No. 36,680, December 30, 1999.
2. It is the first and only Venezuelan constitution approved by the people by voting in a referendum, on December 15, 1999, and received the support of 71.78 percent of the votes counted (3,301,475).
3. Office of the United Nations High Commissioner for Human Rights, "Declaración sobre los principios fundamentales de justicia para las victimas de delitos y del abuso de poder," Office of the United Nations High Commissioner for Human Rights, November 29, 1985.

4. Office of the United Nations High Commissioner for Human Rights, "Principios y directrices básicos sobre el derecho de las víctimas de violaciones manifiestas de las normas internacionales de derechos humanos y de violaciones graves del derecho internacional humanitario a interponer recursos y obtener reparaciones," Office of the United Nations High Commissioner for Human Rights, December 15, 2005.
5. Office of the United Nations High Commissioner for Human Rights, "Derecho Internacional de los Derechos Humanos," Office of the United Nations High Commissioner for Human Rights.
6. UN Human Rights Office, "Derecho Internacional de los Derechos Humanos."
7. "Constitution of the Bolivarian Republic of Venezuela," *Official Gazette* No. 5,453, Extraordinary, March 24, 2000.
8. Constitution of the Bolivarian Republic of Venezuela, Article 31.
9. Constitution of the Bolivarian Republic of Venezuela, Article 26.
10. Universal Declaration of Human Rights, G.A. Res. 217A (III), U.N. Doc A/RES/217(III) (Dec. 10, 1948), art. 2.
11. Amnesty International, *Venezuela: Información para el Comité de Derechos Humanos de las Naciones Unidas: 139° período de sesiones, 9 octubre–3 noviembre de 2023* (London: Amnesty International, 2023).
12. R4V, "Refugiados y Migrantes de Venezuela," Regional Interagency Coordination Platform for Refugees and Migrants of Venezuela.
13. Pedro Nikken, "El concepto de Derechos Humanos," in *Studies on Human Rights, Vol. I,* ed. various authors (San José, Costa Rica: Inter-American Institute of Human Rights, 1994), 27–28.
14. Constitution of the Bolivarian Republic of Venezuela, Article 80.
15. Constitution of the Bolivarian Republic of Venezuela, Article 91.
16. Regarding the concepts that make up the salary in Venezuela, Article 104 of the Organic Law of Labor, Men and Women Workers (LOTTT) establishes that the salary is made up of the following elements: (1) Basic salary, (2) Commissions, (3) Overtime, (4) Night surcharges, (5) Surcharges for work on holidays or weekly rest days, (6) Gratifications, (7) Participation in the benefits or profits of the company, (8) Social Security (public and/or private).
17. This is according to the website Population Today, the United Nations, the World Bank, Nations Geo, Census, and Wikidata as of April 2024; World Bank, "Poblacion active, total–Venezuela, RB," World Bank.
18. Constitution of the Bolivarian Republic of Venezuela, Section III of the National Monetary System, arts. 318–19.
19. Decree with Rank Value and Force of Law of the Statistical Public Function, No. 1,509, published in *Official Gazette* no. 37,321 (2001).
20. Team Anova, "Remesas, Pobreza y Distribucion del Ingreso en Venezuela: Que dice la evidencia?," *Think Nova*, March 30, 2022.
21. Organización International del Trabajo, "Comisión de Encuesta de OIT emitió informe sobre queja presentada contra la Republica Bolivariana de Venezuela," *Organización International del Trabajo*, October 3, 2019.
22. Aryenis Izarra, "La Vida en la Verdad de Aryenis y Alfredo," *Medium*, April 9, 2023.

23. The Bolivarian National Intelligence Service, which was created as defined in the *Official Gazette of the RBV*, No. 39,436 on June 1, 2010. According to the International Convention for the Protection of All Persons from Enforced Disappearances, forced disappearance is understood to be "the arrest, detention, kidnapping or any other form of deprivation of liberty carried out by agents of the State or by individuals or groups of persons who act with the authorization, support or acquiescence of the State, followed by the refusal to recognize said deprivation of liberty or the concealment of the fate or whereabouts of the disappeared person, removing it from the protection of the law."
24. Manuel Tomillo C., "Excarlelan a sindicalista Eudis Girot a pocas horas de llegada de comisión de la OIT," *Efecto Cocuyo*, April 25, 2022.
25. Provea (@_Provea), "Rubén González es un líder sindical que fue sometido injustamente a 2 juicios militares. Encarcelado 17 y luego 21 meses por defender derechos laborales en Venezuela. Rubén tuvo graves problemas de salud sin recibir atención médica, un trato cruel e inhumano," X, July 20, 2023, https://twitter.com/_Provea/status/1682052827470864385?s=20.
26. Venezuela Human Rights Action Education Program is one of the most prominent Venezuelan human rights organizations.
27. Andrés Cañizález, "Poder y medios de comunicación: entre la democratización y el autoritarismo: La sinuosa historia venezolana," *Comunicación Gumilla*, February 24, 2020.
28. Daniella Zambrano, "En Venezuela, cada vez se hace mas difícil defender el derecho a la información," *France 24*, May 1, 2022.
29. Marcelino Bisbal, "Medios de comunicación Social en Venezuela: Notas sobre el nuevo régimen comunicativo," *IPYS*, 2024.
30. Gretal Kahn, "Asi desafían la censura en Venezuela los medios digitales independientes," Reuters Institute, March 15, 2023.
31. CENDAS (@CENDASFVM), "Canasta alimentaria familiar: Enero 2024 $535,23," image, X, February 21, 2024, https://twitter.com/CENDASFVM/status/1760284402079105262.

Chapter 10: Essequibo: Vortex of Confrontations

1. Ricardo Salvador De Toma García, "Geopolítica del petróleo en litigios territoriales: las dimensiones marítimas del Caso Esequibo entre la República Bolivariana de Venezuela y la República Cooperativa de Guyana" (Phd diss., Universidad Federal de Río Grande do Sul, 2023.)
2. Christopher Hernandez-Roy et al., "Miscalculation and Escalation over the Essequibo: New Insights into the Risks of Venezuela's Compellence Strategy," Center for Strategic and International Studies, February 9, 2024.
3. Juan Pablo Álvarez, "Imparable: Un país sudamericano verá crecer 38% su PIB en 2024; al menos eso dicen las proyecciones," *Bloomberg Linea*, April 11, 2024.
4. "PPP no longer Marxist/Leninist—Ramotar," *Stabroek News*, September 6, 2021; Simón Rodríguez Porras and Miguel Sorans, ¿Por qué fracasó el chavismo?: Un balance desde la oposición de *izquierda* (Buenos Aires: CEHuS, 2018).
5. "US Throws Weight Behind Guyana in Territorial Dispute with Venezuela," *Al Jazeera*, December 7, 2023.

6. Reuters, "UK minister visits Guyana amid border dispute with Venezuela," December 17, 2023
7. Arunima Kumar, "Hess says reviewing timeline for closing Chevron's takeover deal," Reuters, March 7, 2024.
8. Gisela Salomón, "Alex Saab fue informante de la DEA, muestran documentos," *AP News,* February 16, 2022.
9. Lucas Pordeus León, "Brasil reforça presença militar na fronteira com Venezuela e Guiana," *Agencia Brasil*, November 30, 2023.
10. Daniel Gallas, "Lula sobre tensão Venezuela-Guiana: 'Referendo obviamente vai dar ao Maduro o que ele quer,'" *BBC*, December 3, 2023.
11. "Lula pide una salida pacífica al conflicto del Esequibo: 'No necesitamos más guerras,'" *Objective*, December 7, 2023.
12. "Guyana acusa a Venezuela de cometer una 'flagrante violación' al promulgar la ley que crea un estado en el Esequibo, territorio en disputa," *CNN Español*, April 4, 2024.
13. Leandro Prazeres, "Essequibo: por que crise ressuscita temor do Brasil sobre presença militar dos EUA na Amazônia," *BBC*, December 8, 2023.
14. Perun, "Venezuela, Guyana and the Essequibo Crisis—Posturing or a New Special Military Operation?," @PerunAU, December 10, 2023, YouTube, www.youtube.com/watch?v=mWSE9dPEx6Y.
15. "Russia Acknowledges Presence of Troops in Venezuela," *Guardian, March 28, 2019; Maria Tsvetkova and Anton Zverev, "Exclusive: Kremlin-Linked Contractors Help Guard Venezuela's Maduro–Sources,"* Reuters, January 25, 2019.
16. Luis González Morales, "Venezuela Is Going To War . . . on TikTok," *Caracas Chronicles*, January 9, 2024.
17. "Venezuela Defends Military Buildup, Accusing Neighboring Guyana of Granting Illegal Oil Contracts," *AP News*, February 11, 2024.
18. Ryan C. Berg and Christopher Hernandez-Roy, "The Entirely Manufactured and Dangerous Crisis over the Essequibo," Center for Strategic and International Studies, December 8, 2023.
19. Simón Rodríguez P., "The Only Fair Way Out of the Essequibo Conflict," *Venezuela Voices*, July 17, 2020.
20. Otto Schoenrich, "El Memorándum de Severo Mallet Prevost," in *Tres momentos en la controversia de límites de Guayana* (Miami: Editorial Cardón, 2023), 169–82.
21. Odeen Ishmael, "The Trail of Diplomacy: A Documentary History of the Guyana-Venezuela Border Issue," Guyana.org, 1998.
22. Department of State, "Action Memorandum From the Assistant Secretary of State for European and Canadian Affairs (Tyler) to Secretary of State Rusk," Office of the Historian, July 10, 1964.
23. Ishmael, "The Trail of Diplomacy."
24. Manuel Alberto Donís Ríos, *El Esequibo: Una reclamación histórica* (Caracas: Universidad Católica Andrés Bello, 2016), 115.
25. Donís Ríos, *El Esequibo*, 123.
26. Ishmael, "The Trail of Diplomacy."

27. Latin American Bureau, *Guyana: Fraudulent Revolution* (London: Practical Action Publishing, 1984), 48–53.
28. Ishmael, "The Trail of Diplomacy."
29. William Neumann, "Nuevos hallazgos de petróleo intensifican la disputa territorial entre Guyana y Venezuela," *New York Times*, November 18, 2015.
30. Latin American Bureau, *Guyana: Fraudulent Revolution*, 77–78.
31. Ishmael, "The Trail of Diplomacy."
32. Donís Ríos, *El Esequibo*, 153.
33. De Toma García, "Geopolítica del petróleo."
34. Jeroen Kuiper, "Relations Between Guyana and Venezuela Have Improved Tremendously Under Chávez," *Venezuelanalysis*, July 4, 2005.
35. De Toma García, "Geopolítica del petróleo."
36. Simón Rodríguez, "Haití: Masiva movilización contra la corrupción con el dinero de Petrocaribe," *Rebelíon*, November 3, 2018.
37. "Maduro reafirma derechos de Venezuela sobre territorio Esequibo," *El Universal*, February 17, 2020.
38. De Toma García, "Geopolítica del petróleo."
39. Neumann, "Nuevos hallazgos de petróleo."
40. Ishmael, "The Trail of Diplomacy."
41. Socialism and Freedom Party, "On the Essequibo Referendum," *Venezuela Voices*, November 28, 2023.

Afterword

1. "Government Forges Undemocratic Elections with Proscriptive Measures," *Venezuelan Voices*, March 26, 2024, https://venezuelanvoices.org/2024/03/26/government-forges-undemocratic-elections-with-proscriptive-measures.
2. "Carter Center Statement on Venezuela Election," The Carter Center, July 30, 2024, www.cartercenter.org/news/pr/2024/venezuela-073024.html.

Contributor Biographies

Anderson M. Bean is an assistant teaching professor of sociology at North Carolina Agricultural and Technical State University in Greensboro, North Carolina. He is the author of *Communes and the Venezuelan State: The Struggle for Participatory Democracy in a Time of Crisis.*

Carlos Carcione was a journalist and researcher of international politics and economy. He was a member of the editorial board of *Revista Comuna*, a social science magazine of the Miranda International Center (CIM). Carcione was the CIM international cooperator for research and dissemination of the productive model proposed during the Chávez government. He was also a coordinator of the Marea Socialista Investigation Team until 2018. He was a journalist at *Periodismo de Izquierda* in Argentina. Carcione was a Trotskyist militant of the Workers' Socialist Movement in the Workers' Left Front-Unity (FIT-U) in Argentina and a member of the International Socialist League.

Juan García has been a revolutionary militant of over fifty years. He was a political prisoner from 1981 until his acquittal in 1987. He is a longtime political organizer of various left-wing social, community, and political organizations, including Marea Socialista, which he cofounded in 2004. He has also edited numerous popular newspapers, including *Referencia Nacional.* García was one of the cofounders of the left-wing website Aporrea, one of the top-four visited political websites in Venezuela. On Aporrea, García published over 150 articles, under a variety of different pen names, from 2010 to 2022. For years, he was a union adviser and currently writes and organizes around the defense of wages and other constitutional labor rights in Venezuela. García is an active member of the Citizen Platform for the Defense of the Constitution. He retired from the human resources department in the National Public Administration in 2015.

Gonzalo Gómez is a psychologist and an education worker. He was a leader of the Socialist Workers Party from the 1970s to the 1990s. He was a key figure in the regroupment of Trotskyism in Venezuela and was a critical supporter of Hugo Chávez and the Bolivarian Revolution. He participated in the Popular Revolutionary Assembly against the 2002 coup. Gómez also was a cofounder of the alternative media site *Aporrea*. He was one of the founders of Marea Socialista, a current that joined the PSUV, of which he was a founding delegate and part of the regional leadership in Caracas. In 2014, Marea was excluded from the PSUV and then broke with the Maduro government. Gómez participated for several years with the Citizen's Platform for the Defense of the Constitution with several former Chávez ministers. Gómez has continued to organize with Marea Socialista as an independent organization and section of the International Socialist League.

Roberto López Sánchez is a historian and revolutionary militant. He was a tenured professor at the University of Zulia from 1994 to 2014. López received his PhD in political science. He has published more than forty articles and papers. López was an activist of the student and teacher movement and has also been linked to the labor, peasant, environmental, Indigenous, and cultural movements since 1977. He participated in the revolutionary armed struggle (1977–88), during which he was a member of the Americo Silva Guerrilla Front and was politically persecuted under Punto Fijismo. He was the founder of the National Union of Workers–Zulia and member of its executive committee (2004–12). He is currently a member of the Consultative Council of the Bolivarian Socialist Federation of Zulia Workers and directs the Diploma in Union Training that is taught at the University of Zulia.

Gustavo Márquez Marín graduated as an electrical engineer from the University of Carabobo (1972), where he later taught. He was the coordinator of Systems Engineering at the National Open University from 1981 to 1985. Márquez has been published in a variety of different national media outlets. He also served as the president of the political party Movement for Socialism (1995–97) as well as the deputy to the Congress of the Republic (1983–99). In the Hugo Chávez administration, he held the following responsibilities: minister of Industry and Commerce (1999), member of the Binational Commission for the delimitation of marine and submarine waters with Colombia (1999), ambassador to the Republic of Austria and permanent representative in United Nations agencies based in Vienna (2001–4), minister of state for Integration and Foreign Trade (2005–7), and ambassador to the Republic of Colombia (2009–10). Márquez is currently a member of the Citizen Platform for the Defense of the Constitution.

Oly Millán Campos is an economist with a master's degree in history from the Universidad Centroccidental Lisandro Alvarado. She is currently a professor at the Faculty of Economic and Social Sciences at Central University of Venezuela. From 2000 to 2006, Millán held various positions in the government of President Hugo Chávez. Some of them included the following: vice president of Economic and Planning Studies, director of the Industrial Bank, vice minister of Financing and Marketing of the Ministry of Popular Economy, director of the Venezuelan Corporation of Guayana, president in charge of the Development Fund Agriculture, Fisheries, Forestry and Related, president in charge of the Fund for the Financing of the Special Zones for Sustainable Development, and minister of Ministry of Popular Economy. From 2007 to 2015, she held various positions as an adviser and facilitator in various programs related to the design and implementation of socio-productive projects, as well as in issues of state planning and with the development of popular power and the promotion and construction of socially owned companies in various states around the country. She has published several opinion articles and research papers in various outlets related to the Venezuelan crisis, the social economy, the connection of the economy with the people, public and citizen audit of the debt, among others. Since 2013, she has, along with other former ministers of President Chávez, leftist leaders, and academics, organized with the Citizen Platform Against Embezzlement of the Nation and the Citizen Platform for the Defense of the Constitution.

Simón Rodríguez is a Venezuelan socialist writer and journalist. He was a student organizer and later became professor at the Universidad de los Andes. When he was a member of the national leadership of the Socialism and Freedom Party, he ran as candidate for the National Assembly in 2015. He is a founding member of Laclase.info and Venezuelanvoices.org and has published articles in *Humania del Sur*, *NACLA*

Report on the Americas, *The New Arab*, and *Rebelión* and on dozens of electronic outlets, and his articles have been translated into six languages. He has given talks and lectures in Argentina, Brazil, Cuba, and the Dominican Republic. He is coauthor with Miguel Sorans of the book *Why Did Chavismo Fail? A Left-Opposition Balance Sheet* (CeHUS, 2018).

Emiliano Terán is a sociologist from the Central University of Venezuela and has a master's degree in ecological economics from the Autonomous University of Barcelona. He is a PhD candidate in environmental science and technology at the same institution. He is also an associate researcher at the Center for Development Studies in Venezuela and a member of the Observatory of Political Ecology of Venezuela.

Omar Vázquez Heredia has a doctorate in social sciences from the University of Buenos Aires, a master's degree in international business relations from the National University Tres de Febrero, and a degree in political science from the Central University of Venezuela. He has been awarded a scholarship to carry out postgraduate studies and academic research by the Gran Mariscal de Ayacucho Foundation of Venezuela, the National Scientific and Technical Research Council of Argentina, the Center for Studies for Labor and Agrarian Development of Bolivia, the Latin American Council of Social Sciences, and the Center for Advanced Latin American Studies. He was a researcher in training at the Institute of Latin American and Caribbean Studies of the University of Buenos Aires. He has taught subjects at the Central University of Venezuela School of Sociology. As a playwright, he has won literary contests for his works *A Reunion at the University Stadium* and *And a Cat Came into Their Lives.*

Ana Sofía Viloria is a social worker and has been a left-wing political activist focused on the defense of human rights in Venezuela for forty-five years. She began her activism in 1978 organizing with the National Association of Human Rights in Venezuela, focusing on freedom for political prisoners. She also cofounded the website *Aporrea*, one of the top four most visited political websites in Venezuela. She continues to organize for the defense of democratic freedoms and human rights in Venezuela.

Index

Bold indicates a map or table; *fn* refers to footnotes.

About Haymarket Books

Haymarket Books is a radical, independent, nonprofit book publisher based in Chicago. Our mission is to publish books that contribute to struggles for social and economic justice. We strive to make our books a vibrant and organic part of social movements and the education and development of a critical, engaged, and internationalist left.

We take inspiration and courage from our namesakes, the Haymarket Martyrs, who gave their lives fighting for a better world. Their 1886 struggle for the eight-hour day—which gave us May Day, the international workers' holiday—reminds workers around the world that ordinary people can organize and struggle for their own liberation. These struggles—against oppression, exploitation, environmental devastation, and war—continue today across the globe.

Since our founding in 2001, Haymarket has published more than nine hundred titles. Radically independent, we seek to drive a wedge into the risk-averse world of corporate book publishing. Our authors include Angela Y. Davis, Arundhati Roy, Keeanga-Yamahtta Taylor, Eve Ewing, Aja Monet, Mariame Kaba, Naomi Klein, Rebecca Solnit, Mohammed El-Kurd, José Olivarez, Noam Chomsky, Winona LaDuke, Robyn Maynard, Leanne Betasamosake Simpson, Howard Zinn, Mike Davis, Marc Lamont Hill, Dave Zirin, Astra Taylor, and Amy Goodman, among many other leading writers of our time. We are also the trade publishers of the acclaimed Historical Materialism Book Series.

Haymarket also manages a vibrant community organizing and event space in Chicago, Haymarket House, the popular Haymarket Books Live event series and podcast, and the annual Socialism Conference.

Also Available from Haymarket Books

Border and Rule: Global Migration, Capitalism, and the Rise of Racist Nationalism
Harsha Walia, afterword by Nick Estes, foreword by Robin D. G. Kelley

Brazil's Dance with the Devil
The World Cup, the Olympics, and the Fight for Democracy
Dave Zirin

Coup: A Story of Violence and Resistance in Bolivia
Thomas Becker and Linda Farthing

Environmentalism from Below
How Global People's Movements Are Leading the Fight for Our Planet
Ashley Dawson

In the Red Corner: The Marxism of José Carlos Mariátegui
Mike Gonzalez

The Last Day of Oppression, and the First Day of the Same
The Politics and Economics of the New Latin American Left
Jeffery R. Webber

The Long Honduran Night
Resistance, Terror, and the United States in the Aftermath of the Coup
Dana Frank

Radicals in the Barrio: Magonistas, Socialists, Wobblies, and Communists in the Mexican American Working Class
Justin Akers Chacón

www.ingramcontent.com/pod-product-compliance
Lightning Source LLC
Jackson TN
JSHW080227090126
96708JS00014B/87

* 9 7 9 8 8 8 8 9 0 4 6 4 0 *